WORLD BANK STAFF OCCASIONAL PAPERS □ NUMBER THIRTY

Enzo R. Grilli, Barbara Bennett Agostini,
and Maria J. 't Hooft-Welvaars

•⦁•

The World Rubber Economy
Structure, Changes, and Prospects

•⦁•

Published for the World Bank
The Johns Hopkins University Press
Baltimore and London

The Johns Hopkins University Press
Baltimore, Maryland 21218, U.S.A.

Copyright © 1980 by The International Bank
for Reconstruction and Development / THE WORLD BANK
1818 H Street, N.W., Washington, D.C. 20433 U.S.A.
All rights reserved
Manufactured in the United States of America

Library of Congress Cataloging in Publication Data

Grilli, Enzo R
  The world rubber economy.

  (A World Bank staff occasional paper ; 30)
  Bibliography: p.
  1. Rubber industry and trade. I. Agostini, Barbara
Bennett, 1934–   joint author. II. Hooft-Welvaars,
M. J. 't, joint author. III. Title. IV. Series: World
Bank staff occasional papers ; 30.
HD9161.A2G73   338.4'76782   80–554
ISBN O–8018–2421–4 (pbk.)

World Bank Staff Occasional Papers

(continued)

Contents

•●•

TABLES

FIGURES

Foreword

I would like to explain why the World Bank does research work and why this research is published. We feel an obligation to look beyond the projects that we help finance toward the whole resource allocation of an economy and the effectiveness of the use of those resources. Our major concern, in dealings with member countries, is that all scarce resources—including capital, skilled labor, enterprise, and know-how—should be used to their best advantage. We want to see policies that encourage appropriate increases in the supply of savings, whether domestic or international. Finally, we are required by our Articles, as well as by inclination, to use objective economic criteria in all our judgments.

These are our preoccupations, and these, one way or another, are the subjects of most of our research work. Clearly, they are also the proper concern of anyone who is interested in promoting development, and so we seek to make our research papers widely available. In doing so, we have to take the risk of being misunderstood. Although these studies are published by the Bank, the views expressed and the methods explored should not necessarily be considered to represent the Bank's views or policies. Rather, they are offered as a modest contribution to the great discussion on how to advance the economic development of the underdeveloped world.

ROBERT S. MCNAMARA
President
The World Bank

Preface

This study represents the result of joint research between the World Bank and the United Nations Food and Agriculture Organization (FAO) on the future prospects for natural rubber. It was begun after a seminar at the Bank on the effects of the energy crisis on the competitive position of natural rubber. The authors worked closely throughout the entire period of the research and did field work in all the major rubber producing and consuming countries.

In completing this study the authors received help and advice from a great number of organizations, private individuals, and government officials throughout the world. This study would not have been possible without their direct and generous help, which is here gratefully acknowledged. Thanks are also due to many in the World Bank, FAO, and the Economic and Social Institute of the Free University in Amsterdam (ESI), particularly to Vera Klein, Werner A. Lamade, Charles W. Brookson, Maurizio de Negris, Enrico Oppes, and Luciana Cattaneo of FAO; to Shamsher Singh, Peter Pollak, Pee Teck Yew, Ray Helterline, Gajinder Ahuja, and Stephen Huete of the World Bank; and to Paul J. Vennedal of ESI Amsterdam, who made substantial contributions. Finally, acknowledgements are due to Jean Lombardo and Barbara Thompson for their patience and skills in typing the various drafts of this study.

Virginia deHaven Hitchcock edited the manuscript for publication and coordinated production of the book, Raphael Blow prepared the figures, and Chris Jerome (through the Word Guild) read and corrected proof.

Enzo R. Grilli
Barbara Bennett Agostini
Maria J. 't Hooft-Welvaars

Acronyms and Definitions

ANRPC, Association of Natural Rubber Producing Countries
BR, polybutadiene rubber
c.i.f., cost-insurance-freight
CR, polychloroprene rubber
EPM, EPDM, ethylene-propylene rubbers
FAO, United Nations Food and Agriculture Organization
FELDA, Federal Land Development Authority (Malaysia)
f.o.b., freight-on-board
GDP, gross domestic product
GNP, gross national product
IISRP, International Institute of Synthetic Rubber Producers
IR, polyisoprene rubber
IRR, butyl rubber
IRSG, International Rubber Study Group
MBER, Michigan Bureau of Economic Research
MITI, Ministry of International Trade and Industry (Japan)
MRRDB, Malaysian Rubber Research and Development Board
NBR, nitrile rubber
NR, natural rubber
OECD, Office of Economic Cooperation and Development
OPEC, Organization of Petroleum Exporting Countries
RRIM, Rubber Research Institute of Malaysia
SBR, styrene-butadiene rubber
SIR, Standard Indonesian Rubber (technically specified rubber)
SMR, Standard Malaysian Rubber (technically specified rubber)
SR, synthetic rubber
UNCTAD, United Nations Conference on Trade and Development

The World Rubber Economy

Structure, Changes, and Prospects

1

Introduction and Summary

After twenty-five years of profound but relatively orderly structural changes, caused for the most part by technological evolution, the world rubber economy has been subjected in the past few years to severe exogenous shocks: first the oil crisis and then a deep economic recession in industrialized countries. The supply of rubber has been affected directly and indirectly by the quadrupled real prices of oil, which have changed the cost structures of both synthetic and natural rubbers.[1] The demand for rubber has been affected by the economic recession in industrialized countries, which has severely dampened the growth optimism of the rubber industry.[2] For the first time in more than two decades, there are serious doubts about the future of this industry, which depends so heavily on the growth of the automotive sector.[3]

The World Rubber Economy from 1945 to 1973

From the end of World War II to 1973 the growth of the world rubber economy was rapid, but relatively steady and orderly. Profound structural changes resulted mostly from technological evolution. Synthetic rubber (SR), which was developed under wartime needs, not only continued to be produced in increasing quantities, but gained a predominant position in the world market, dissolving

1. Throughout this study, where not otherwise qualified, the terms "rubber" and "elastomer" imply both natural and synthetic rubbers.
2. Developed countries use about 70 percent of all the rubber in the world.
3. Over 65 percent of all rubber produced in the world is directly used by the automotive industry in tires and in other automotive parts, such as hoses, belts, strips, bumper parts, seat cushions, and mounts.

the near-monopoly position continuously enjoyed by natural rubber (NR) in the first half of the 1900s. Production of synthetic elastomers became more and more diversified in terms of kinds, geographical location, and product performance. Forward integration by petro-chemical producers and backward integration by tire manufacturers also became a prevalent characteristic of the production process.

The consumption of rubber grew also. The extremely rapid growth of the use of motor vehicles in Western Europe and Japan, coupled with the continuous expansion of automotive production and use in North America (where levels were already comparatively high) created a strong and steady demand for elastomers. Nonautomotive elastomer demand also increased rapidly, following closely the fast expansion in world production of other industrial and consumer goods in which rubber was used. Between 1948 and 1973 total consumption of elastomers increased 6.3 percent a year.

The World Rubber Economy since the Oil Crisis

In 1973 the world rubber economy suffered its first severe exogenous shock: the oil crisis and subsequent sharp rise in crude oil prices. For an industry whose major component—SR—depends so heavily on petrochemical feedstocks, the sudden drastic increase in crude oil prices in 1973–74 represented a major change in cost structures and production economics. The other component of the industry—NR— was less affected directly, but was still subject to all the indirect effects of the oil crisis: acceleration of world inflation, changes in consumer expectations, and rising doubts about the long-term future of world elastomer demand in the energy-intensive automotive sector.

In 1974–75 the serious economic recession that affected the indus-trialized countries deepened the already existing doubts concerning the long-term future of the rubber industry. Industrial production in general and the output of the automotive industry in particular fell drastically, and so did world demand for elastomers. The growth optimism that had long characterized the world rubber economy received another serious jolt. In 1978–79 the price of crude oil again increased sharply in real terms, bringing the cumulative increase since 1973 to more than 400 percent. Actual investments and new invest-ment planning in the synthetic rubber sector have come virtually to a halt outside the centrally planned economies. The industry fore-casts emerging in the second half of the 1970s clearly show the underlying pessimism regarding future growth of demand for elastomers. This pessimism has been created both by the expected low growth in world economic activity and by the expected medium-to-long-term decrease in the demand for elastomers, because of increasing use of smaller and lighter vehicles and of longer-wearing radial tires and because of the decreasing use of private transport.

Increased Production Costs
of Natural and Synthetic Rubbers

The sharp rise in crude oil prices in 1973–74 affected the production cost of SR much more than that of NR. The production cost of SR depends heavily (as much as 70 percent of the total) on the costs of chemical feedstocks and energy inputs (such as steam and electricity), which are closely related to the costs of oil and gas. Between 1973 and 1975 the cost of the basic chemical monomers used in synthetic rubber production—styrene, butadiene, and isoprene—and of other chemical and energy inputs more than doubled. In addition, labor and overhead costs also increased substantially. As a result, the average total direct cost of producing general purpose SR from existing facilities increased by an estimated 75 to 100 percent in all major industrialized countries.

The direct effect of the oil price change on the production cost of NR was relatively small (an increase of less than 10 percent), since energy-related inputs account for only about 15 percent of the total cost of producing NR from existing trees. If the change in labor cost, which accounts for about 55 percent of the total cost of producing NR from trees already in the ground, is also considered, the total effect was large, but still less than one-half of that experienced by general purpose SR.

In Malaysia, the country for which the most accurate cost comparisons before and after the oil crisis could be made, the average direct cost of producing NR increased by only about 30 percent between 1971 and 1974, measured in terms of the local currency. Moreover, even this relatively modest increase overstates the full effect of the oil crisis on the cost of producing NR, since it was largely due to higher labor cost, which in Malaysia is at least in part related to rubber market prices. Measured in U.S. dollars, the overall cost increase between 1971 and 1974 was about 70 percent, caused by the strong appreciation of the Malaysian dollar during this period.

The long-term cost competitiveness of NR appears to have been strengthened even further by the recent drastic change in energy prices. It is estimated, for example, that to have invested profitably in styrene-butadiene rubber (SBR) production in Western Europe in 1977, the industry would have needed future expected real prices of at least about 40¢ per pound, whereas investments in NR in Malaysia at the same level of profitability would have required an expected future real price of about 35¢ per pound, c.i.f. The relative profitability of natural rubber investments would have been even greater in relation to other kinds of SR, such as polyisoprene. The 40 percent increase in the real price of oil between 1977 and 1979 added at least another 5¢ per pound to the future expected price necessary to invest profitably in SBR. The crude oil price increases expected in the 1980s will further improve the long-run competitiveness of NR.

Future Growth of Demand for Rubber

Changes in consumer preferences together with technological changes are likely to slow down the future growth of world elastomer demand. The results of forecasting exercises based on both a modified regional income elasticity framework, and on a more disaggregated end-use demand model for the developed countries (which account for about 70 percent of the world market for elastomers) clearly point to this conclusion. Under World Bank assumptions concerning the future growth of the world economy, world demand for elastomers can be expected to grow an average of 5 to 5.5 percent a year between 1976 and 1990, which is at about 1 percent a year below the historical rate.

This slowdown in the expected future growth of rubber demand is likely to be stronger in developed countries, where the major structural changes in demand are expected to occur and where rubber use is already high, than in the centrally planned economies, where the elasticity of demand for rubber with respect to income and industrial production is higher and where, given the relatively low levels of rubber use, strong growth is expected in the future. Rubber consumption is also expected to continue to expand in developing countries, particularly in high-income developing countries where the use of motor vehicles is increasing.

Despite the expected slower growth of elastomer demand compared with the performance of the past twenty-five years, the world rubber economy is still facing relatively favorable overall prospects which should leave to both the natural and synthetic rubber sectors ample scope for future expansion. Particularly from the standpoint of natural rubber producers, a potential export market for a primary commodity that is expected to expand at about 5 percent a year presents a rather uncommon opportunity for future growth.

Prospects for Growth in the Synthetic Rubber Industry

In the synthetic rubber sector, the scope for future productivity gains appears to be limited. Outside the field of specialty rubbers, technological innovations in production and economies of scale, which were the major factors behind the exceptionally fast growth of general-purpose rubbers in the post-war period, appear to have run much of their course. Their future effect is likely to be much less strong than in the 1950s and 1960s, although by no means negligible. The synthetic rubber industry outside the centrally planned economies is reaching a mature stage where emphasis is likely to be on rationalization, consolidation, and more planned growth. Inside the centrally planned economies strong expansion will be pursued for self-sufficiency, almost irrespective of any other consideration.

Apart from serious economic constraints to further rapid growth represented by the high and possibly rising real cost of energy, the synthetic rubber industry will have to face greater uncertainties concerning the availability and prices of chemical feedstocks and mounting pressures over environmental and health issues.

Prospects for Growth in the Natural Rubber Industry

The natural rubber industry is in a favorable position to take advantage of the present good market opportunities. Although still faced with difficult problems connected with its diversity, fragmentation, and location, the natural rubber industry is just emerging from a period of profound internal transformation and rationalization. The benefits of the long-term research and development efforts pursued vigorously during the past twenty years and of the increased use of technical innovations in production and processing (such as high yield varieties of trees, chemical stimulation, crumb rubber, and technically specified and specialty rubbers) are still to be fully reaped by the industry.

Productivity increases of enormous proportions can be achieved over the next thirty years by diffusion of existing tree breeding and selection technologies. By using chemical stimulants, yields of existing low-yielding trees can be substantially increased, the escalating labor costs can be contained, and the responsiveness of supply to changing market price conditions can be enhanced.

Despite the solid premises for a period of strong expansion of the world natural rubber economy during the next fifteen to twenty years, natural rubber producers will have to fulfill several important conditions to take full advantage of the future market potential.

(a) Natural rubber supply will have to keep pace with the expected growth of isoprenic rubber demand, and a secure supply will have to be assured.

(b) Existing production technologies will have to be adopted both within and across countries.

(c) Research, development, marketing, and technical assistance programs will have to be maintained and strengthened.

Maintaining a supply of NR to meet world market demand for isoprenic rubbers is clearly the most important and, at the same time, the most uncertain condition that needs to be fulfilled. Natural rubber supply is expected to increase in line with market needs until the end of the 1970s. On the basis of current information on areas under rubber, on projected yield profiles of trees already in the ground, and on expected rates of replanting and new plantings, however, it appears likely that beyond the early 1980s natural rubber supply will grow at below potential market needs. Even on the basis of relatively conservative assumptions concerning the growth of isoprenic rubber demand outside the centrally planned economies and a relatively optimistic assessment of the likely growth of natural rubber supply from existing plantings and from plantings scheduled to come into production, a potential natural rubber demand gap of 0.5 million tons is likely by the end of the 1980s.

If not met by increased natural rubber supplies, this demand gap will be most likely filled by synthetic polyisoprene. Given the relatively long lags that characterize investments in NR, new investment decisions will have to be made immediately in the key producing countries to increase supply in the late 1980s. Synthetic polyisoprene producers outside the centrally planned economies now have ample spare capacities and, more importantly, much shorter investment lags. Their production can be increased more rapidly and investment risks are, therefore, lower. Yet analysis shows quite clearly that natural rubber producers have a substantial competitive cost advantage over polyisoprene (at least under known production technologies) and that with its technical and economic potential, NR can fill the potential demand gap for isoprenic rubber in the late 1980s.

Within the framework of each country's comparative advantage in natural rubber production, attention should, therefore, be focused on:

(a) The possibility of speeding up current replanting and rehabilitation plans, particularly in countries such as Indonesia, Sri Lanka, and Nigeria, where existing smallholder yield levels are relatively low and where current replanting rates can be increased substantially;

(b) The possibility of rehabilitating the rubber industries of Vietnam and Cambodia;

(c) The possibility of stepping up investments in newly planted rubber in countries such as India, the Philippines, the West African countries, and Brazil, depending on the relative availability of production factors; and

(d) The feasibility of accelerating the use of chemical stimulants, in conjunction with the most recent tapping techniques, on existing mature and old trees in all producing countries.

This last option could well be, at least in the short-to-medium term, the most feasible one.

Enough private and public investment capital should be available to expand natural rubber production. The technology for expansion is not only available, but also reasonably well proven. International organizations can play an important catalytic role in mobilizing the financial and managerial resources that are necessary to initiate the expansion of natural rubber production capacity. The experience accumulated by both the World Bank and the Food and Agriculture Organization of the United Nations (FAO) in preparing and implementing suitable and viable production schemes should be used to the fullest extent possible to help bring substantial economic benefits to the developing countries which produce natural rubber.

Structure of the Study

In order to put in perspective some of the choices that natural rubber producing countries will have to make, this study assesses the magnitude and scope of the changes that have recently occurred in the rubber economy throughout the world and the likely consequences of these changes on the future of the world natural rubber industry. The first section reviews the structure of the rubber economy and examines the production, consumption, trade, and price trends of the past twenty years. The second section examines in detail the market interaction between NR and SR. The third part analyzes the short- and long-term effects of the oil crisis on the competitive relation between NR and SR. The fourth part gives the possible growth scenarios for rubber demand, the supply prospects of NR and SR, and the balances of supply and demand for NR over the next decade. Finally, the study focuses on the policy implications of the analysis from the point of view of the natural rubber producers. Production planning, price competitiveness, price stabilization, and profitability of new investments are discussed in this context. Six appendixes contain details of the technical analyses on which much of this study is based. The basic statistics of the world rubber economy are contained in a statistical appendix.

2

•-•--•-•--•-•--•-•--•-•--•-•--•-•--•-•--•-•--•-•--•-•--•-•--•-•--•-•--•-•--•-•--•-•--•-•--•-•--•-•-•

Development and Structure
of the World Rubber Economy

The world rubber industry began to develop in the 1800s.
The impetus came from technological innovations: the invention of
the masticator, which enabled solid natural rubber (NR) to be soft-
ened, mixed, and shaped, and of the vulcanization process, which
drastically improved the physical properties of NR. Throughout the
1800s and most of the first half of the 1900s, important changes
took place within the world natural rubber economy.[1] Wild rubber
from Brazil and Africa gave way to plantation rubber from East Asia
(Ceylon, Malaya, and the Netherlands East Indies). These changes
in the mode and geographic location of natural rubber production
led to vast improvements in productivity. The dramatic increase in
natural rubber yields was aided not only by the spread of modern
production practices, but particularly by continuous research in tree
breeding and tree care, which was applied to rubber production.

The growth of the natural rubber industry in the early 1900s was
helped also by the emergence of production by smallholders, and, by
and large, supply kept pace with the growing demand, which was
spurred by the use of motor vehicles in the United States and
Western Europe. In the late 1920s and early 1930s, however, the
world economic recession drastically reduced the demand for rubber
in automotive uses, and excess capacity developed. The industry
responded with a supply regulation scheme that lasted until 1943.[2]

1. P. W. Allen, *Natural Rubber and the Synthetics* (London: Crosby Lockwood, 1972), pp. 31–44.

2. The International Rubber Regulation Agreement was, in essence, an export
quota scheme, backed up by limitations on plantings and replantings. For a
detailed account and evaluation of this scheme and its operations, see Peter T.

Despite some troublesome periods, the world natural rubber economy continued to grow between the wars. The monopoly position of NR, as the only kind of elastomer used by the world industry, remained virtually unchallenged. Some synthetic rubber (SR) began to be produced in Germany, the U.S.S.R., and the United States, but even as late as 1939 these rubbers accounted for only 2 percent of total world rubber consumption.

World War II gave the main impetus to the development of SR on a large scale. Western Europe and the United States were cut off from their main sources of NR, so they turned to the domestic chemical industry to meet their large and expanding need for elastomers. This effort was particularly successful in the United States, where a crash development program was launched by the government. By 1945 the United States produced about 1 million tons of SR a year. Considerable production capacity was also established in Canada, Germany, and the U.S.S.R. After a brief period of retrenchment following the end of World War II, the expansion of SR started again and has continued unabated throughout the past three decades. Synthetic rubbers now account for about 70 percent of all elastomer consumption, and NR accounts for the remaining 30 percent.

Over the past thirty years, therefore, the world rubber economy has come to be based on two broad types of elastomers, natural and synthetic. Their relative importance has changed drastically, however: NR has lost its near monopoly position, and the share of the natural rubber sector in the world rubber economy has decreased progressively and is now the smaller one.

The Synthetic Rubber Industry

The production of SR is concentrated in a few countries. The United States, Japan, and the European Community (EC) account for 65 percent of world production.[3] The U.S.S.R. and the other centrally

---

Bauer, *The Rubber Industry: A Study in Competition and Monopoly* (Cambridge, Massachusetts: Harvard University Press, 1948), pp. 88–215.

3. In this study the term European Community is used in its current meaning, implying membership by nine countries: France, the Federal Republic of Germany, Italy, Belgium, the Netherlands, Luxemburg, the United Kingdom, Ireland, and Denmark.

planned economies of Europe account for another 28 percent of the total (Table 2-1). Consumption is distributed in roughly the same fashion: 64 percent in developed countries, 28 percent in centrally planned economies, and the remainder in developing countries. Within each area, SR is produced in only a few firms. In the United States the four largest synthetic rubber producers account for about 65 percent of total shipments. In Italy, the United Kingdom, the Federal Republic of Germany, Belgium, the Netherlands, and Canada, the largest firms account for 50 percent or more of total capacity. In France and Japan, the two largest firms account for more than 40 percent of total productive capacity. Because of the relatively small size of domestic markets in relation to the minimum economic size of mainstream synthetic rubber plants (that is, styrene-butadiene rubber, SBR), SR is also produced by only a limited number of firms in developing countries.

Backward and forward integration is another important structural characteristic of the synthetic rubber industry. The dependence of tire manufacturers on SR encouraged them to integrate backward into the rubber industry, whereas the similarity between the technical processes of synthetic rubber production and those of petrochemical production offered chemical producers a considerable incentive for forward integration. Tire manufacturers and petrochemical producers dominate the production of SR outside the centrally planned economies. The petrochemical industry alone appears to control over 50 percent of the existing production capacity of SR, and the rubber manufacturing industry owns another 40 percent of total capacity. The remainder appears to be in the hands of various industrial concerns, most of which are owned or supported by a national government. If the centrally planned economies are included, more than 55 percent of total world production capacity of SR is in one way or another captive, because of backward or forward integration in the industry.

Substantial differences in the pattern of integration exist, however, between the main synthetic rubber producing countries and regions. In the United States backward integration is predominant. The tire manufacturers have developed SR's largely for their own consumption and, in some instances, have moved even further back into the production of basic petrochemicals. Five large tire companies control more than 55 percent of total existing U.S. synthetic rubber capacity. The remainder is split roughly equally between petrochemical firms and independent producers. In Western Europe, however, petro-

Table 2–1. *World Synthetic Rubber Production,*
by Main Countries and Economic Regions,
1955 to 1977, Selected Averages and Growth Rates
(thousands of metric tons)

Economic region and country	1955–57		1966–68	
	Average	*Percentage of world total*	*Average*	*Percentage of world total*
Developed countries	1,205.0	73.0	3,483.3	77.5
North America	1,193.6	72.3	2,236.4	49.8
Japan	. . .	—	298.0	6.6
Western Europe	11.4	0.7	900.7	20.0
Others	. . .	—	48.2	1.1
Developing countries	. . .	—	110.6	2.5
Africa	. . .	—	. . .	—
Asia	. . .	—	20.9	0.5
Latin America	. . .	—	89.7	2.0
Centrally planned economies	445.0	27.0	901.7	20.0
U.S.S.R.	374.2	22.7	651.0	14.5
Eastern Europe	70.8	4.3	224.0	5.0
China	. . .	—	26.7	0.5
World total	1,650.0	100.0	4,495.6	100.0

— Not applicable.
. . . Zero or negligible.

1972–74		1975–77		Growth rate (annual percentage)		
	Percent-age of world		Percent-age of world	1955–57 to	1966–68 to	1972–74 to
Average	total	Average	total	1966–68	1972–74	1975–77
5,351.8	72.7	5,203.7	67.3	10.1	7.4	−0.9
2,697.7	36.6	2,465.5	31.9	5.9	3.2	−2.3
881.6	12.0	900.4	11.6	—	19.8	0.8
1,699.2	23.1	1,763.3	22.8	—	11.1	1.2
73.3	1.0	74.5	1.0	—	7.2	0.5
265.9	3.6	328.8	4.2	—	15.7	7.3
. . .	—	. . .	—	—	—	—
31.4	0.4	58.9	0.8	—	7.0	23.0
234.5	3.2	269.9	3.5	—	17.4	4.8
1,748.1	23.7	2,204.1	28.5	6.6	11.7	8.0
1,332.3	18.1	1,700.0	22.0	5.2	12.7	8.5
377.5	5.1	445.5	5.8	11.0	9.1	5.7
38.3	0.5	57.6	0.7	—	6.2	14.6
7,365.8	100.0	7,736.6	100.0	9.5	8.6	1.7

Sources: International Rubber Study Group, *Statistical Bulletin*, various issues.

chemical firms dominate synthetic rubber production, whereas tire manufacturers and independent producers account for only about 20 and 10 percent, respectively, of the total. In Japan production of SR is, for all practical purposes, controlled exclusively by petrochemical companies.[4]

Multinational corporations play an important role in the world synthetic rubber industry. Synthetic rubber is produced largely by tire and petrochemical firms that operate simultaneously in several developed countries. Manufacturers of tires and other rubber products, moreover, have set up producing facilities in developing countries, but have so far shown little inclination to establish synthetic rubber plants in these countries. The precise effect of multinational corporations on the world market for SR is difficult to assess now with any degree of precision. Undoubtedly technical and economic factors tend to limit the number of synthetic rubber plants that can be established in any single market, whereas the availability of production technology (particularly for the newer types of SR) tends to favor large existing producers. The present world market for SR is clearly oligopolistic in structure and is characterized normally by only limited price competition among the large producers.

The Natural Rubber Industry

The production of NR, like that of SR, is concentrated in only a few countries. Three major Asian producers—Malaysia, Indonesia, and Thailand—account for 80 percent of the world total. Two other Asian producers—Sri Lanka and India—and two African producers—Liberia and Nigeria—account together for another 12 percent of the world total (Table 2–2).

Within each country, however, a large number of small units produce the NR. Despite its original commercial development as a plantation crop, NR production soon became attractive to smallholders. By the mid-1930s production was split evenly between estates and small-holdings. Today smallholdings account for about 80 percent of the rubber-producing area in the four major Asian rubber-producing countries taken together: about 95 percent of the total rubber area in Thailand, about 80 percent in Indonesia, 65 percent in Malaysia, and

---

4. The single largest independent producer of SR has integrated backward into petrochemicals.

53 percent in Sri Lanka.[5] Smallholdings are also predominant in India and Nigeria. Statistically estates and smallholders are differentiated by an arbitrary cutoff point: holdings of over 40 hectares are usually considered estates. The typical rubber smallholding is only 3 to 5 hectares. Therefore, despite its strong geographic concentration, world natural rubber production is actually spread out over perhaps 1.5 million small units, plus thousands of larger units. In contrast, world production of SR (excluding specialty rubbers) is controlled by just over 100 firms that operate about 300 plants.

Natural rubber production is a technically and economically suitable operation on both estates and smallholdings.

There is no question of rubber being "better" produced by estates than by smallholdings, or vice versa. Both sectors have their distinctive attributes and both are capable of producing rather economically, while providing their owners with fair returns. Estates, because of their size and organization, tend to be the innovators, risk takers, and trend setters; they possess appropriate managerial skills and may be able to take some advantage of economies of scale (though these economies are nowhere near as predominant as the case with the synthetics). Smallholdings, especially when of adequate size and when provided with proper support (advice plus, perhaps, central processing and marketing facilities) can make a vital contribution to the national well-being.[6]

Estate rubber was originally almost totally owned by European companies, but is now mostly nationally owned and operated. European business concerns control about 12 percent of total world production of NR. Another 4 to 5 percent is controlled by the major U.S. tire manufacturers. On the whole, although the major U.S. and Western European tire manufacturers have maintained a sizeable interest in NR, they have not integrated backward into natural rubber production to the extent that they have into synthetic rubber production.

---

5. These percentages were derived from estimates of total area under rubber in 1974–75. During the same years, production statistics, which are more reliable than area statistics, showed that smallholders accounted for 56 percent of total production in western Malaysia, 70 percent in Indonesia, and about 90 percent in Thailand. In these three countries, smallholders accounted for about 65 percent of total production of rubber in 1974–75.

6. Allen, *Natural Rubber and the Synthetics*, p. 74.

Table 2–2. *World Natural Rubber Production,*
by Main Countries and Economic Regions,
1955 to 1977, Selected Averages and Growth Rates
(thousands of metric tons)

Economic region and country	1955–57		1966–68	
	Average	Percent- age of world total	Average	Percent- age of world total
Developing countries	1,823.1	94.9	2,422.0	96.3
Asia[a]	1,682.5	87.6	2,222.7	88.4
Malaysia	691.5	36.0	1,021.2	40.6
Indonesia	714.0	37.3	743.8	29.6
Thailand	134.0	7.0	227.6	9.1
Sri Lanka	97.3	5.0	141.0	5.6
India	23.6	1.2	61.4	2.4
Other[a]	22.1	1.1	27.7	1.1
Africa	111.3	5.8	169.4	6.7
Liberia	39.8	2.1	59.7	2.4
Nigeria	36.6	1.9	61.6	2.4
Zaïre	31.0	1.6	30.0	1.2
Other	3.9	0.2	18.1	0.7
Latin America	29.3	1.5	29.9	1.2
Brazil	23.3	1.2	22.9	0.9
Other	6.0	0.3	7.0	0.3
Centrally planned economies	99.1	5.1	91.8	3.7
China	. . .	—	. . .	—
Vietnam	68.7	3.5	39.7	1.6
Cambodia	30.4	1.6	52.1	2.1
World total[b]	1,922.2	100.0	2,513.8	100.0

— Not applicable.
. . . Zero or negligible.
a. Including Oceania.
b. Including allowance for discrepancies in available statistics.

1972–74		1975–77		Growth rate (annual percentage)		
Average	Percentage of world total	Average	Percentage of world total	1955–57 to 1966–68	1966–68 to 1972–74	1972–74 to 1975–77
3,230.4	98.4	3,423.1	98.0	2.6	4.9	1.6
2,973.5	90.6	3,176.9	90.9	2.6	5.0	1.7
1,457.0	44.4	1,576.9	45.1	3.6	6.1	2.7
838.2	25.5	835.0	23.9	0.4	2.0	−0.1
366.0	11.1	389.2	11.1	4.9	8.2	2.0
142.4	4.3	149.0	4.3	3.4	0.1	1.5
120.2	3.7	145.1	4.2	9.1	11.8	6.5
49.7	1.5	81.7	2.3	2.1	10.2	13.2
224.3	6.8	209.8	6.0	3.9	4.8	−2.2
85.0	2.6	81.7	2.3	3.8	6.1	−1.3
67.2	2.0	59.9	1.7	4.8	1.5	−3.8
39.4	1.2	29.7	0.9	−0.3	4.7	−9.0
32.7	1.0	38.5	1.1	15.0	10.4	5.6
32.6	1.0	36.4	1.0	0.2	1.5	3.8
22.6	0.7	20.7	0.6	−0.2	−0.2	−2.9
10.0	0.3	15.7	0.4	1.4	6.1	5.0
52.5	1.6	70.7	2.0	−0.7	−8.9	10.4
15.0	0.5	26.6	0.8	—	—	21.0
21.0	0.6	29.1	0.8	−4.9	−10.1	11.5
16.5	0.5	15.0	0.4	5.0	−17.4	−3.1
3,356.7	100.0	3,493.8	100.0	2.5	4.5	2.1

Sources: International Rubber Study Group, *Statistical Bulletin*, various issues; FAO, *Production Yearbook*, various issues; and World Bank, Economic Analysis and Projections Department.

Recent Trends in the World Rubber Economy

From 1948 to 1973 total world consumption of rubber increased steadily at an average rate of 6.3 percent a year (Figure 2–1). This growth followed closely the growth of world industrial production, especially in industrialized countries. The recovery of industrial production in general, and of automotive production in particular, after the end of World War II created a strong demand for elastomers and propelled the world rubber economy into a period of rapid and steady growth.

Figure 2–1. *World Consumption of Rubber, 1946 to 1978*

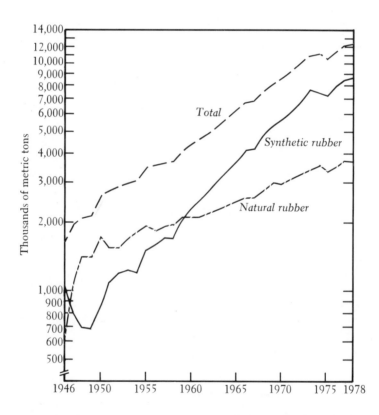

Note: Semilog growth rates for 1948–73: synthetic rubber, 9.3 percent per year; natural rubber, 3.3 percent per year; and natural and synthetic rubber, 6.3 percent per year.

Consumption and production

In the developed countries rubber use during the past thirty years grew about 6 percent a year. Rubber demand grew at an even faster rate in centrally planned economies and developing countries—7 and 10 percent a year, respectively—but from a much smaller initial base. Developed countries now account for 63 percent of total world rubber consumption, centrally planned economies for 25 percent, and developing countries for the remaining 12 percent (Table 2–3).

Within the developed countries, the use of rubber increased faster in Japan and Western Europe than in North America, closely reflecting the different rates of the increase of motor vehicle use in these regions.[7] During the past thirty years, the use of motor vehicles advanced more rapidly in Japan and Western Europe than in North America, where the process had started much earlier and had achieved high levels by the end of World War II.[8] Within the centrally planned economies, rubber use increased faster in Eastern Europe than in the U.S.S.R., although this trend has been reversed in the past few years, following the decision in the U.S.S.R. to increase automobile production for private use. Apparently, rubber consumption also increased quite rapidly in China during the 1950s and the 1960s, but the available data show that both the aggregate and the per capita levels of rubber use are still rather low. Despite the uncertainty that surrounds the available statistics on China, it is clear that both automotive and industrial use of rubber in this country are strictly controlled by the government and are kept to a bare minimum to save foreign exchange.[9]

---

7. Throughout this study the term "North America" refers to the United States and Canada only.

8. In 1950, for example, the number of cars for every 1,000 inhabitants was 265 in the United States, 139 in Canada, 21 in Western Europe, and 1 in Japan. By 1973 the number of cars for every 1,000 inhabitants had increased to 481 in the United States, 355 in Canada (at an average annual rate of 2.6 and 4.3 percent, respectively), 216 in Western Europe, and 134 in Japan (an average annual rate of 10.7 and 23.5 percent, respectively).

9. Domestic production of both NR and SR is very small in China: an estimated 25,000 metric tons a year of NR and 60,000 metric tons a year of SR. This country relies on imports of SR and, most importantly, of NR to meet its domestic needs. Efforts are now being made to expand the domestic production of rubber, but actual and potential needs appear to be much too high to be met totally by domestic production.

Table 2–3. *World Elastomer Use,*
by Main Countries and Economic Regions,
1955 to 1977, Selected Averages and Growth Rates
(thousands of metric tons)

	1955–57		1966–68	
Economic region and country	*Average*	*Percentage of world total*	*Average*	*Percentage of world total*
Developed countries	2,639.6	75.0	4,895.0	69.5
North America	1,590.1	45.2	2,460.0	34.9
Japan	118.2	3.4	519.0	7.4
Western Europe	837.5	23.8	1,765.0	25.1
Other	93.8	2.7	151.0	2.1
Developing countries	207.2	5.9	598.7	8.5
Latin America	125.6	3.6	295.0	4.2
Asia	74.9	2.1	246.2	3.5
Africa	2.0	0.1	12.5	0.2
Middle East	4.7	0.1	45.0	0.6
Centrally planned economies	673.0	19.1	1,517.0	21.5
U.S.S.R.	460.0	13.1	900.0	12.8
Eastern Europe	156.0	4.4	410.0	5.8
China	57.0	1.6	207.0	2.9
World total	3,518.0	100.0	7,044.0	100.0

Sources: International Rubber Study Group, *Statistical Bulletin,* various issues; FAO, *Trade Yearbook,* various issues; and World Bank, Economic Analysis and Projections Department.

1972–74		1975–77		Growth rate (annual percentage)		
Average	Percent-age of world total	Average	Percent-age of world total	1955–57 to 1966–68	1966–68 to 1972–74	1972–74 to 1975–77
7,121.0	67.0	7,084.0	62.5	5.8	6.5	−0.2
3,268.1	30.7	3,203.5	28.3	4.0	4.8	−0.7
957.3	9.0	946.7	8.4	14.4	10.7	−0.4
2,655.8	25.0	2,699.3	23.8	7.0	7.0	0.5
239.8	2.3	234.5	2.0	4.4	8.0	−0.7
1,147.3	10.8	1,339.2	11.8	10.1	11.4	5.3
541.5	5.1	606.7	5.4	8.1	10.6	3.9
471.5	4.4	570.5	5.0	11.4	11.4	6.5
48.2	0.5	64.3	0.6	18.1	25.0	10.1
86.1	0.8	97.7	0.8	22.8	11.4	4.3
2,366.7	22.2	2,883.3	25.5	7.7	7.7	6.8
1,465.8	13.8	1,796.2	15.9	6.3	8.5	7.0
634.2	5.9	777.1	6.9	9.2	7.5	7.0
266.7	2.5	310.0	2.7	9.2	4.3	5.1
10,635.0	100.0	11,327.8	100.0	6.5	7.1	2.1

After recovering rapidly from the slump induced by war, world production of NR more than doubled between 1946 and 1950, and then grew during the next twenty years at the modest rate of slightly less than 3 percent a year. The years between the wars had left the natural rubber industry with a production capacity that was well below the needs of the postwar market. The rapid expansion in the use of motor vehicles in Western Europe and Japan, as well as its spread to practically all areas of the world in the 1950s and 1960s, created a demand for elastomers that NR was unable to meet. World elastomer demand increased more than 6 percent a year between 1948 and 1973, whereas natural rubber production grew less than 3 percent a year during the same period. The gap in demand was filled by the synthetic rubber industry, whose output, after some initial adjustment difficulties in the period immediately following the war, expanded rapidly from 1949 onward and continued to grow about 9 percent a year until the early 1970s (Figure 2–2).

The onset of the Korean War and the consequent renewed fears of a possible rubber shortage similar to the one experienced during World War II stimulated the recovery of synthetic rubber produc-

Figure 2–2.   World Production of Rubber, 1946 to 1978

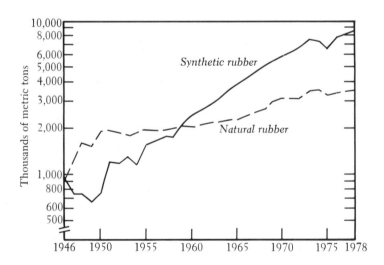

Note: Semilog growth rates for 1948–73: synthetic rubber, 9.3 percent per year; and natural rubber, 2.8 percent per year.

tion in North America. It also reinforced the U.S. government's decision to maintain a large domestic synthetic rubber industry under private ownership. Technological breakthroughs in SBR production and processing in the early 1950s, namely cold polymerization and oil extension, improved the quality and production profitability of this major type of general purpose SR.

The major reason for the rapid expansion of the synthetic rubber industry throughout the 1950s, however, was the growth of world demand for elastomers, which NR could not meet. Once launched on a large scale and firmly placed under private ownership, the world synthetic rubber industry continued to grow at a fast rate, supported by a massive research, development, and marketing effort.

Commercial production of SR spread from the United States to Western Europe, and subsequently to Japan. Until the mid-1950s practically all SR outside the centrally planned economies was produced in North America (see Table 2–1). Western Europe began to produce SR on a large scale in the early 1960s, whereas Japanese production began on a significant scale only in the mid-1960s. By 1966–68, North America, with about 50 percent of the total, still dominated world synthetic rubber production, but its share had dropped more than 20 percent below the levels of the mid-1950s. By then Western Europe produced 20 percent of world total, and Japan about 7 percent. These trends continued into the late 1960s and early 1970s. By 1975–77 North America's share of world synthetic rubber production had dropped to 32 percent, whereas that of Western Europe and Japan had risen to 23 and 12 percent, respectively.

Within the centrally planned economies, which account together for about 29 percent of world total production, the U.S.S.R. still holds the predominant position, followed by Eastern Europe, and then by China, whose production is still extremely small. Synthetic rubber production did not spread to developing countries until the middle-to-late 1960s. It began in Brazil and India almost at the same time, and subsequently spread to Argentina and Mexico. Developing countries today still produce only about 4 percent of the world total of synthetic rubber, and production is still concentrated in a few countries: Brazil, Mexico, Argentina, India, and Korea.

On a global basis, the trends in consumption of NR and SR after World War II closely reflected trends in production: natural rubber use increased at an average annual rate of 3.3 percent between 1948 and 1973, whereas the use of SR increased during the same period

Figure 2-3. *Natural Rubber Market Shares, 1950 to 1978*

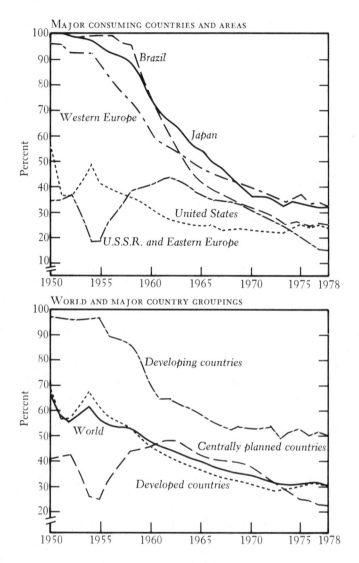

at 9.3 percent a year (see Figures 2–1 and 2–2).[10] Consequently the share of NR in the world market for new rubbers decreased from 57.3 percent in 1951–53 to 32.7 percent in 1971–73. The market share of NR declined sooner and farther in the United States than in Western Europe or Japan, but the advances of SR were common to developed countries, centrally planned economies, and developing countries (Figure 2–3).[11]

Compared with the dynamic growth of the synthetic rubber industry in terms of volume, geographic spread, and innovation (several new types of SR were developed and produced commercially during the postwar period), the 3 percent a year growth of the world natural rubber industry in the postwar period may appear to have been quite modest. The Asian countries, which shaped this trend, maintained their predominant position as the major source of natural rubber supply, and no new large-scale producer emerged on the world scene.[12] Yet, despite the appearance of only modest growth and of no major change in the location of the industry, the postwar period was one of steady progress for the natural rubber industry.

The advances of synthetic rubbers eventually were slowed. The natural rubber industry, far from shrinking passively under the burden of a seemingly overwhelming challenge, reacted positively to it in several ways. Research into high-yielding varieties of trees continued, as well as replanting with higher-yielding clones in some key producing countries of Asia, such as Malaysia, Indonesia, and Thailand. Cultural practices were improved, and the natural rubber production process was rationalized.

As a consequence of replantings, new plantings with more productive varieties of rubber trees, and improvements in cultural practices, natural rubber yields increased dramatically from the mid-1950s to the mid-1970s. Although the productivity gains were not evenly distributed among producers, they were widespread enough across coun-

10. Although production apparently increased only 2.8 percent a year during the same period, in actual fact the rates of growth of production and consumption must have been virtually the same. The discrepancy is attributed to inaccuracies in the data, particularly in the earlier years.

11. The problem of competition between the two rubber industries is examined in detail in Chapter 3.

12. Asia (including the Asian centrally planned economies) accounted for 92.9 percent of world production in 1955–57, Africa for 6 percent, and Latin America for 1.1 percent. In 1975–77 the production share of Asia still was 91 percent, that of Africa 6.0 percent, and that of Latin America 1.0 percent (see Table 2–2).

Table 2–4. *Natural Rubber Yields in Major Producing Countries, 1930 to 1973, Selected Years* (pounds per acre)

Year	Malaysia		Indonesia, estates[a]	Thailand, total	Sri Lanka, total	India	
	Estates	Small-holders				Estates	Small-holders
1930[a]	380	n.a.	375	n.a.	350	205	n.a.
1950	510	n.a.	560	n.a.	412	n.a.	n.a.
1955	490	385	527	n.a.	361	n.a.	n.a.
1960	677	389	450	312	417	440	187
1965	850	526	495	337	560	603	257
1970	1,060	671	631	393	707	781	467
1973	1,273	826	612	475	694	899	564

n.a. Not available.
a. Imputed yields are calculated on the basis of volume of production and area in tapping.
Sources: Bauer, *The Rubber Industry: A Study in Competition and Monopoly;* World Bank, Economic Analysis and Projections Department.

tries and producing sectors (estates and smallholders) (Table 2–4) to allow NR to withstand the market pressures caused by continuously falling synthetic rubber prices. The long-term payoffs of the research into the development of higher-yielding varieties of trees and of the effort made to ensure their acceptance and commercial adoption are still to be reaped to a large extent. The success of this process of technical innovation and of its continuing spread throughout the industry is clear, however, and demonstrates the enormous potential of research and development to ensure a future for agricultural products that compete against synthetic substitutes.

The competitive standing of NR in relation to SR was also improved by the introduction in the mid-1960s of technically specified rubber grades for NR: that is, rubber whose quality is determined by rigorous technical tests. At the same time new processes for producing dry rubber were introduced, which generally involved the mechanical conversion of the artificial or natural rubber coagulum into granules instead of the traditional sheets. This produced block rubber, which was then graded by the new method. In less than ten years exports of technically specified block rubber accounted for over one-third of total rubber exports.[13] Apart from being rigorously specified in its quality, which facilitates the choice of the user, the new block rubber also began to be packaged in small bales (much like SR) usually bulked into pallets and often was transported in container ships. These rubbers save transport, handling, and storage costs for both producers and users. Aside from the direct economic and commercial advantages that natural rubber exporters gained by introducing technically specified rubber, the credibility of NR as a dependable raw material capable of being transformed and improved to meet market needs was also increased. The natural rubber industry clearly demonstrated its ability to meet the changing requirements of the marketplace.

Chemical yield stimulation of rubber trees was another important technical innovation. The possible use of synthetic vegetal hormones (principally 2-4-D and 2-4-5-T acid-based stimulants) to increase rubber yield was researched for a long period. A breakthrough came with the discovery of chemical ethylene-based stimulants that increase cellular permeability and therefore prolong the flow of latex.[14]

---

13. See the next section, "Trade," and Table SA-7.

14. Ethrel (2-chloroethyl phosphoric acid-CEP) is the most common kind of ethylene-generating stimulant now in use.

The effect of ethylene-based stimulants on yield is quite dramatic, particularly on low-yielding material, where yield is increased by as much as 100 percent. The commercial use of ethylene-generating stimulants has proceeded rather slowly since their discovery in the early 1970s, both because of the uncertainties that still exist about the possible influence of the continuous use of these stimulants on the productive life of the tree and because of the organizational problems connected with their widespread use. As a result, chemical stimulants have so far been applied to relatively old trees (fifteen years old or older), and almost exclusively by estates.[15] Although the total potential effect of chemical stimulation on natural production is not yet known, the use of chemical stimulants offers a further possibility for productivity increases, particularly in the smallholders' sector. It also gives natural rubber producers a greater measure of short-term supply flexibility, which should reduce the volatility of natural rubber prices.

Practically all these changes—as well as many others in internal marketing, technical assistance to natural rubber producers and users, and promotion—were initiated by Malaysia, which also led in implementing them. Other producing countries contributed directly or indirectly, and so did international organizations. Throughout this period natural rubber producers showed a remarkable degree of mutual cooperation and singlemindedness in their efforts to conserve and restructure their industry. The world natural rubber economy went through a period in which retrenchment and reorganization proceeded together, and during which real long-term progress was made despite enormous difficulties.

Trade

Natural rubber is a typical export commodity: about 90 percent of the world production is exported. Only a small—even if growing—percentage of total production is used in the main producing countries: 8.5 percent in 1972–74, compared with 2.5 percent in 1952–54.

---

15. In 1973 about 400,000 acres of Malaysian estate rubber (more than 30 percent of mature acreage) was reported to be under Ethrel stimulation. As a consequence of a ban imposed by the government to reduce output in order to stabilize rubber prices, estate rubber acreage under chemical stimulation dropped substantially in 1975. Use of Ethrel is also reported to be widespread in the Indonesian estate sector. In Thailand and Sri Lanka, on the contrary, the use of chemical stimulants is still extremely limited.

On the contrary, synthetic rubbers are used mostly in the producing countries: only about 25 percent of world production is exported.

The major natural rubber producers—Malaysia, Indonesia, Thailand, and Sri Lanka—are also the major exporters. Malaysia accounts for 50 percent of world total exports, Indonesia for 26 percent, Thailand for 12 percent, and Sri Lanka for 5 percent. Export trends for NR in the post-war period have paralleled production trends. Within the Asia exporters' group, Malaysia and Thailand, whose production of NR grew faster than the average, increased their export shares at the expense of Indonesia and Sri Lanka. On the whole, Asia maintained its predominant position as the main source of natural rubber exports, with 94 percent of world total. The remainder continued to come from Africa (Table 2–5).

Developed countries are still the main importers of NR, but their import share has decreased substantially during the past twenty years, from 82 percent in 1955–57 to 67 percent in 1972–74. This declining trend, however, appears to have abated in recent years, largely because of the increased demand for NR resulting from the introduction of radial tires in North America and Japan; the share of the world total declined only fractionally in those two regions between 1972–74 and 1975–77.[16] Developing countries, on the other hand, continuously increased their relative intake of natural rubber imports, from 6 percent in 1955–57 to 11 percent in 1975–77. The share of total world imports of NR by centrally planned economies doubled between the mid-1950s and the mid-1960s. This increase in imports has slowed down considerably in recent years, however, because of a strong drive toward more domestic production of isoprenic synthetic rubber (polyisoprene).[17] The share of NR imports to centrally planned economies, after increasing from 12.6 percent in 1955–57 to 26.8 percent in 1966–68, declined to 22 percent in 1975–77 (see Table 2–5).

World trade of SR is not only relatively small in relation to production, but is also heavily concentrated in developed producing countries. Developed countries account for 84 percent of world exports and 69 percent of world imports. Most of world trade in SR is among developed producers. The United States, traditionally the

16. Radial tires were first developed and commercially introduced in Western Europe in the mid-1960s. They were introduced in North America and Japan on a large scale only in the early 1970s. Radial tires require a higher percentage of NR in the total rubber mix than bias-ply or bias-belted tires. See Chapter 3 and Appendix A.

17. This trend seems to be particularly strong in the U.S.S.R.; see Chapter 5.

Table 2–5. *World Natural Rubber Exports and Imports,*
by Main Countries and Economic Regions,
1955 to 1977, Selected Averages and Growth Rates
(thousands of metric tons)

Economic region and country	1955–57		1966–68	
	Average	Percent-age of world total	Average	Percent-age of world total
Exports				
Developing countries	1,758.6	94.9	2,304.6	96.4
Asia	1,645.4	88.8	2,138.4	89.5
Malaysia	701.0	37.8	1,076.7	45.1
Indonesia	696.4	37.6	686.5	28.7
Thailand	133.2	7.2	221.9	9.3
Sri Lanka	94.2	5.1	135.0	5.6
Others	20.6	1.1	18.3	0.8
Africa	111.2	6.0	165.2	6.9
Latin America	2.0	0.1	1.0	—
Developed countries	. . .	—	. . .	—
Centrally planned economies	95.4	5.1	85.1	3.6
World total	1,854.0	100.0	2,389.7	100.0
Imports				
Developing countries	107.2	5.8	176.3	7.4
Asia	26.1	1.4	78.2	3.3
Africa	5.0	0.3	19.7	0.8
Latin America	76.1	4.1	78.4	3.3
Developed countries	1,516.1	81.7	1,563.3	65.8
Western Europe	697.4	37.6	763.2	32.1
North America	633.4	34.1	485.6	20.4
Japan	112.5	6.1	243.3	10.2
Others	72.8	3.9	71.2	3.0
Centrally planned economies	233.4	12.6	636.9	26.8
Eastern Europe	86.8	4.7	167.8	7.1
U.S.S.R.	87.4	4.7	287.4	12.1
China	59.2	3.2	181.7	7.6
World total	1,856.7	100.0	2,376.5	100.0

— Not applicable.
. . . Zero or negligible.
a. Including allowance for discrepancies in available statistics.
Sources: International Rubber Study Group, *Statistical Bulletin*, various issues; and
FAO, *Trade Yearbook*, various issues.

1972–74		1975–77		Growth rate (annual percentage)		
Average	Percentage of world total	Average	Percentage of world total	1955–57 to 1966–68	1966–68 to 1972–74	1972–74 to 1975–77
2,980.6	98.8	3,058.2	98.7	2.5	4.4	0.9
2,779.3	92.1	2,878.0	92.9	2.2	4.5	1.2
1,484.3	49.1	1,537.0	49.6	4.0	5.5	1.2
790.0	26.2	800.0	25.8	−0.1	2.4	0.4
352.6	11.7	370.6	12.0	4.7	8.0	1.7
132.3	4.4	144.1	4.7	3.3	−0.3	2.9
20.1	0.7	26.3	0.8	−1.1	1.6	9.4
201.3	6.7	180.2	5.8	3.7	3.3	−3.6
. . .	—	. . .	—	—	—	—
35.6	1.2	39.8	1.3	−1.0	−13.5	3.8
3,033.7[a]	100.0	3,097.5[a]	100.0	2.3	4.1	0.9
281.7	9.3	341.1	10.9	4.6	8.1	6.6
125.8	4.1	119.1	3.8	10.5	8.2	−1.8
23.3	0.8	67.2	2.2	13.3	2.8	42.0
132.6	4.4	154.8	4.9	0.3	9.1	5.3
2,046.2	67.4	2,097.4	67.1	0.3	4.6	0.6
923.0	30.4	906.6	29.0	0.8	3.2	−0.6
691.0	22.8	787.1	25.2	−2.3	6.0	4.4
321.8	10.6	298.9	9.6	7.3	4.8	−2.5
109.5	3.6	104.8	3.3	−0.2	7.8	−1.4
706.3	23.3	686.5	22.0	9.5	1.7	1.0
223.2	7.4	233.8	7.5	6.2	4.9	1.6
268.6	8.8	216.4	6.9	11.4	−1.1	−7.0
214.5	7.1	236.3	7.6	10.7	2.8	3.3
3,034.2	100.0	3,125.0	100.0	2.3	4.2	1.0

Figure 2–4. *Price Trends of Rubber, 1947 to 1978*

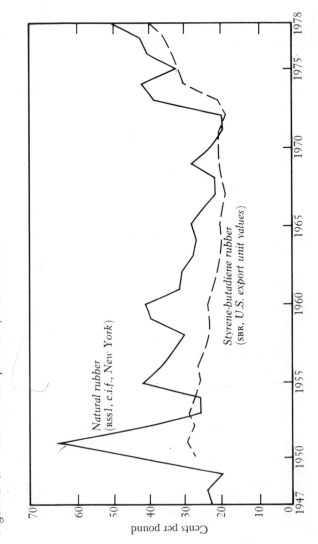

largest single net exporter of sr, has in recent years been replaced by Japan. The ec is also a net, although small, exporting area. Developing countries are the only net importing group. Centrally planned economies are largely self-sufficient in sr. The U.S.S.R. and the German Democratic Republic, the two largest single producers, are also the main net exporters within the centrally planned economies. China is a small net importer of sr (Table 2–6).

Prices

Natural rubber prices fluctuated considerably after World War II.[18] Natural rubber is sold in international markets under conditions approaching perfect competition. Changes in the balance of supply and demand, as well as in expectations which may be affected by strikes in the major consuming industries (automobile and tire industries), transport difficulties, and political uncertainties influence the market price of nr. Natural rubber demand is quite insensitive to price changes in the short term,[19] but is more sensitive to changes in economic activity.[20] Natural rubber supply, moreover, is also very insensitive to price movements in the short term.[21] This low price elasticity of demand and supply causes natural rubber prices to fluctuate widely in the short term whenever changes in economic activity induce even relatively small shifts in demand or when the flow of supply is reduced temporarily.

After World War II there were four major price peaks when natural rubber prices rose substantially above trend: 1950–51, 1955, 1959–60, and 1973–74 (Figure 2–4). The 1950–51 and 1973–74 peaks can largely be attributed to "exogenous" factors: the Korean War and the oil crisis.[22] The 1955 and 1959–60 price peaks, however, represent a

18. Between 1955 and 1977 the average percentage deviations from the three- and five-year moving average were 8.5 and 13.4 percent, respectively (annual price data in constant 1977 U.S. dollars were used to derive the fluctuation index).

19. Short-term price elasticities of natural rubber demand are of the order of from −0.2 to −0.3.

20. Income elasticities of natural rubber demand are of the order of from 0.6 to 0.8.

21. Short-term price elasticities of natural rubber production are of the order of from 0.1 to 0.2.

22. Import demand for nr was strong in 1973, because of the simultaneous boom in industrial production in all the major developed countries. In 1974, however, prices remained high, even though world demand remained stagnant.

Table 2–6. *World Synthetic Rubber Exports and Imports,*
by Main Countries and Economic Regions,
1955 to 1977, Selected Averages and Growth Rates
(thousands of metric tons)

Economic region and country	1955–57		1966–68	
	Average	Percentage of world total	Average	Percentage of world total
Exports				
Developed countries	234.7	78.9	925.3	87.2
Western Europe	1.8	0.6	431.3	40.7
North America	232.9	78.3	424.8	40.0
Japan	. . .	—	65.2	6.1
Other	. . .	—	4.0	0.4
Developing countries	. . .	—	9.0	0.9
Centrally planned economies	62.9	21.1	126.7	11.9
Eastern Europe	40.4	13.6	74.3	7.0
U.S.S.R.	22.5	7.5	52.4	4.9
World total	297.6	100.0	1,061.0	100.0
Imports				
Developed countries	198.3	67.7	761.1	73.3
Western Europe	151.9	51.8	584.4	56.3
North America	15.5	5.3	91.4	8.8
Japan	9.6	3.3	52.4	5.0
Other	21.3	7.3	32.9	3.2
Developing countries	23.1	7.9	142.3	13.7
Asia	3.6	1.2	29.7	2.9
Africa	1.0	0.4	24.4	2.3
Latin America	18.5	6.3	88.2	8.5
Centrally planned economies	71.6	24.4	134.9	13.0
Eastern Europe	46.1	15.7	90.6	8.7
U.S.S.R.	25.5	8.7	34.7	3.4
China	. . .	—	9.6	0.9
World total	293.0	100.0	1,038.3	100.0

— Not applicable.
. . . Zero or negligible.
Sources: International Rubber Study Group, *Statistical Bulletin,* various issues; and
OECD, *Trade by Commodities: Exports,* various issues.

1972–74		1975–77		Growth rate (annual percentage)		
Average	Percentage of world total	Average	Percentage of world total	1955–57 to 1966–68	1966–68 to 1972–74	1972–74 to 1975–77
1,570.5	85.9	1,590.2	83.7	13.3	9.2	0.4
936.0	51.1	969.9	51.0	64.5	13.8	1.2
374.6	20.6	343.1	18.1	5.6	−2.1	−2.9
254.1	13.9	273.0	14.4	—	25.4	2.4
5.8	0.3	4.2	0.2	—	6.4	−10.2
43.5	2.3	33.5	1.7	—	30.0	−8.3
215.1	11.8	277.1	14.6	6.6	9.2	8.8
128.2	7.0	151.6	8.0	5.7	9.5	5.7
86.9	4.8	125.5	6.6	8.0	8.8	13.0
1,829.1	100.0	1,900.8	100.0	12.3	9.5	1.3
1,347.2	73.6	1,328.1	69.3	13.0	10.0	−0.5
1,053.8	57.6	1,034.9	54.7	13.0	10.3	−0.6
205.3	11.2	211.3	11.2	17.5	14.4	1.0
25.5	1.4	21.9	1.2	16.7	−11.3	−4.9
62.6	3.4	60.0	2.2	4.0	11.3	−1.4
301.1	16.5	322.5	17.1	18.0	13.3	2.3
100.5	5.5	122.8	6.5	21.1	22.0	6.2
77.5	4.2	85.1	4.5	33.7	21.0	3.2
123.1	6.8	114.6	6.1	12.8	5.7	−2.4
181.7	9.9	258.1	13.6	5.9	5.1	12.4
139.7	7.6	189.8	10.0	6.3	7.5	10.8
27.2	1.5	57.1	3.0	2.8	−3.9	28.0
14.8	0.8	11.2	0.6	—	7.5	−8.8
1,830.0	100.0	1,890.0	100.0	12.2	9.9	1.1

more direct market response to boom conditions of demand: world motor vehicle production increased by 34 percent in 1955, by 22 percent in 1959, and by 18 percent again in 1960.

In the oligopolistic market for synthetic rubber prices are very stable in the short run. This price stability has been an additional factor that has helped these rubbers to penetrate the market. Prices of SBR and of most other SR's have steadily declined over time. The only break in this long-term trend occurred in 1973–74, when the oil crisis drastically increased the cost of the chemical monomers used to produce SBR. Prices have since risen moderately following the pace set by input costs. The prices of SR are still stable in the short term.

From the early 1950s, when production of SR began on a large scale, to the early 1970s, the trend in natural rubber prices continued to decline. The main cause was the steady fall of synthetic rubber prices brought about by economies of scale and by technical progress in the world synthetic rubber industry. As SR became progressively more and more important in world markets, its prices set the overall trend, and natural rubber producers became, to a large extent, price takers. The structure of the synthetic rubber industry is such that prices can be quite differentiated between regional and specific use markets. For this reason, a "world price," even for a specific type of SR, is almost impossible to reconstruct. For SBR, however, the long-run trend in world prices is approximated reasonably well by the trend in U.S. export unit values (see Figure 2–4). The available empirical evidence confirms the hypothesis that the declining trend in natural rubber prices from the early 1950s to the early 1970s was influenced by the decline in general purpose synthetic rubber prices.[23]

As previously observed, a sharp break in the natural rubber price trend occurred in 1973–74 as a consequence of the oil crisis and the subsequent sharp rise in crude oil prices. Both the short- and the long-run cost curves of the natural and synthetic rubber industries were affected substantially, and the interaction between the prices of NR and SR has now shifted to a different and higher trend level.

23. See I. Haque, "Analysis of Natural Rubber Market," World Bank Staff Working Paper, no. 133 (Washington, D.C.: The World Bank, August 1972), pp. 6–8; and more recently Charles River Associates and Wharton Econometric Forecasting Associates, *Forecasts and Analysis of the Rubber Market* (submitted to the Office of Stockpile Disposal, GSA, Washington, D.C., 1974) (processed), p. 60; and Enzo Grilli, Ray Helterline, and Peter Pollak, "An Econometric Model of the World Rubber Economy," World Bank Commodity Staff Paper, no. 3, January 1979, pp. 27–29.

3

•❉••

Market Interaction between Natural and Synthetic Rubbers

In order to analyze the market interaction between natural rubber (NR) and synthetic rubber (SR), it is necessary first to know the similarities and differences between the two kinds of rubber and to be familiar with their major uses. Then the particular factors affecting their demand, the competitive relation between the two, and the behavior of the market share of NR can be better understood.

The Main Kinds of Rubber

All rubbers are (high) polymers and possess distinctive chemical structures that enable them to be transformed into materials having the property of "rubberiness." They differ, however, in their basic properties (such as tensile strength, elongation at break, and resilience) and, above all, in their processing behavior and end-product performance.

Natural rubber

Natural rubber is a fairly homogenous commodity. Its qualities and product performance are well known, and it still is the reference point for man-made elastomers. Natural rubber has high resilience and tensile strength and low heat buildup. Its resistance to impact, abrasion, and tear are excellent. Natural rubber, however, is not very resistant to environmental factors, such as oxidation and ozone. It also has low resistance to chemicals, such as gasoline, kerosene, benzol, degreasers, solvents, synthetic lubricants, and hydraulic fluids. Because of its physical and resistance properties, NR is preferred for the manufacture of products that require high strength and low heat generation (for example, airplane tires, giant truck tires, and off-the-road vehicles' tires) and engineering products which require high fatigue resistance.

Traditionally, NR has been traded in sheets whose quality is evaluated by visual inspection. There are six different grades of ribbed smoked sheets: RSS1 to RSS6. The no. 1 grade (RSS1) is the highest quality variety of traded rubber sheets, followed by RSS2, RSS3, and so on. Historically, RSS1 was also the most widely traded variety of rubber. In the past two decades, however, its relative importance has diminished considerably, particularly in relation to RSS3, which is the standard kind of NR used in tires. In addition to sheets, NR is also traded as crepes. There are six standard kinds of crepes: pale, estate brown, thin brown, thick blanket, flat bark, and pure smoked blanket. Each kind of crepe, except the last one, is subdivided into different grades.[1] All rubber crepes, like the sheets, are visually graded. Sheets and pale crepes are prepared from coagulated field latex. Estate brown, thin brown, thick blanket, and flat bark crepes are prepared from remilled sheets.

As previously mentioned, block rubber was introduced by Malaysia in the mid-1960s. The quality of block rubber is determined by more rigorous and technical tests, and unlike rubber sheets and crepes, the quality of block rubber is specified and guaranteed. The example of Malaysia was followed by other countries: Singapore, Indonesia, and more recently Sri Lanka, Thailand, Liberia, Nigeria, Ivory Coast, and Cameroon. In 1977 exports of technically specified rubber accounted for 39 percent of total world exports (see Table SA–7).

According to the Standard Malaysian Rubber (SMR) scheme, there are four basic grades of block rubber (SMR5, SMR10, SMR20M, and SMR50) and two special grades (SMR5L and SMREQ). For each grade, the dirt content, ash content, volatile matter content, nitrogen content, plasticity, and color are rigorously specified.[2] The SMR scheme

---

1. See "International Standards of Quality and Packing for Natural Rubber," International Rubber Quality and Packing Conference, 1969. (This publication is commonly known as "The Green Book.")

2. The numbers refer to the maximum allowable dirt content expressed in percentages: 0.05 percent, 0.10 percent, 0.20 percent, and 0.50 percent. In the recently revised SMR scheme (see revisions to SMR scheme 1979, SMR Bulletin no. 9) improvements in all the specified properties have been introduced to provide for more uniform processability; raw materials for each grade have been specified,

also specifies the size of the rubber block, as well as its packaging.[3] Following the Malaysian example, various countries now use standardization and quality control schemes. After the SMR scheme, the largest of these schemes are the Standard Indonesian Rubber (SIR), followed by the Specified Singapore Rubber and the Thai Technical Rubber. In addition to the basic and special grades of technically specified rubber, several kinds of modified natural rubber have also become available.[4]

Although most natural rubber is shipped as dry rubber, it can also be shipped in the liquid latex form. In 1975 about 8.5 percent of total world rubber exports were latex. Latex is used mostly in carpets, dipping, adhesives, thread, and foam.

Synthetic rubber

There are many kinds of synthetic rubber available on the market.[5] The detailed statistics on worldwide consumption, which have become available in recent years, clearly show that seven main kinds of SR dominate the market in terms of tonnage, accounting for about 98 percent of all SR and for about 66 percent of all rubber consumed

---

and regrading of rubbers under the scheme has been carefully restricted. The specifications for top quality rubbers would include an additional cure feature, which will be more helpful to the customer. Finally, the revised scheme introduces a completely new grade of SMR: the general purpose, or GD, rubber. This grade will have specified raw materials (including latex, sheet, and field coagulum), low levels of dirt content, controlled Mooney viscosity levels, and declared vulcanized features.

3. The literature on the SMR scheme is vast. See Rubber Research Institute of Malaysia, *Proceedings of the RRI Planters' Conferences* (Kuala Lumpur: RRI, 1971–75). The processing and grading of NR in Malaysia is well described and analyzed in Pee Teck Yew and Ani bin Arope, *Rubber Owners' Manual* (Kuala Lumpur: RRIM, 1976), pp. 161–77.

4. The two most important kinds, from the standpoint of volume, are viscosity stabilized natural rubber (SMRCV), developed to deal with the hardening of NR, and superior processing natural rubber (SP), developed to improve the mixing properties of NR. Other kinds are: a special tire rubber, which does not require mastication before mixing and was specifically designed for the tire industry, and an oil-extended natural rubber (OENR), which contains from 20 to 40 percent oil and which is used in winter tires.

5. A more detailed analysis of the technical, economic, and end-use characteristics of the seven most important kinds of SR is included in Appendix A.

Table 3–1. *World Rubber Consumption, by Kind of Rubber, 1977*

Kind of rubber	Thousands of metric tons	Percentage of synthetic rubber	Percentage of total rubber
Synthetic rubber			
Styrene-butadiene (SBR)	3,328	58.3	38.3
Polybutadiene (BR)	895	15.7	10.3
Polyisoprene (IR)	208	3.6	2.4
Ethylene-propylene (EPM-EPDM)	290	5.1	3.3
Polychloroprene (CR)	318	5.6	3.7
Butyl (IIR)	386	6.8	4.4
Nitrile (NBR)	190	3.3	2.2
Other synthetic	91	1.6	1.1
Total	5,706	100.0	65.7
Natural rubber	2,984	—	34.3
Total rubber	8,690	—	100.0

Note: Excluding centrally planned economies.
— Not applicable.
Sources: International Institute of Synthetic Rubber Producers (IISRP), private communication; and International Rubber Study Group, *Statistical Bulletin.*

outside the centrally planned economies (Table 3–1).[6] Styrene-butadiene (SBR), polybutadiene (BR), and polyisoprene (IR) are commonly classified as the general purpose SR.[7] Ethylene-propylene rubbers (EPM-EPDM), polychloroprene rubber (CR), nitrile rubber (NBR), and butyl rubber (IIR), together with the large number of rubbers manufactured in small tonnage amounts and grouped under "other synthetic," are classified as specialty rubbers.[8] This classifica-

6. The International Institute of Synthetic Rubber Producers (IISRP) began to publish world production and consumption figures in 1973.
7. The other general purpose rubber is NR.
8. In terms of historical development, these seven main kinds of SR can be divided into two main classes: (a) first generation synthetic rubbers (styrene-butadiene, polychloroprene, butyl, and nitrile) developed before World War II; (b) second generation or stereoregular rubbers (polybutadiene, polyisoprene, and ethylene-propylene) developed in the 1950s. The development of solution SBR, which also is stereoregular, is more recent. See American Chemical Society, *Chemistry in the Economy* (Washington, D.C.: American Chemical Society, 1973), pp. 126–37.

tion, although quite accepted in practice,[9] is far from being unambiguous: how "special" EPM-EPDM rubbers are is still uncertain, and how "general" BR is, is certainly a matter of interpretation.[10]

Another classification was recently adopted by P. W. Allen, and distinguishes rubbers by the tonnage consumed.[11] Large-tonnage SR's include SBR, BR, IR, and EPM-EPDM; medium-tonnage rubbers are CR, IIR, and NBR, and small-tonnage rubbers include all the remaining types. The only ambiguity in this classification is that two of the large tonnage rubbers—IR and EPM-EPDM—have lower levels of world consumption than the two other kinds of SR's classified as medium tonnage—CR and IIR. The reason for this apparent contradiction is that IR and EPM-EPDM are thought to have the potential for becoming large tonnage rubbers. Even though no unique classification will be adopted in this study, the one proposed by Allen is quite useful for the purpose of examining the competition between NR and SR, since the prices of the four large-tonnage SR's historically have been in the range of natural rubber prices, and their markets have overlapped those of NR to a greater or lesser extent.

In terms of tonnage, styrene-butadiene rubber (SBR) is by far the single most important kind of rubber in the world. It represents 38 percent of total rubber consumption outside the centrally planned economies. Its share in total synthetic rubber consumption is even higher, about 58 percent (Table 3–1). SBR has some important technical advantages over NR, but also some inferior properties. It has lower resilience and tensile strength, but its resistance to mechanical, temperature, and environmental factors is roughly comparable to that of NR. SBR, however, can be easily extended with oil, giving it good wear resistance and excellent grip. For this reason SBR is used mostly in automobile tire treads where good resistance to wear and low propensity to skid on wet surfaces are necessary performance characteristics. Worldwide, more than 60 percent of all SBR is consumed in tires. Other uses include footwear, conveyor belts, cable insulation, hoses, battery containers, and adhesives. Physical proper-

9. See, for example, C. F. Ruebensaal, *Changing Markets and Manufacturing Patterns in the Synthetic Rubber Industry* (New York: IISRP Inc., 1975), p. 17; and David Dworkin, "Changing Markets and Technology for Specialty Elastomers," *Rubber World* (February 1975), pp. 43–46.

10. See further Chapter 3 and Appendix A.

11. P. W. Allen, *Natural Rubber and the Synthetics* (London: Crosby Lockwood, 1972), pp. 17–24.

ties alone, however, cannot explain the outstanding commercial success of SBR; its low production cost is also important. When demand for rubber—especially in tires—started to increase after World War II at a rate that was well beyond the capacity of natural rubber producers, SBR producers filled this gap in demand with a product that had good physical and end-use properties. But above all SBR had relatively low production costs and could, therefore, be sold at competitive prices.

Polybutadiene rubber (BR) is the second most important kind of SR and the third most important kind of rubber in terms of volume: BR consumption accounted in 1977 for 15.7 percent of total consumption of SR outside the centrally planned economies and 10.3 percent of total rubber consumption (Table 3–1). Because of its high resilience and low heat buildup, BR is used to improve the performance of SBR and NR in tire treads, sidewalls, and carcasses. BR is, therefore, almost exclusively a tire rubber and is hardly ever used alone.

Polyisoprene (IR) is the closest synthetic approximation of the natural elastomer. On the basis of its physical and processing characteristics it has found uses in areas where NR was previously chosen, such as car, truck, and bus tires, and pharmaceutical and mechanical goods. Despite its excellent properties and high manufacturers' expectations of its market potential, IR has found it difficult to compete with NR on a relative price basis. IR still is a costly SR to produce, since both the derivation of the isoprene monomer and the polymerization process are technically more complex and costly than those of SBR. The market penetration of IR has been slow over the past ten years. In 1977, IR accounted for only 3.6 percent of all SR and 2.4 percent of all rubber consumed outside of the centrally planned economies.[12]

Ethylene-propylene rubbers (EPM and EPDM) are the fifth most important group of SR's in terms of tonnage. They have excellent resistance to environmental factors, high tensile strength, and resistance to heat. When first introduced, EPM rubber was expected to become a new general-purpose rubber. The low cost of the basic monomers (ethylene and propylene), the ability of EPM to accept high loadings of oil, and its processing ease were thought to be strong assets. EPM

---

12. In 1973 the IR share of total SR consumed outside the centrally planned economies was 5.1 percent. On a world basis, the market share of IR is probably higher than indicated in Table 3-1 due to the relatively higher market penetration reached by IR in the U.S.S.R. and Eastern Europe. No precise figures are available for these countries, however.

was difficult to vulcanize, however, and the solution to this problem—
the addition of diene, a costly material—counteracted much of the
initial relative cost advantage and prevented the modified EPM
(EPDM) from entering the tire market, except for some specific uses
(tire sidewalls, cover strips, and off-the-road vehicle tires). EPDM is
now used mostly in automotive parts other than tires, where resistance
to ozone and weather is necessary.

Polychloroprene (CR), butyl rubber (IIR), and nitrile rubber (NBR)
are the three remaining important kinds of SR from the standpoint
of world consumption. They all are expensive and are used only in
products that require their special technical properties. Because of its
excellent weather, ozone, and fire resistance, CR is used in automotive
parts other than tires, mechanized goods, and wire cables. CR competes with EPDM in automotive goods and with NR in some mechanical
applications, but for the most part it competes with other specialty
rubbers, particularly NBR. IIR, because of its impermeability to gas,
is used mostly in inner tubes where it has displaced NR. NBR, which
has an excellent resistance to oil and chemical solvents, is mostly
used in oil hoses, oil seals, gaskets, belts, tubing, and sealants.

Other SR's include a large number of specialty rubbers which meet
specific needs of certain manufactured products. There are at least
170 distinct kinds of specialty rubbers, which can be classified in
three broad groups: castable elastomers, such as urethane, silicones,
and polysulfides; thermoplastic rubbers; and powdered elastomers.[13]

The Main Uses of Rubber

The breakdown of world rubber consumption by main uses is not
known precisely. The only estimated breakdown is between tire and
nontire uses, in which each accounts for about 50 percent of the total.

Uses in the major economic regions

A greater percentage of rubber is used in tires in developed countries (57 percent of the total) than in developing countries and centrally planned economies (38 and 27 percent, respectively, of the
total).[14] The percentage of rubber that is used in tires also reflects

13. See Appendix A.
14. These percentage shares refer to 1972–74.

Table 3–2. Elastomer Consumption in Developed Countries, by Major Uses, 1970

Use	United States Thousands of metric tons	United States Percent	European Economic Community Thousands of metric tons	European Economic Community Percent	Japan Thousands of metric tons	Japan Percent
Tire						
Passenger car	855	34.0	420	22.6	110	14.1
Truck/bus	445	17.7	325	17.5	192	24.6
Tractor/industrial	100	4.0	75	4.0	21	2.7
Bicycle/motorcycle	3	0.01	25	1.4	13	1.7
Aircraft	9	0.04	3	0.02	0.3	—
Retreading	130	5.1	75	4.0	10	1.3
Inner tubes	45	1.8	50	2.7	39	5.0
Other products	20	0.07	20	1.1	15	1.9
Total	1,607	63.8	993	53.4	400	51.3
Nontire						
Latex products	203	8.1	195	10.5	74	9.5
Belting	30	1.2	40	2.2	43	5.5
Hose	50	2.0	45	2.4	15	1.9
Footwear	90	3.6	75	4.0	68	8.7
Wire and cable	30	1.2	40	2.2	12	1.6
Other products	507	20.1	471	25.3	167	21.5
Total	910	36.2	866	46.6	379	48.7
Total consumption	2,517	100.0	1,859	100.0	779	100.0

Sources: Industry sources (interview data); International Rubber Study Group, Statistical Bulletin, various issues; and Malaysian Rubber Research and Development Board, The Techno-Economic Potential of Natural Rubber, MRRDB Monograph 1 (Kuala Lumpur: MRRDB, 1974).

the degree of motor vehicle use in each country, ranging from 64 percent in the United States to about 10 percent in the People's Republic of China.

In developed countries, the uses of rubber are known in much greater detail, even though category classifications are often different between countries and comparisons are quite difficult, especially for uses other than tires. Table 3–2 summarizes the situation in the United States, the EC, and Japan. Rubber is used for tires in all three areas, but there are substantial differences among areas in the pattern of use. Rubber use in passenger-car tires is higher in the United States than in Europe or Japan, because of the higher levels of per capita automobile ownership and use as well as the relatively larger average size of automobiles (and thus tires) in the United States. After car tires, the largest single market for rubber is tires for commercial vehicles, such as trucks and buses. Japan uses more rubber for commercial vehicle tires than other countries. In Japan, however, many commercial vehicles are small buses and small and midget trucks, whose tires are categorized as commercial vehicle tires but which are really more similar to passenger-car tires. After tires, latex products, footwear, belts and hoses, and wire cables are the most important uses for rubber.

Uses and market shares of natural rubber

Statistics on consumption by use and on market shares in each use for NR have been almost totally unavailable until recently for most countries. In 1973 a pioneer study by the Malaysian Rubber Research and Development Board (MRRDB) provided much needed empirical evidence on the uses and the market shares of NR.[15] Additional data made available to the World Bank and the Food and Agriculture Organization of the United Nations (FAO) by industry sources confirm—with some minor modification—the distribution of uses first given by the MRRDB. Table 3–3 summarizes the uses of NR in the United States, the EC, and Japan.

Commercial-vehicle tires represent the largest single outlet for NR in all three areas, followed by passenger-car tires. Commercial-vehicle

---

15. P. W. Allen, P. O. Thomas, and B. C. Sekhar, *The Techno-Economic Potential of Natural Rubber in Major End-Uses* (Kuala Lumpur: MRRDB, 1973), pp. 27–30.

Table 3–3. Natural Rubber Consumption in Developed Countries, by Major Uses, and Natural Rubber Share in Each Use, 1970

Use	United States Thousands of metric tons	Share of total (percent)	NR share (percent)	European Economic Community Thousands of metric tons	Share of total (percent)	NR share (percent)	Japan Thousands of metric tons	Share of total (percent)	NR share (percent)
Tire	400	70.4	24.9	384	54.8	39.0	154	54.4	38.5
Passenger car	124	21.8	14.5	110	15.7	26.0	31	11.0	27.0
Truck/bus	222	39.1	50.0	190	27.1	58.0	90	31.8	45.0
Tractor/industrial	30	5.3	30.0	45	6.4	60.0	10	3.5	45.0
Bicycle/motorcycle	...	...	—	7	1.0	30.0	8	2.8	60.0
Aircraft	8	1.4	90.0	3	0.04	90.0	0.3	...	100.0
Retreading	13	2.3	10.0	25	3.6	33.0	5	1.8	55.0
Inner tubes	2	0.03	5.0	2	0.03	5.0	4	1.4	10.0
Other products	1	0.02	5.0	2	0.03	10.0	6	2.1	04.0
Nontire	168	29.6	19.0	317	45.2	36.6	129	45.6	34.0
Latex products	67	11.8	33.0	65	9.3	33.0	21	7.4	28.0
Belting	12	2.1	15.0	12	1.7	30.0	22	7.8	51.0
Hose	...	—	—	11	1.6	5.0	6	2.1	40.0
Footwear	22	3.9	25.0	26	3.7	35.0	30	10.6	44.0
Wire and cable	1	0.01	3.0	6	0.09	15.0	4	1.4	33.0
Other products	66	11.6	13.0	197	28.1	42.0	46	16.3	27.5
Total consumption	568	100.0	22.6	701	100.0	37.7	283	100.0	36.0

— Not applicable.
.... Zero or negligible.
Sources: Industry sources (interview data); and MRRDB, The Techno-Economic Potential of Natural Rubber.

tires generally require more NR in the blend. The larger the tire, the greater the share of NR, since high resistance to wear-and-tear and cracking as well as low heat buildup are needed. Natural rubber has high resilience and, therefore, minimum heat buildup. Giant tires are made almost entirely with NR (about 95 percent), large truck tires usually contain about 65 percent NR, and small truck tires have only from 17 to 25 percent NR.[16] The relatively greater importance of small and midget trucks in Japan partially explains the lower share of NR in commercial-vehicle tires in that country.

Passenger-car tires are the second largest market for NR despite the heavy losses in market share suffered by NR in the 1950s and 1960s. SBR and BR are now the dominant rubbers in this market. Comparison of natural rubber consumption shares in passenger-car tires shows an interesting difference between the United States and Europe. The share of NR is much higher in the EC than in the United States, largely because of the higher percentage of radial tires on passenger cars there. Radial tires, which require more NR than other tires, were pioneered by Michelin in France, and gained consumer acceptance much earlier in Western Europe than in the United States, where the industry went from cross-ply to bias-belted tires before getting into radial-tire production. Radial tires for passenger cars were introduced on a large scale in the U. S. market only in the early 1970s.[17] The situation in Japan is more similar to that in the United States than to that in Europe. Radial tires were introduced in Japan in the late 1960s and early 1970s, and therefore the share of NR in passenger-car tires is lower than in Europe. The data in Table 3–3 show a somewhat distorted picture of the market share of NR in passenger-car and commercial-vehicle tires in Japan. The reported share in passenger-car tires is higher and that in truck or bus tires is lower than it would be if the small- and mini-truck tires were categorized as passenger-car tires.

The third largest market for NR is in latex products, where its market share is about 30 percent in all three major consuming areas. Industrial tires, footwear, hoses, and belting are other important

16. See, for example, E. H. Sonneken, *Statement to the United States Cost of Living Council* (Akron, Ohio: Goodyear Tire and Rubber Co., September 1973).

17. It is significant that the natural rubber share of the market for tires and tire products increased steadily in the United States from 23.6 percent in 1971 to 29.8 percent in 1977, whereas in the world market it rose only from 21.6 percent to 24.5 percent.

markets. An extreme illustration of the importance of technical and performance requirements that constrain the choice of rubber inputs is the market for airplane tires, in which NR has an absolutely predominant share. It is the only material that has the strength at very high temperatures and the resistance to fatigue during repeated flexing that are necessary in aircraft tires.

Factors Affecting the Demand for Rubber

Demand for rubber originated from the use of various kinds of elastomeric materials in a large number of manufactured products. Rubber demand is, by its nature, a derived demand. The usual difference between rubber uses related to tires and uses not related to tires highlights the importance of tires as the leading outlet for rubber, but does not indicate the large variety of other manufactured products in which rubber is used, such as latex products, beltings, hoses, footwear, wire and cables, medical articles, and glues and adhesives.

The kind of rubber to be used in manufacturing a product is chosen on the basis of technical factors (performance needs of the products and process technology), economic factors (product economics, which depend on relative input prices and processing costs), and factors related to the market (ease of input availability, market structures, marketing and service needs, and capabilities). Although the choice of rubber to be used can be assumed to be based (at a given level of process technology) on the usual criteria of minimum cost, in practice several technical and nontechnical factors constrain the ease of substituting one kind of rubber for another. Rubber users tend to delay changes in the mix of inputs in response to changes in relative prices because of the technical adjustment costs that are often involved. Moreover, the largest users of rubber, the tire makers, have large captive production capacities of SR and tend to use their own supplies whenever possible. Other users of rubber, who do not have captive production capacities, are often tied to specific domestic synthetic rubber suppliers by contractual and other customary relations, which are hard to break. This limits their ability or willingness to switch from one kind of rubber to another in response to changes in relative market prices. Government policies to save foreign exchange tend to favor the use of domestically produced rubbers, most often SR's. Security reasons also weigh in favor of protecting and encouraging domestic synthetic rubber production instead of importing

NR. Of these two political factors that interfere with a choice of rubber inputs that is usually based only on technical and economic considerations, the former—foreign exchange saving—applies mostly to developing countries, whereas the latter—security—generally applies to industrialized countries. In centrally planned economies both factors apply simultaneously.[18]

The Competitive Relation between Natural and Synthetic Rubbers

The analysis of the nature of the demand for the main kinds of rubber and for their main uses clearly illustrates the complexity of the market interaction between NR and SR. The competitive relation between natural and synthetic elastomers hinges upon a set of related factors, which are difficult to evaluate individually. The study of this relation, moreover, has been clouded by emotions, political considerations, and self-serving attitudes, which are often heavily influenced by conflicting economic interests. In the end, a clear understanding of the issues involved can come only from careful analysis aimed at obtaining much-needed empirical evidence on this subject.[19]

Study of the technical and economic characteristics of the main kinds of rubber and of the uses of rubber has shown that NR and SR are close substitutes for each other in many product applications where relative price and availability are the main determinants of the choice of elastomers. Natural rubber, SBR, and IR compete in all applications for which a general purpose rubber with standard characteristics is needed. Even isolating these applications is a difficult task, however. It is equally difficult to identify the uses in which any one of the main kinds of rubber has clear-cut technical advantages over another, given the fact that careful compounding can yield almost innumerable combinations of rubbers with a given set of

18. A lucid analysis of the process of choice between rubber inputs is presented in Allen, Thomas, Sekhar, *The Techno-Economic Potential of Natural Rubber in Major End-Uses*, pp. 17–23. The manufacturers' problems of choice have also been reexamined recently by J. G. Anderson of Avon Processed Polymers Ltd. See J. G. Anderson, "The Rubber Manufacturers' Choice: Natural or Synthetic Rubber?," *Plastics and Rubber International* (July/August 1977), pp. 169–72.

19. The last section of this chapter offers some new empirical evidence; see further Appendix B.

properties. The economic choice in these cases would have to depend not only on relative input costs but also on relative compounding costs.

The opinions of the experts in this field are widely divergent, often because all of the details of the technical and economic options have not been (and probably cannot be) explored simultaneously. At one end of the spectrum is the view that the potential for switching from sr to nr on technical or commercial grounds is quite limited, probably only about 5 percent of total elastomer use, even given continued assurance of economic advantage. According to this view, political factors could be more important than economic factors in determining whether this potential will be realized or not.[20] At the other end of the spectrum, in a carefully reasoned and finely documented study of the competition between nr and sr, the mrrdb concludes that, apart from the markets accounted for by specialty rubbers (about 15 percent of the total) and the market for sbr/br blends in passenger-car tires (another 15 percent of the total), the remainder of the world rubber market is technically open to isoprenic rubbers (nr and ir).[21] After allowing for differences in processability and price between nr and ir, the potential market share of nr is reduced to 50 percent. In a further realistic assessment of the technoeconomic market share for nr, based on an analysis of its uses, the mrrdb study concludes that the normal share of nr in total elastomer use is 43 percent; the actual market share of nr was 35 percent in 1970.

Our direct research on rubber uses outside the centrally planned economies indicates that the possibilities of switching from sr to nr under favorable conditions of price and availability vary a great deal from country to country and from industry to industry. It appears, however, that at least 15 percent of the sbr and 50 percent of the ir market could go to nr. Using consumption figures for 1977, this means that, outside the centrally planned economies, 3.6 million metric tons of nr could have been used compared with the 3 million metric tons actually consumed. Natural rubber had, therefore, a

20. See D. A. Bennett, "Changes in Markets for Synthetic Rubber and Its Raw Materials," *Proceedings of the ECMRA Conference*, Madrid, 1976; processed. A similar view is taken by the irsg Ad Hoc Advisory Panel in a recent study on the prospects for rubber. See irsg, "Report of the Ad Hoc Advisory Panel on the Prospects for Rubber," Jakarta, October 1975, p. 7; processed.

21. See Allen, Thomas, and Sekhar, *The Techno-Economic Potential of Natural Rubber*, pp. 23–27.

potential market share of about 42 percent as opposed to an actual market share of 34.3 percent. On a world basis, its market share would probably be lower, since centrally planned economies have policies of self-sufficiency in rubber and would not shift back to NR on as large a scale as that implied for developed countries.

Estimates of the Market Share Elasticities of Natural Rubber

The relation between the share of NR in total rubber consumption and the import prices of NR relative to prices of competing SR in North America, Western Europe, and Japan was examined using a market share model. Because of the lack of reliable data on synthetic rubber prices, this model could not be applied to other developed consuming countries, developing countries, or centrally planned economies. North America, Western Europe, and Japan, however, are the largest consuming areas, accounting together for about 60 percent of total world rubber consumption and for 95 percent of total rubber consumption in developed countries.

The model assumes that rubber consumers can use both NR and SR; that NR and SR are close, but not perfect, substitutes; and that changes in the relative prices of these two inputs affect relative use only gradually, given the uncertainties about the nature of price changes (temporary or permanent) and given the time and cost involved in shifting from one input to the other. The economic rationale for these assumptions stems from the analysis presented above.

The market share of NR is hypothesized to be a function of the prices of NR and SR and of technology. If rubber users adjust their consumption patterns gradually in response to changes in relative prices and technology, only a fraction of the projected share of NR in total rubber use can be expected to be reached within a certain period. A Nerlovian partial adjustment model was postulated, and a reduced form equation was used to obtain the statistical estimates of the short- and long-term elasticities of the natural rubber market share with respect to relative prices. The results are shown in Table 3–4.[22]

22. Appendix B contains the details of the analysis of the natural rubber market share.

Table 3–4. *Estimates of the Market Share Elasticities of Natural Rubber in North America, Western Europe, and Japan*

Area	Rate of adjustment $\delta = 1 - a_2$	Short-term elasticity[a]	Long-term elasticity
North America	0.504	−0.18[b]	−0.36[b]
Western Europe	0.587	−0.13[b]	−0.46[b]
Japan	0.568	−0.14[b]	−0.25[b]

a. Computed at the mean values of the relevant variables.
b. Significant at the 95 percent confidence level.
Source: Table B–1.

The estimated short-term elasticities are, as expected, much smaller in absolute value than long-term elasticities. In the short run relative prices influence only slightly the choice of rubber inputs. This is consistent with a priori expectations, given the technical adjustment cost that is involved when a rubber user switches from one kind of input to another. In the longer run, however, the choice of rubber inputs is clearly and more strongly influenced by changes in relative prices. Another interesting finding is that the values of long-term market share elasticities are higher for Western Europe than for North America and Japan. This again confirms expectations, since in Western Europe there is less vertical integration of the tire industry than in the United States. In addition, despite the similar production structures in Western Europe and Japan, informal ties linking SR manufacturers and tire makers, as well as institutional pressures in favor of domestically produced SR, are much weaker than in Japan.

4

•◦•

Effect of the Oil Crisis on the Competitive Relation between Rubbers

The drastic increase in crude oil prices since 1973 has fundamentally changed the competitive relation between natural and synthetic rubbers. The relative market position of natural rubber (NR) has improved substantially in the short term, but has improved even more in the longer term. After more than two decades of experiencing serious difficulties in meeting the price challenge of synthetic rubbers (SR), NR now faces a market situation in which relative cost advantages seem to have turned strongly in its favor.

The effect of the oil price change on the relative market position of rubbers is examined here, differentiating the short-term effects from the long-term effects. Although this approach is somewhat schematic, it brings out the crucial difference between the changes that the oil price increase has caused in the cost of producing rubber from existing facilities—trees already in the ground and production plants already in operation—and the cost of producing more rubber from new facilities—newly planted trees and new synthetic rubber production units.

Short-Term Effects on Operating Costs

Assessing the effects of the oil crisis on the production costs of NR and SR is conceptually easier in the short term than in the long term. In practice both exercises are difficult and somewhat risky.

Natural rubber

Natural rubber is a perennial crop. The rubber tree does not begin to produce until the fifth or sixth year after planting. The costs incurred during this immaturity period include: (a) land clearing; (b) new planting (or replanting); (c) field care and upkeep (for example, pest and disease control, pruning, weeding, and fertilizing); and (d) management and overhead (prorated). These are essentially investment costs similar in nature to those incurred in building a synthetic rubber plant. After maturity is reached and the tree is exploited, the costs incurred in producing rubber include: (a) tapping and collection of latex and cup-lumps; (b) processing into sheets, blocks, or concentrate latex; (c) field care and upkeep (for example, pest and disease control, chemical stimulation, and fertilizing where applicable); and (d) management and overhead.[1] These are essentially operating costs. In addition to the direct cost of producing rubber, a charge for depreciation is normally included. This charge, however, should also include an allowance for interest on capital. Traditional compilations of production cost do not include such allowances in addition to depreciation. Therefore the cost estimates presented below omit interest charges and allowances for possible changes in the replacement cost of the rubber holdings.[2]

To deal with the cost of NR in global as well as in sectoral terms is quite difficult. Rubber production is a labor-intensive operation; about two-thirds of total operating costs are direct labor charges. In addition, in all the major producing countries small farmers produce the bulk of the rubber. Valuing labor—especially family labor—in the production of any agricultural commodity in developing countries

1. Applicable to estates.
2. For a recent detailed examination of the natural rubber production process and production economics, see I. Haque, "Efficiency in Resource Allocation: The Case of Natural Rubber," World Bank report no. EC-179 (a restricted-circulation document) (Washington, D.C.: World Bank, July 1971), pp. 19–37, processed; and Maria 't Hooft-Welvaars, "Profitability of New Investments in Rubber Plantings in Malaysia," UNCTAD document TD/B/C.1/SYN/52 (Geneva, June 1971). I. Haque's paper also contains the most important references to the existing literature on this subject, which is very extensive. A new and comprehensive analysis of natural rubber production economics and marketing has recently become available from the Rubber Research Institute of Malaysia (RRIM). See Pee Teck Yew and Ani bin Arope, Rubber Owners' Manual (Kuala Lumpur: RRIM, 1976), pp. 24–183. This manual is destined to become the standard reference on most aspects of rubber production economics and marketing.

is notoriously difficult, both conceptually and practically. There are also serious difficulties in ascertaining the average cost of producing rubber on estates. Estate costs depend to a great extent on yields, and in some countries wage rates are linked to market prices of rubber.[3] Government policies—taxes, cesses, levies, and subsidies on planting and/or replanting—complicate the assessment of operating costs and make comparisons between countries and years extremely difficult.

The analysis considered here, however, does not require definitive statements about average natural rubber cost. The direct short-term effect of the energy crisis on the cost of producing NR from existing capacity can be ascertained by looking at input prices related to energy—such as fertilizers, chemical stimulants, and pesticides—and at other energy costs—such as fuel and electricity—in the processing and transport of rubber. The indirect effect of the energy crisis is more difficult to determine. At the micro level, wages on estates and imputed returns to labor on smallholdings (which are a critical variable) are affected by domestic inflation rates, which depend in part on international inflation and exchange rates. In some cases the domestic effect of international inflation on imported agricultural and industrial inputs (including capital goods and energy) are offset partially by changes in exchange rates, whereas, in other cases, such changes reinforce the cost-push effect of international inflation. These effects, moreover, differ according to the degree of dependence of the major rubber-producing countries on imports.

The cumulative effect of these factors on the direct cost of rubber production can be observed in the case of Malaysia. The estimates presented in Table 4–1 refer to average direct costs on estates and smallholdings.[4] Malaysia is the only rubber-producing country in which the average costs for these producing sectors can be derived with a reasonable degree of confidence. In terms of the local currency, the total operating cost of rubber estates (exclusive of export duties and other taxes) apparently has increased about 30 percent between 1971 and 1974, roughly paralleling increases in labor cost (which are

3. See, for example, Ng Choong Sooi, Colin Barlow, and Chan Chee-Kheong, "Factors Affecting the Profitability of Rubber Production in West Malaysian Estates," *Proceedings of Natural Rubber Conference*, Kuala Lumpur, 1968; and Pee Teck Yew, "Economics of Field Collection," *Planters' Bulletin of the Rubber Research Institute of Malaysia* no. 110 (September 1970), pp. 164–79.

4. Weighted averages by yield ranges for both estates and smallholders.

Table 4–1. *Estimated Average Direct Costs of Production of Natural Rubber in Malaysia, 1971 and 1974*

Producing sector and process	1971 (Malaysian cents per kilogram)	1974 (Malaysian cents per kilogram)	Increase, 1971–74 (percent)
Estates			
Tapping and collecting[a]	34.5	45.0	
Management	7.5	8.5	
Processing	7.5	8.5	
Weeding and fertilizing	7.2	11.5	
Others[b]	8.8	11.7	
Amortization	6.5	10.0	
Total[c]	72.0	95.2	32.2
(Total in U.S. cents per pound)[d]	(10.8)	(17.9)	(65.7)
Smallholdings			
Tapping and collecting[e]	30.0	39.0	
Processing	14.8	17.0	
Weeding and fertilizing	4.6	8.0	
Others	6.6	10.6	
Total[f]	56.0	74.6	33.2
(Total in U.S. cents per pound)[d]	(8.4)	(14.1)	(67.9)

a. Tapping costs on estates depend to some extent on rubber prices, which were taken as an average of 100 M¢/kg in 1971 and 150 M¢/kg in 1974.

b. Includes field maintenance, latex stimulation, pest and disease control, land taxes, insurance, and sundry items.

c. Excludes research tax and export tax, which depends on rubber prices.

d. Converted in US$ at average exchange rate of year shown: US$1 = M$3.02 in 1971, and US$1 = M$2.407 in 1974.

e. Mostly unpaid family labor, the cost of which is imputed at the going wage rate.

f. Excludes amortization, marketing charges, research tax, and export duty, which depends on rubber prices.

Source: Industry sources (interview data).

most clearly shown by tapping and collection costs). The effect on total operating cost of the much larger relative change in the cost of inputs related to energy which are included in weeding and fertilizing costs, is quite small, since their share in total cost is only about 15 percent. The overall cost changes in the smallholders' sector are roughly of the same order of magnitude as in the estate sector. This results from calculating tapping and collection costs for smallholders at market wage rates, which is not an unreasonable assumption, given the labor market in Malaysia.[5] Measured in terms of U.S. dollars, operating costs on estates and smallholdings apparently increased by about 65 percent between 1971 and 1974 because of the appreciation of the Malaysian dollar in relation to the U.S. dollar.

Synthetic rubber

The direct effect of the oil crisis was much stronger on the cost of SR than on the cost of NR. The production cost of SR depends heavily on the cost of chemical monomers and of other energy inputs (such as steam and electricity), which are in turn related to that of oil and gas. The quadrupling of crude oil prices more than doubled the cost of the basic rubber monomers (styrene, butadiene, and isoprene) and of the other chemical and energy inputs, pushing up quite drastically the cost of producing SR between 1973 and 1975. The amount of increase in production costs depended on the specific kind of SR and on the reliance of the various petrochemical and rubber industries on different kinds of chemical feedstocks. In Western Europe and Japan, where oil (or naphtha) is the basic feedstock of the chemical industry and where the industries depend almost totally on imported crude, the cost and price of rubber monomers increased more than in the United States. The U.S. petrochemical industry depends much more on domestically produced gas (natural gas and gas liquids such as ethane, propane, and butane) than on oil (or naphtha) for producing the basic rubber monomers. In the United States, moreover, both gas and crude oil prices were subject to government regulation and were not allowed to increase as much as world market prices (Table SA–9).

Before the oil crisis, synthetic rubber monomers accounted, on the average, for about 45 percent of the total production cost of SBR-1500, 50 percent of the total of BR, and 55 percent of the total cost of high-*cis* IR.[6] Other energy-related inputs (chemicals, steam, and electricity) accounted for another 20 to 25 percent of total cost, depending on the kind of rubber. The dependence of the synthetic

---

5. In other rubber-producing countries this assumption would probably be less appropriate.

6. Costs of isoprene are particularly difficult to ascertain and vary quite substantially between the three main producing areas (Western Europe, United States, and Japan) according to the different methods of isoprene recovery and polymerization processes. See Appendix A.

Figure 4–1. *Estimated* SBR-*1500 Prices and Raw Material Costs, 1960 to 1976*

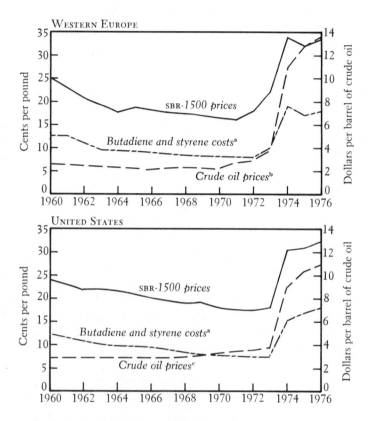

a. Taken at 76 percent butadiene and 24 percent styrene.
b. Landed crude oil import value for Western Europe.
c. Average price at well until 1972; refiner acquisition cost since 1973.

rubber industry on chemical feedstocks and other input costs related to energy was, therefore, overriding. Also, the oil crisis came at a time when economies of scale and technological improvements had already run much of their course in reducing the production cost of most rubber monomers (with the possible exception of isoprene) as well as the cost of polymerization (again with the possible exception of IR).

One of the reasons for the commercial success of the synthetic rubber industry in the postwar period has been the availability of chemical monomers at continuously declining prices. The petrochemical industry is highly capital intensive; capital requirements and, therefore, related manufacturing costs are less than proportional to plant capacity, whereas productivity (in the sense of use of labor, energy, and materials) is generally better in large-scale plants. The costs and prices of the two most important chemical monomers for the synthetic rubber industry—butadiene and styrene—decreased substantially until the early 1970s as a result of economies of scale, and synthetic rubber producers thus were able to secure the basic raw materials at continuously diminishing prices. The close relation that existed between falling monomer costs and prices of SBR in the 1960s and early 1970s is illustrated clearly in Figure 4-1.

Between 1973 and 1975 crude oil prices increased from an average of $3.75 to $12.10 per barrel in Western Europe, from $3.30 to $11.90 per barrel in Japan, and from $4.10 to $10.40 per barrel in the United States.[7] The prices of olefin chemicals increased drastically: ethylene prices trebled, and propylene and butadiene prices more than doubled. The prices of aromatics (for example, styrene) also more than doubled. Butadiene prices increased from about 8¢ to 16–18¢ a pound, and styrene prices from 7¢ to 19–20¢. SBR-1500 prices increased from 18¢ to about 30¢ a pound in the United States, from 20¢ to 32¢ a pound in Western Europe, and from 21.5¢ to 35.5¢ a pound in Japan. SBR provides a good example of the effects of the drastic change

7. Western European and Japanese prices are (landed) crude oil import unit values. U.S. prices are refiner's acquisition prices (a weighted average of domestic and imported crude); domestic oil prices are, in turn, a weighted average of "old" and "new" oil. "Old" oil prices were fixed until 1976 at $5.03 per barrel, whereas "new" oil prices are in line with world market prices. See Federal Energy Administration, *Monthly Energy Review*, December 1976, pp. 66–69 and explanatory notes in the appendix. All prices—oil, chemicals, and rubber—are in U.S. dollars.

Table 4–2. *Estimated Average Direct Costs of Production of* SBR-1500 *in the Main Producing Areas, 1973 and 1975*
(U.S. cents per pound)

	United States			Western Europe[a]			Japan[a]		
Cost	1973	1975	Percent-age change	1973	1975	Percent-age change	1973	1975	Percent-age change
Energy	10.4	21.0		11.5	23.5		10.6	22.0	
Monomer	7.5	17.0		7.8	18.0		} 9.7	20.5	
Other chemical	2.5	3.4		2.7	3.7				
Utilities	0.4	0.5		1.0	2.2		0.9	1.5	
Other	5.0	6.0		4.9	6.3		6.5	9.4	
Labor	2.4	2.8		1.9	2.5		1.8	2.3	
Overhead	1.2	1.4		1.3	1.6		1.7	2.4	
Depreciation	1.0	1.2		1.7	2.2		1.7	1.9	
Others	0.4	0.6		n.a.	n.a.		1.3	2.8	
Direct costs[b]	15.4	27.0	75.3	16.4	29.8	81.7	17.1	29.4	71.9

n.a. Not available separately.
a. Costs are converted into U.S. cents at the average exchange rate of year shown.
b. Excludes packaging and selling costs and return on investment.
Source: Industry sources (interview data).

in oil prices on the direct costs of production of sr (Table 4–2). Allowing for the differences in cost accounting procedures and exchange rate changes between 1973 and 1975, both of which complicate comparisons of production costs between countries, the average direct cost of producing sbr-1500 increased by some 70 to 80 percent over this period.[8] Oil- and energy-related costs more than doubled in all synthetic rubber producing areas, and other manufacturing costs increased by 20 to 40 percent. The production cost of other kinds of rubber (br and ir) increased between 1973 and 1975 by roughly the same order of magnitude (70 to 90 percent) in response to the oil crisis.

The most important conclusion emerging from the comparative analysis of the changes in the cost structure of nr and sr since the oil crisis is that the short-term cost competitiveness of nr improved considerably. The cost (in U.S. dollars) of producing nr from existing capacity in Malaysia increased less than the cost of producing sbr from existing plants in the United States, Western Europe, and Japan, notwithstanding the appreciation of Malaysian currency over the U.S. dollar by more than 25 percent between 1971 and 1974. The short-term cost effectiveness of nr also improved quite substantially in relation to synthetic ir.

The effects of this improvement in the cost competitiveness of nr relative to sbr and ir are best illustrated by what happened in world markets during 1975. When world demand for all elastomers dropped quite drastically in 1975 as a consequence of the economic recession in industrialized countries, natural rubber prices declined to an average of 30¢ a pound, c.i.f. At this price level neither ir nor sbr could compete with nr. In a declining total market, the share of nr increased, whereas that of ir and sbr declined correspondingly. The world market share of ir dropped 0.5 percent and that of sbr 1.0 percent, whereas the world market share of nr increased 1.5 percent.[9] The substantial improvement in the cost advantage of nr compared with both ir and sbr seems to have made the synthetic rubber industry—especially the general purpose rubber producers—more vulnerable to drops in market demand than in the past. The sharp cutbacks

---

8. These estimates of average direct costs of production of sbr, like those for nr presented in Table 4–1, do not include allowances for interest on capital and for possible increases in the replacement value of the plants.

9. Excluding the centrally planned economies.

in synthetic rubber production that had to be implemented in 1975 clearly illustrate this point.[10]

Long-Term Effects on the Profitability of New Investments

The total production capacity of NR for roughly the next ten years is by and large already determined by the planting decisions made in the late 1960s and early 1970s.[11] The planting decisions made from now to the early 1980s, however, will begin to influence the output trend only toward the end of the next decade. Their full effect will not be felt until the mid-1990s. In the case of SR, production on a world basis is well below total capacity, with only about 73 percent of total capacity used in 1976.[12] Even allowing for the possibility of a strong pickup in synthetic rubber demand outside the centrally planned economies in the early-to-mid-1980s, it is clear that no substantial expansion of production capacity is needed before 1980–81.[13] It is only in the centrally planned economies that expansion is expected to continue in line with demand growth.[14]

Whereas additions to the production capacity in SR can be imple-

---

10. The utilization rate of capacity in the synthetic rubber industry outside the centrally planned economies dropped from 75 percent in 1974 to 62 percent in 1975. See Chapter 5, Table 5–4.

11. Natural rubber producers now have more control over output in the short term than they had in the past, since they can more quickly increase yields through a more intensive use of fertilizers and chemical stimulants. As the use of chemical stimulants spreads from estates to smallholders—not only in Malaysia, but also in other producing countries—the short-term responsiveness of natural rubber output to price changes should increase. Presently the total maximum capacity of natural rubber producers to increase output in the short term can be estimated at roughly 250,000 metric tons (about 7 percent of total output).

12. The utilization to capacity ratio for the seven main types of synthetic rubbers—SBR, BR, IR, NBR, IIR, EPM-EPDM, and CR—was about 73 percent in the developed and developing countries taken together. It appears, from the available data, that in the centrally planned economies there was almost full utilization of existing capacity. Data on both production and capacities for specialty rubbers are not available on a world basis with any sufficient degree of precision.

13. This view is shared by the synthetic rubber industry as well. For an example, see D. A. Bennett, "Changes in Markets for Synthetic Rubber and Its Raw Materials," *Proceedings of the ECMRA Conference*, Madrid, 1976, processed, pp. 5–6 and IRSG, "Report of the Ad Hoc Advisory Panel on the Prospects for Rubber," Jakarta, October 1975, processed, pp. 7–8.

14. See further Chapter 5.

mented fairly quickly (from two to three years), additions to the production capacity of NR have to begin much more in advance (six to seven years). This difference in "gestation periods," coupled with the fact that synthetic rubber producers outside the centrally planned economies are likely to have spare capacity until the early 1980s, highlights the basic asymmetry in decisionmaking needs that exists now between the two sectors of the world rubber economy. Whereas synthetic rubber producers can afford to wait until the early 1980s before deciding to expand capacity for the next decade, natural rubber producers will have to make critical planting decisions almost immediately. These decisions will only begin to produce results in the late 1980s and, given the length of maturation of these investments, must necessarily be based on relatively weaker estimates of profitability.

Comparative analysis of investment profitability

To shed some light on the critical decisions which confront natural rubber producers, an in-depth comparative analysis of investment profitability in NR and SR was undertaken to determine whether developments in prices are likely to favor investment in NR.[15] The profitability of new investments in NR was examined for Malaysia, and the profitability of new investments in SBR was examined for Western Europe. These two areas were chosen as case studies for several reasons. Malaysia was selected not only because of the relatively greater ease with which reliable cost information can be obtained, but also because the new calculations can be compared with similar estimates made before the oil crisis.[16] SBR was chosen also on the grounds of greater data availability and reliability of results, as well as because SBR—being the cheapest and most widely used kind of SR—represents a "base case" against which the profitability of new investments for NR can be compared.[17] Western Europe was chosen

15. This analysis of investment profitability is purely financial in nature. Analysis of social and economic profitability would have to take into account other contributions of natural rubber production to national well-being that are not considered here (for example, benefits accruing from employment and tax receipts).

16. Maria 't Hooft-Welvaars, "Profitability of New Investments in Rubber Plantings in Malaysia," pp. 1–16.

17. The analysis of investment in IR which was undertaken separately is much more speculative given the uncertainty about the economics of isoprene production and the uncertainty about the effects of economies of scale in polymerization.

because the chemical feedstock situation there is less complex and more representative of world conditions than that in the United States.[18] For SBR, the analysis was conducted in terms of 1973, 1975, and 1977 input prices and capital-labor costs to capture the effect of the oil crisis on the profitability of new SBR investments.

Creating new capacity in NR means either establishing new plantations or replanting existing areas under rubber with higher-yielding trees. Only new planting of rubber is examined here. Creating new capacity in SR means either maximizing capacity of existing facilities (sometimes called debottlenecking) or setting up a new production facility (in isolation or as part of an integrated operation that includes the production of the monomers). Setting up a new SBR production facility as a part of an integrated chemical operation was considered as the more likely future case, and is the only alternative examined here.

For the production firm—be it a natural rubber plantation or a SBR plant—the decision to add new production capacity depends, other things being equal, on the expected rate of return on investment relative to the opportunity cost of capital. In evaluating the rate of return on the prospective investment, all the expenditures that can be expected during the working life of the project are listed. These include fixed investment expenditure, as well as variable expenditures connected with the production operation. At the same time, an estimate is normally made of both the volume of production during the working life of the project and the price at which this production can be sold: that is, an estimate of all receipts. If both expenditures and receipts are entered in constant prices, then the discount rate that would equate the present value of expenditures to the present value of receipts represents the real interest rate that the capital used for the project will earn, if the estimates of receipts and expenditures are correct.

A slight adaption of this common technique of project evaluation allows calculation of the price which, if received over the entire working life of the project, would cover all expenditures and would provide a desired real rate of return on all capital involved in the production operation. This price is called here the "full supply price." In essence, instead of forecasting output and real prices (that is, receipts in real terms), and then finding the discount rate that equates

18. See Chapter 3. The situation in Japan is similar to that of Western Europe.

the present value of receipts to that of expenditure, the desired real rate of return is here taken as the discount rate. The price that equalizes the present value of expenditure to the present value of revenue from the sale of the (forecast) output is then calculated.[19] The full supply price measured in this way not only includes actual expenditures incurred in production, but also a charge for interest that is either incurred or foregone by investing in the production of NR or SR and a risk premium, if the discount rate used is higher than the real rate of interest.

This method of calculating a full supply price has two clear advantages: it can take into account the changes in the production capacity of the project during its economic life and, above all, it clearly brings out the importance of interest. Both these factors are very important in examining investment decisions in NR, since the output of a rubber project changes over time because of the yield cycle of the trees and so do costs and revenues.[20] Moreover, despite the fact that planting and producing NR is labor intensive, the role of capital—and thereby of interest—is nevertheless important, since the plantings take six years to reach maturity and because substantial expenditures are incurred before any returns from planting become available. The influence of the rate of interest can be seen clearly from the differences in supply prices at various discount rates.

Full supply price of natural rubber

The estimates of the full supply price of NR in Malaysia shown in Table 4–3 are based on the expenditures required to establish and to exploit an "estate" of 3,000 hectares. The specific structure of this "estate" is such that it can fit a cooperative kind of arrangement among small farmers settling on a unit of newly planted land with government support.[21] It was assumed that: (a) planting would take place in three installments of 1,000 hectares a year; (b) immaturity would last for six years; (c) the economic lifetime of the project would last for twenty-eight years; (d) the latest available technology,

19. The full supply price, P, is $\Sigma \dfrac{E_i}{(1+\delta)^i} \ / \ \Sigma \dfrac{Q_i}{(1+\delta)^i}$, where E_i = expenditures, Q_i = output, δ = discount rate, and i = year.

20. Natural rubber yields increase rapidly after tapping. They reach a peak ten years after tapping, and then begin to decline slowly. This decline, however, can now be stemmed by the use of chemical stimulants.

21. The details of the calculations, as well as the rationale for selecting this cooperative type of estate production structure, are given in Appendix C.

in terms of proven high-yielding varieties, tapping systems, fertilizers, and chemical stimulation, would be used; and (e) the latex from the plantation would be processed into crumb rubber using a facility that is an integral part of the production unit. The calculations of the full supply prices are based on 1974 input costs. The full supply price in 1974 can be compared with the full supply price in 1970 (at a real discount rate of 8 percent) calculated for Malaysia using a similar methodology (see Table 4–3).[22]

Between 1970 and 1974 the Malaysian supply price of NR (at a real discount rate of 8 percent) increased by 39 percent in local currency and by 72 percent in U. S. dollars. The increase in the supply price in Malaysia can be attributed only to a small extent to the direct influence of the rise in oil prices. The prices of fertilizers and chemicals used in weeding and stimulation did increase considerably; their relative share of the full supply price rose from 8.5 percent in 1970 to 13.5 percent in 1974. A major reason for the increase in the supply price between 1970 and 1974, however, was the rise in wages, which amounted to about 45 percent. Part of this increase was mere compensation for imported inflation. Consumer prices in Malaysia had increased by 36 percent between 1970 and 1974, mainly due to the high price of food, especially rice. Another part of the wage increase

---

22. The methodology used to calculate the 1970 full supply price differs somewhat from that for the 1974 calculations. The 1970 full supply price was computed for three discount rates, assuming that the gazetted rubber price was given independently. The 1974 calculations, on the contrary, put the gazetted price equal to the full supply price. The wage system in Malaysia allows for wage bonuses that increase in line with the level of gazetted natural rubber prices. Export duty and surcharge increase steeply when the gazetted price increases. Thus, when a higher discount rate is used, especially the investment items in the supply price will rise, and this, in turn, will influence tapping cost and export levies. In the 1970 calculations, where the gazetted price was regarded as exogenous, wages and export levies did not increase with a higher discount rate. The best comparison between 1970 and 1974 is therefore between figures at an 8 percent discount rate. The details of the 1970 calculations can be found in Maria 't Hooft-Welvaars, "Profitability of New Investments in Rubber Plantings in Malaysia." Some details of the 1974 calculations are given in Appendix C to this paper. Full information can be found in Maria 't Hooft-Welvaars, "The Profitability of NR and SBR Investments," World Bank Staff Commodity Paper (draft) (Washington, D.C.: The World Bank, 1978). Although these calculations were based on actual input costs and the currently available production technology, both the size and the nature of the "estate" taken as the model make the results only broadly indicative of the real situations which are, by their nature, much more complex.

Table 4–3. *Full Supply Prices of Natural Rubber in Malaysia at Real Discount Rates of 8, 10, and 12 Percent, 1970 and 1974*

	Percentage					
	8	10	12	8	10	12
Real discount rate	(Malaysian cents per pound)			(U.S. cents per pound)		
1970[a]						
f.o.b. Malaysia	42.5	46.7	51.6	13.7	15.1	16.7
c.i.f. Western Europe	47.0	51.2	56.2	15.2	16.5	18.1
c.i.f. New York	48.5	52.7	57.6	15.7	17.0	18.6
1974[b]						
f.o.b. Malaysia	59.1	71.5	89.9	23.6	28.6	36.0
c.i.f. Western Europe	66.8	79.2	97.7	26.7	31.7	39.1
c.i.f. New York	68.6	81.0	99.5	27.4	32.4	39.8

Note: Natural rubber in crumb rubber form.

a. The calculation of wages in supply prices has been based on a gazetted price range of 55.1–60 M¢ a pound in 1970. The exchange rate has been taken at US$1.00 = M$3.10.

b. For 1974 the element of wage and export levies in the supply price has not been calculated on the basis of an independently fixed gazetted price. The gazetted price has been assumed equal to the supply price, showing the interdependency between wage cost, export levies, and final supply price. (For full explanation, see Appendix C.) As a result, the 1970 and 1974 figures, especially at the discount rates of 10 and 12 percent, are not fully comparable.

The exchange rate in 1974 has been taken at US$1.00 = M$2.50.

Sources: 1970 calculations, Maria 't Hooft-Welvaars, "Profitability of New Investments in Rubber Plantings in Malaysia," 1974 calculations, Appendix C.

was connected with the rise during this period of the gazetted price of NR.[23] Finally, wages also contained increases for productivity, but this is not reflected in the supply price. The higher gazetted price led to higher export levies. Prices of other material inputs also rose considerably, especially those for imported inputs, such as vehicles. The cost of housing estate workers more than doubled during the same period, again not only because of inflation, but also because of improvements in living standards.

The 1974 natural rubber supply price estimates are updated to 1976/77 values in Appendix A. The price increase since 1974 is about

23. The gazetted price is the official reference price, which is the basis for calculating export duties.

15 percent, if the high 1976/77 estimate is accepted (at the lower estimate, there is no price increase at all). The 1976/77 supply price of NR c.i.f. New York is calculated to be around 36¢ a pound at a real discount rate of 10 percent.

Full supply price of synthetic rubber

A set of full supply prices (that is, prices required to make it worthwhile to invest in synthetic rubber production) was also calculated for the synthetic rubber industry. These supply prices are obviously theoretical, since the overcapacity in the industry throughout most of the industrialized countries tends to discourage new investments. Supply prices were calculated only for SBR-1500, the major competitor of NR, using the same method as that used for NR. It was assumed that a butadiene extraction plant with a capacity of 60,000 tons a year; a styrene plant, based on ethylene and benzene, with a capacity of 250,000 tons a year; and an SBR plant with a capacity of 60,000 tons a year, using the emulsion process, all would be part of a large petrochemical complex. Full supply prices were calculated first for the basic inputs, styrene and butadiene, and then for SBR.

The information on capital investments and on input requirements were collected partly from industry interviews and partly from a review of the literature. Because of a lack of comparable figures on recent new investments other than for debottlenecking operations, figures for the capital cost index from U.S. publications were used to estimate the supply prices for 1975 and 1977. Nevertheless, the estimated supply prices are considered to be representative of those in Western Europe for three reasons. First, the free market price of crude in Western Europe has been used throughout, and, therefore, the input prices used are higher than those which would apply to the United States. Second, butadiene was assumed to be extracted from a naphtha cracker, and not by the Houdry process still used in the United States. Finally, marketing, research, and development costs are included in the SBR supply price. The inclusion of marketing costs implies that the rubber-production firm has no captive markets, a situation which is more common in Western Europe than in the United States.[24]

---

24. The details about method and actual figures used in these calculations are given in Appendix D.

The supply prices of sbr-1500 over the years are determined by the changes in capital costs, labor costs, the price of crude, and the relation each year between naphtha and fuel oil prices on the one hand, and the price of crude on the other.[25] Given investments and labor costs for 1973 and assuming unchanged production technology over the estimation period, prices were estimated for 1975 and 1977 by using published index figures for capital and labor cost changes and actual crude oil prices. Supply prices of sbr-1500, and its components butadiene and styrene, were calculated for three desired real rates of return: 8, 10, and 12 percent.[26] The valuation of the C_4 stream from the naphtha cracker as an input into the butadiene extraction presented a difficult problem, since the value of the C_4's depends more on the market value of butadiene than the value of butadiene depends on that of C_4.[27] By taking a lower and a higher value for the C_4 stream, a lower and a higher butadiene price was arrived at. This in turn resulted in a low and a high supply price for sbr-1500.

Table 4–4 shows the calculated supply prices of sbr-1500 in 1973, 1975, and 1977. They include marketing cost and expenses for research and development, taken at 10 percent of the supply price. The low alternative of sbr supply prices is entirely the result of the low valuation of the C_4 stream used in butadiene extraction. It is, of course, quite possible, even likely, that when market conditions are depressed, sbr-1500 will be sold at prices even below the low prices in Table 4–4. Such prices would simply mean a lower rate of return on investments or, expressed differently, that full interest and depreciation at replacement value would not be covered by market prices.

The increase in the supply prices of sbr between 1973, 1975, and 1977 also depends, of course, on the discount rate used. The higher the discount rate, the greater the proportion of investment expenditure in the final supply price. Investment expenditure occurs during the first years, whereas expenditure for labor and chemical input, as well as receipt from sales, occur later. At a lower discount rate, the

25. This relation is by no means stable.

26. In a country with, for example, 8 percent inflation, this would mean nominal rates of return of 16, 18, and 20 percent if all expenditures and receipts were inflated by the same percentage.

27. Cracking naphtha (or gas oil) yields ethylene, propylene, and fuel oil. In addition it yields C_4 and C_5 fractions, which include a variety of chemicals. Separation of the C_4 fraction yields butadiene and other C_4's.

Table 4–4. *Full Supply Prices of* SBR-*1500 in Western Europe at Real Discount Rates of 8, 10, and 12 Percent, 1973, 1975, and 1977*

Real discount rate	Percentage		
	8	10	12
1973 (first half)			
SBR, low	19.4	20.6	21.7
SBR, high	21.2	22.4	23.6
1975			
SBR, low	31.7	33.3	34.9
SBR, high	36.3	37.9	39.6
1977			
SBR, low	38.1	39.9	41.8
SBR, high	43.4	45.4	47.4

Note: The following basic data inputs underlie the supply price estimates:

	1973 (first half)	1975	1977
Price of crude			
—dollars per ton	23.50	87.50	98.00
—dollars per barrel	3.22	11.99	13.42
Price of crude—index	100.0	372.3	417.0
Capital cost index	100.0	127.0	152.8
Labor cost index	100.0	135.0	162.6

Source: Appendix D.

increase in feedstock prices resulting from the increase in oil prices thus weighs more heavily. As the increase in the price of crude far outweighed the increase in capital cost, supply prices at a lower discount rate show a sharper increase than those at a higher discount rate. Thus, at a real discount rate of 8 percent, the low supply prices of SBR are estimated to have risen by 63.4 percent between 1973 and 1975 and by 96.4 percent between 1973 and 1977. At a real discount rate of 12 percent, the supply price increases over the two periods are 60.8 and 92.6 percent, respectively. The increases in the high SBR supply price estimates are even larger, since the high estimates are based on higher values for butadiene, which makes them even more sensitive to the oil price increase.

These calculations show that, to invest profitably in SBR production in 1977, the Western Europe industry would have had to price the SBR twice as high as in 1973. In absolute figures, a real rate of return of 10 percent would have been achieved only by investing in SBR-1500 if future expected real prices were at least about 40¢ a pound (low estimates of feedstock costs). Investment in NR in Malaysia, at the same real rate of return of 10 percent, would, on the contrary, have been possible in 1977 if a future real price of 36¢ a pound c.i.f. in Europe had been expected. Moreover, this supply price for NR contains an export duty element equal to 14 percent of the f.o.b. price, whereas the tax element in the SBR-1500 supply price is about 4 percent. The relative profitability of natural rubber investments would have been even greater in relation to IR, since its supply prices are at least 3¢ to 5¢ a pound higher than those of SBR-1500. It seems, therefore, that NR can compete effectively with both IR and SBR in the long term. Greater investments in NR would ensure greater future supply, which would allow NR to blunt any further substantial development of IR and to slow down the expansion of SBR production capacity, at least outside the centrally planned economies.

The question of how generally applicable these conclusions are deserves some further comment. First, the calculated supply price of NR is on the conservative side, so that the estimates presented here possibly overstate cost by as much as 2¢ to 3¢ a pound.[28] Second, the comparison between the expected future prices that would make investments in NR and SBR profitable in 1977 were made between the high estimate for NR and the low estimate for SBR. This was done to factor in the possibility of slightly higher natural rubber investment costs outside Malaysia, even though recent evidence from projects in Thailand and Indonesia financed by the World Bank indicates that investment costs in these two countries do not differ much from those of Malaysia. Third, although the estimated SBR supply price is still more representative of the situation in Western Europe, it is not likely to be significantly different from the prices in the United States and Japan. Although the U.S. supply price in 1977 would have been from 1 to 1.5¢ a pound lower than that in Western Europe, this difference resulted mostly from the relatively lower cost of oil in the United States due to the price regulations in effect during that period. The thrust of U.S. energy policy, however, clearly indicates that prices in the United States will fall in line with world prices. They have already begun to do so in the past year. Most of the difference in SBR supply

28. See 't Hooft-Welvaars, "The Profitability of NR and SBR Investments."

Table 4–5. *Sensitivity of Full Supply Prices of* SBR
to Crude Oil Price Changes at a Real Discount Rate of 10 Percent

Price	A	B	C	D
Real crude oil price				
U.S. dollars per barrel	13.42	15.43	16.77	18.79
Index (1977 = 100)	100.0	115.0	125.0	140.0
SBR full supply price—low				
U.S. cents per pound	39.9	41.7	42.8	44.6
Index (1977 = 100)	100.0	104.5	107.3	111.8
SBR full supply price—high				
U.S. cents per pound	45.4	48.0	49.7	52.3
Index (1977 = 100)	100.0	105.7	109.5	115.2

Source: Appendix D.

prices between Western Europe and the United States should, therefore, disappear in the near future.

Furthermore, the relative importance of the most important variable affecting SBR supply prices and, thus, the future profitability of any investments in SBR—the price of oil—needs to be examined separately, since the implicit assumptions made about crude oil prices are quite slanted in favor of SBR. In 1973 the part of the cost of base materials and utilities which was related directly to crude oil prices represented about 16 percent of the total supply price of SBR (at a 10 percent discount rate). In 1977 the share of total had risen to about 30 percent. The substantial changes in the real price of crude oil that have occurred since have already substantially increased the supply prices of SBR by at least 5¢ a pound.[29] Therefore, the benchmark year (1977) used to compare the long-term profitability of natural and synthetic rubber investments understates appreciably the relative advantage of NR. At 1979 real oil prices such relative advantage is already much greater than it was in 1977.

The sensitivity of SBR supply prices to changes in real crude oil prices is shown in Table 4–5. The basis of the sensitivity analysis is the 1977 estimated SBR supply prices. To ensure the same real rate of return on SBR investments (for example, 10 percent)—other things remaining equal—the low supply price of SBR would have had to in-

29. Between 1977 and 1979 the real price of crude oil in international markets has increased an average of about 40 percent.

crease by about 4.5 percent if the real price of oil increased by 15 percent; by about 7 percent if the real price of oil increased by 25 percent; and by about 12 percent if the real price of oil increased by 40 percent. For the high SBR supply price, these percentage increases would have had to have been even higher. Each additional increase of $1 a barrel in the real price of crude oil adds 0.87¢ a pound to the low SBR supply price and 1.27¢ a pound to the high SBR supply price.

The future cost competitiveness of NR is likely to improve further if energy prices continue to rise above their 1979 levels. The available indications are that the real prices of oil will have to increase in real terms to ensure equilibium between world energy supply and demand by the end of the century.[30] Current World Bank projections of real oil prices in the medium term point to a possible increase of 30 percent between 1980 and 1990.[31]

30. See, for example, Workshop on Alternative Energy Strategies (WAES), *Energy: Global Prospects to 1985 and 2000* (New York: McGraw-Hill, 1977), pp. 8–17 and 40–41.

31. These projections incorporate a substantial upward adjustment in real oil prices during 1980. The average OPEC price for oil, in 1977 U.S. dollars, is expected to be $19.30 per barrel in 1980, as opposed to $15.20 per barrel in 1979.

5

•−•··•−•·

Future Balance
of Supply and Demand

Forecasting the demand for, and supply of, rubber is a difficult endeavor. Future growth of demand depends on the evolution of a complex set of technological and economic variables with which the world energy situation interacts strongly. Future growth of supply is also quite uncertain, but the uncertainty is greater with synthetic than with natural rubber, at least during the 1980s.[1]

Outlook for the World Demand for Rubber

During the next ten years the pattern of growth of the world demand for rubber will continue to be shaped to a large extent by the growth of the world automotive industry. In industrialized countries, where the use of motor vehicles has already reached high levels and where energy conservation can be expected to be pursued vigorously, through higher prices and other changes in the mode and structure of transport induced by the government, the growth of motor vehicle production and use is likely to be slower than in the past. In the centrally planned economies (with the possible exception of China), the negative effect of energy conservation measures and of higher energy prices on the future increase in the use of motor vehicles can be expected to be much smaller than in developed countries, since the present levels of vehicle ownership and use in the centrally planned economies are still relatively low, and growth of individual income will continue to generate strong demand for motor vehicles, especially

---

1. See Appendixes D and E for details.

automobiles. In developing countries with high average incomes the same situation is likely to occur. In the poorer developing countries, however, reliance on public transport is likely to predominate for the foreseeable future, and the growth of the automotive sector is expected to be much smaller than in the high-income developing countries.

The other component of rubber demand—demand for uses other than tires—is, on the contrary, expected to continue to grow in all major consuming areas, as in the past, in some fixed relation to real income or industrial production.

Because of the historical dominance of the automotive sector in the total demand for rubber and the close relation that existed between growth of real income and the production and use of motor vehicles, past forecasts of rubber demand were usually based on the historical link between total elastomer use and real growth in the gross national product (GNP). This relation has remained strong and stable during the past twenty-five years. However, the expected changes in the structure of motor vehicle demand in developed countries (caused by declining rates of expansion of per capita vehicle ownership as real per capita income grows; decreased use of vehicles because of higher operating costs; and shifts in consumers' tastes toward smaller, lighter, and more fuel-efficient vehicles) have raised serious doubts about the traditional method of forecasting rubber demand in these countries. It was felt, therefore, that the forecasting approach based on historical income elasticities needed some important modifications before it could be applied to the present situation.

In this study a modified aggregate income elasticity forecasting framework and a more disaggregated demand model are used to estimate future levels of rubber demand. The former, applied to all major consuming areas—developed, developing, and centrally planned economies—relies upon scaling down the historical income-elasticity coefficients of total rubber demand over the forecast period. The latter, applied to the major developed consuming areas—North America, Western Europe, Japan, and Oceania—is based upon dividing rubber demand into demand for use in tires and demand for use other than in tires (nontire uses). It relates rubber demand for tires to motor vehicle production (and various technical factors, such as vehicle size, tire size, and tire type); motor vehicle use to real GNP growth, fuel prices, and technological factors; and nontire demand to real GNP growth. The results obtained from the disaggregated demand model provide a useful check on the results derived from the

Table 5-1. World Elastomer Demand, Actual Averages, Projected, and Growth Rates, 1955 to 1990, Selected Years

Economic region	Actual averages (thousands of metric tons)			Projected (thousands of metric tons)		Growth rates (annual percentage)			
	1955–57	1972–74	1975–77	1985	1990	1956–73	1976–85	1985–90	1976–1990
Developed countries[a]—I	2,640	7,121	7,084	10,900	13,000	6.0	4.9	3.6	4.4
—II				10,500	12,500				
Developing countries	207	1,147	1,339	2,800	4,000	10.6	8.6	7.4	8.1
Centrally planned economies	673	2,367	2,883	5,300	7,000	7.7	7.0	5.7	6.5
World total—I	3,520	10,635	11,327	19,000	24,000	6.7	5.9	4.8	5.5
—II				18,600	23,500		5.7	4.8	5.4

a. Alternative I refers to projections based on income elasticity; alternative II refers to projections derived from end uses.
Source: Actual data, International Rubber Study Group.

modified aggregate forecasting approach for rubber demand in the developed countries, where the forecast uncertainties are greatest.[2]

Under the current World Bank assumptions about the future growth of the world economy, world demand for rubber is projected to grow an average of 5.5 percent a year between 1976 and 1990 (Table 5–1), that is at about 1 percent a year below the historical rate. The future growth of elastomer demand is projected to decrease more in developed and developing countries than in the centrally planned economies. In developed countries rubber demand is forecast to grow 4.4 percent a year, compared with an historical annual rate of about 6 percent. In both developing countries and centrally planned economies, rubber consumption is expected to grow at much higher rates than in developed countries: at 8.1 and 6.5 percent a year, respectively, between 1976 and 1990, compared with historical annual rates of about 10.6 and 7.7 percent, respectively.

On the whole, even under conservative assumptions regarding the growth of the world economy during the next ten years and the relatively unfavorable built-in assumptions concerning the changes in the structure of demand, world consumption of rubber should continue to grow at a healthy rate. This would offer both the natural and the synthetic rubber industries ample scope for future expansion.

Projections of Natural Rubber Production

The potential for natural rubber production between now and the end of the next decade is, to a large extent, already determined by the yield profile of the trees that are already in the ground. Those planted during the first half of the 1970s have begun to produce, and will reach maximum yields toward the end of the next decade. New planting and replanting during the late 1970s have had—in terms of incremental production—only a limited effect on world natural rubber output in the second half of the 1980s. Its full effect will be felt in the 1990s.

Under such circumstances, the projections of natural rubber production presented here simply quantify the likely normal output in

2. Appendix E provides detailed explanations of both models, of the methodologies used to make the forecasts, of the assumption made concerning the exogenous variables, and of the results that were obtained.

Table 5–2. *World Natural Rubber Production, Actual, Projected, and Growth Rates, 1955 to 1990, Selected Years*

Economic region and country	Actual (thousands of metric tons)					Projected (thousands of metric tons)		Growth rates (annual percentage)			
	1955	1960	1970	1976	1977	1985	1990	1955–76	1976–85	1985–90	1976–90
Developing countries	1,857	1,883	2,902	3,492	3,511	5,035	5,875	3.1	4.1	3.1	3.8
Malaysia	708	765	1,269	1,640	1,613	2,400	2,700	4.1	4.3	2.4	3.6
Indonesia	750	620	815	847	835	1,010	1,100	0.6	2.0	1.7	1.9
Thailand	133	171	287	392	425	785	1,140	5.3	8.0	7.7	7.9
Sri Lanka	95	99	159	152	146	185	195	2.3	2.2	1.1	1.8
India	23	25	90	148	152	200	220	9.3	3.4	1.9	2.9
Others	148	203	282	313	340	455	520	3.6	4.2	2.7	3.7
Centrally planned economies	93	114	42	78	80	210	260	−0.8	11.6	4.4	9.1
Vietnam	66	77	29	33	35	100	120	−3.3	13.1	3.7	9.7
Cambodia	27	37	13	20	15	35	40	−1.4	6.4	2.7	5.1
China	..	..	..	25	30	75	100	—	13.0	5.9	10.4
World total[a]	1,950	2,035	3,102	3,565	3,600	5,245	6,135	2.9	4.4	3.2	4.0

— Not applicable.
.. Zero or negligible.
a. For 1955, 1960, 1970, 1976, and 1977 the world total is not the sum of the two sub-totals. The differences are caused by the statistical discrepancies shown in IRSG data.
Source: Actual data, International Rubber Study Group.

1985 and 1990, based on existing acreage, age of existing trees, composite yield profiles, and likely rates of replanting and new planting in the major producing countries. The norm projections are not, therefore, based on specific price assumptions; they simply assume that natural rubber prices will remain high enough to ensure continuous tapping of existing productive trees and moderate use of chemical stimulation on relatively old trees.[3] Obviously, depending on the price trend, both the intensity of tapping and the use of chemical stimulants can be varied, and, correspondingly, the actual output trend can deviate from the projected norm.

The level of normal production was derived individually for all the five major and the eight smaller producing countries.[4] The best information available to both the Food and Agriculture Organization of the United Nations and the World Bank was used to make the projections. For Malaysia, Thailand, Sri Lanka, and India, future production was derived from specific information about areas under rubber, age distribution of trees, yield profiles, and assumptions about rates of replanting, likely new planting, and the use of chemical stimulants. For Indonesia and the smaller producing countries, the production projections are based on a much less rigorous model. They contain a larger element of judgment, even though past trends, national plans, and information specific to each country were considered as much as possible.[5]

The projections show that world output of natural rubber (NR) can be expected to grow about 4 percent a year between 1976 and 1990, which is slightly over 1 percent a year above the historical rate. The pattern of growth of natural rubber production, however, is likely to be quite uneven: after growing 4.4 percent a year until 1985, the annual rate of expansion is expected to fall to about 3 percent in the second half of the 1980s (Table 5–2). In Thailand, in the smaller producing countries, and possibly in Indonesia, however, rubber production is projected to grow at rates above the historical trend be-

3. A price for rss1, c.i.f. New York, of about 40¢ per pound (in 1977 constant U.S. dollars) would probably fulfill these assumptions.

4. The major producing countries are Malaysia, Indonesia, Thailand, Sri Lanka, and India; the smaller producing countries are Liberia, Nigeria, Zaïre, Vietnam, Cambodia, Brazil, the Philippines, and the Ivory Coast.

5. Appendix F sets out in detail the methodology by country, showing the specific assumptions upon which the natural rubber production projections were made.

tween 1976 and 1990. Malaysia and Sri Lanka are, on the contrary, expected to increase their rubber production at rates below those experienced from the mid-1950s to the mid-1970s. In Malaysia, this stems from the slowdown in new planting and replanting in the late 1960s and early 1970s, when oil palm production became more attractive than rubber production, particularly to estates. The lack of a vigorous rubber replanting policy in the 1960s and 1970s is also the main cause of the expected slowdown of growth in Sri Lanka during the 1980s.

Although it is expected, with a reasonable degree of confidence, that natural rubber production will increase during the next ten years at a faster pace than during the past twenty years, the accuracy of the projections presented here depends to some extent on the future production profiles of Indonesia and of the smaller producers, both of which are subject to considerable uncertainty. Indonesia might not reach the production shown in Table 5–2, particularly during the second half of the 1980s. The short-term production potential of some of the smaller producers may also be overstated.

Capacities for Synthetic Rubber Production

World producing capacity for synthetic rubber (sr) increased at roughly the same rate as actual production in the 1960s, about 9 percent a year. The rate of expansion was faster in the developed countries than in the centrally planned economies. Developing countries did not begin to produce sr until the mid-1960s (Table 5–3). During the 1960s an average of 80 percent of existing world production capacity was utilized.

This rapid pace of expansion began to slow down in the early 1970s and was further retarded by the uncertainties created by the oil crisis and by the subsequent downturn in world economic activity in the mid-1970s. Expansion of production capacity for sr has now virtually ceased in industrialized countries, but is continuing at a rapid pace in the developing countries and in the centrally planned economies of Eastern Europe and the U.S.S.R.

Little growth in world production capacity is foreseen until 1981, the latest year for which estimates are quite firm. Practically all of the projected expansion—about 22 percent with respect to 1976 levels—will take place in the centrally planned economies (U.S.S.R. and Eastern Europe) and in developing countries (Brazil, Argentina,

Korea, and India). Synthetic rubber production in Middle Eastern countries is not expected to begin on a significant scale until the mid-1980s. On the whole, world capacity for synthetic rubber production is not expected to grow much more than 4 percent a year until the early 1980s.

Outside the centrally planned economies, the rates of capacity utilization are bound to increase appreciably in the late 1970s, when the synthetic rubber industry will probably have to operate at close to full capacity (Table 5–4).[6]

Although firm projections of production capacities cannot be made much beyond 1980, it is apparent that major investment decisions will have to be taken in the next two to three years—particularly in developed countries—to begin the production facilities necessary to meet the growth in demand that is expected in the 1980s.

In the centrally planned economies of Eastern Europe and the U.S.S.R. expansion of production capacity for sr is expected to continue to increase at a fast pace. China has almost completed a large petrochemical complex, which will generate substantial additional capacity for producing sr.

In the U.S.S.R. in particular, the production of synthetic *cis*-polyisoprene (ir) is expected to continue to expand rapidly. Growth of about 10 percent a year between 1976 and 1985 is planned. According to an International Rubber Study Group report, ir production capacity in centrally planned economies (excluding China) will reach 1.1 million metric tons by 1980 and 1.8 million metric tons by 1985, from an estimated capacity of 0.63 million metric tons in 1978.[7] Other authoritative estimates of ir production in the centrally planned economies of Eastern Europe and the U.S.S.R. discount somewhat the published expansion plans and implicitly place production of ir in these countries at about 0.8 million metric tons by 1980 and 1.2 million metric tons by 1985.[8] On balance, however, it

6. Use of about 90 percent of total rated capacity can be considered to be full capacity utilization.

7. International Rubber Study Group (irsg), "The Polyisoprene Rubber Situation: A Report by the Ad Hoc Advisory Panels," London, March 1977 (processed), p. 5.

8. See for example, C. F. Ruebensaal, *Changing Markets and Manufacturing Patterns in the Synthetic Rubber Industry* (New York: iisrp Inc., 1977), pp. 6–10. These estimates are consistent with the projections of ir capacity by the sources in Table 5-3.

Table 5–3. *World Synthetic Rubber Capacities (Net Rubber), Estimated, Projected, and Growth Rates, 1960 to 1982, Selected Years*

Economic region and country	Estimated (thousands of metric tons)				Projected (thousands of metric tons)		Growth rates (annual percentage)			
	1960	1965	1970	1976	1978	1982	1960–65	1965–70	1970–76	1976–82
Developed countries										
North America[a]	1,900	2,454	3,009	3,355	3,323	3,366				
Japan	28	246	742	1,355	1,327	1,462				
Western Europe	318	866	1,584	2,583	2,647	2,930				
Others[b]	...	60	92	124	125	125				
Total	2,246	3,626	5,427	7,417	7,422	7,883	10.1	8.4	5.3	1.2
SBR	1,765	2,437	3,371	4,513	4,476	4,697				
BR	20	359	749	998	1,079	1,151				
IR	...	123	210	359	280	280				
NBR	117	161	253	290	300	312				
IIR	174	286	349	465	493	575				
EPM/EPDM	...	47	149	391	385	426				
CR	170	213	346	400	409	439				
Developing countries										
Latin America[c]	...	138	205	368	389	599				
Asia	...	30	30	56	165	235				
Africa	...	...	...	...	—	—				
Middle East	...	...	...	...	—	—				
Total	...	168	235	424	554	834	—	6.9	10.3	14.5
SBR	...	140	205	377	475	633				
BR	...	28	28	38	67	138				
IR	...	...	...	...	—	—				

NBR	...	...	2	8	12	13				
IIR	...	...	...	...	...	50				
EPM/EPDM	...	...	...	...	—	—				
CR	...	...	...	...	—	—				
Centrally planned economies										
Total	682	801	1,201	2,048	2,605	3,388	3.3	8.4	9.3	10.6
SBR	607	696	871	1,258	1,420	1,720				
BR	...	30	65	185	215	285				
IR	...	...	100	375	625	940				
NBR	20	20	30	65	80	88				
IIR	25	25	30	90	105	120				
EPM/EPDM	...	...	30	...	...	—				
CR	30	30	75	75	160	235				
World total	2,928	4,595	6,863	9,889	10,581	12,105	9.4	8.4	6.3	4.1
SBR	2,372	3,273	4,447	6,148	6,371	7,050	6.7	6.3	5.5	2.7
BR	20	417	842	1,221	1,361	1,574	85.0	15.1	6.4	5.2
IR	...	123	310	734	905	1,220	—	20.0	15.4	10.7
NBR	137	181	285	363	392	413	5.7	9.5	4.1	2.6
IIR	199	311	379	555	598	745	9.3	4.0	6.6	6.1
EPM/EPDM	...	47	179	391	385	426	—	31.0	13.9	1.7
CR	200	243	421	475	569	674	4.0	11.6	2.0	7.2

Note: Totals may not add up because of rounding.
— Not applicable.
... Zero or negligible.
a. Excludes Mexico.
b. Australia and South Africa.
c. Includes Mexico.
Source: For 1960 and 1965, C. F. Ruebensaal, "World Synthetic Rubber—Its Manufacture and Markets," Rubber and Plastic Age (various issues); for 1970, 1976, and projections to 1978 and 1981, C. F. Ruebensaal, "The Rubber Industry Statistical Report," International Institute of Synthetic Rubber Producers, New York, annual report (1971 and 1977).

Table 5–4. *Utilization of Synthetic Rubber Production Capacity in Developed and Developing Countries, Actual and Projected, 1974 to 1980, Selected Years*
(percentage)

Economic region or country	Actual			Projected, 1980
	1974	1975	1976	
Developed countries				
North America	81	66	75	87
Western Europe	73	60	72	83
Japan	65	54	69	80
Others	68	59	64	85
Developing countries	88	76	76	88
Total	75	62	73	85

Source: Industry sources (interview data).

seems quite likely that these countries will continue to pursue policies of self-sufficiency in rubber and that their relatively favorable situation concerning energy supply will give additional impetus to their plans. The possibility of substantial IR exports from the U.S.S.R. to Western Europe also cannot be totally discounted.

Outside the centrally planned economies the expansion of IR production capacity is likely to be quite modest over the next nine to ten years. Some expansion will take place in North America and Japan. Greater uncertainty exists in Western Europe. Total production capacity could expand from the 1976 level of 360,000 metric tons to 500,000 metric tons in 1985.[9] Should natural rubber prices—in 1977 U.S. dollars—increase substantially in the 1980s above 1979 levels (48.7¢ a pound), reflecting relative scarcities of NR, IR production would be stimulated, and production capacity in industrialized countries would expand much faster than projected. The analysis in Chapter 4 indicates that expected prices of NR (in 1977 U.S. dollars) in the neighborhood of 50¢ a pound would trigger new substantial investments in IR in industrialized countries.

This situation is not very likely, since full natural rubber production from existing trees is almost guaranteed at c.i.f. prices of about 40¢ a pound (in 1977 U.S. dollars) and since the expansion of exist-

9. IRSG, "The Polyisoprene Rubber Situation," p. 5.

ing production capacity through replanting and new plantings would be economically justified. The long lags between investments in NR and actual production, however, complicate considerably the process of investment synchronization. This increases the risk of temporary price increases that could lead to price expectations different from those warranted by the analysis of supply prices. These price expectations about future natural rubber prices could give impetus to investments in IR.

The Balance of Demand and Supply

Between 1976 and 1990 total world consumption of elastomers is projected to grow 5.2 to 5.4 percent a year. Production of NR over the same period is likely to grow less than 4 percent a year. Even using the lower growth projection for elastomer demand, it is apparent that the market share of NR is likely to continue to decline during the next fifteen years because of insufficient supply. The world market share of NR is projected to fall from 30 percent in 1977, to 28 percent in 1985, and to 26 percent in 1990 (Table 5–5). Excluding the centrally planned economies, the market share of NR is likely to remain at about its 1976 level (33.5 percent) until the end of the current decade, but to fall to about 32 percent in the mid-1980s, and to 31 percent in 1990. If the higher growth projection for elastomer demand is used, the projected fall in natural rubber market share would be greater.

As indicated above, the centrally planned economies (particularly Eastern Europe and the U.S.S.R.) seem to be developing a large indigenous production of synthetic cis-IR. If this happens, the market share of NR in these countries will drop irrespective of the levels of supply and price. Demand for NR in the centrally planned economies will then increase slowly over the next fifteen years, and it will likely be used only in products for which substitution with IR is technically difficult.[10] Yet, despite the consequent availability of more NR to both developed and developing countries, and without a concentrated program to increase production even further, the market

---

10. The importance attached to the maintenance of trade relations with some of the natural rubber producing countries is also likely to play a role in determining how much NR is used by the centrally planned economies.

Table 5-5. *World Elastomer Balance of Supply and Demand, Actual Averages, Projected, and Growth Rates, 1955 to 1990, Selected Years*

Item	Actual averages (thousands of metric tons)				Projected (thousands of metric tons)		Growth rates (annual percentage)		
	1955–57	1966–68	1972–74	1975–77	1985	1990	1976–85	1985–90	1976–90
Production of elastomers									
Synthetic rubber	1,650	4,496	7,366	7,737	13,355	17,365	6.3	5.4	5.9
Natural rubber	1,935	2,533	3,357	3,493	5,245	6,135	4.6	3.2	4.1
Total	3,585	7,029	10,723	11,230	18,600	23,500	5.8	4.8	5.4
Consumption of elastomers									
Synthetic rubber	1,616	4,425	7,251	7,792	13,355	17,365	6.2	5.4	5.9
Natural rubber	1,902	2,619	3,384	3,536	5,245	6,135	4.5	3.2	4.0
Total	3,518	7,044	10,635	11,328	18,600	23,500	5.7	4.8	5.4
Consumption of natural rubber									
Developed countries	1,498	1,669	2,113	2,128	3,240	3,795	4.8	3.2	4.2
Developing countries	184	345	564	703	1,050	1,300	4.6	4.4	4.5
Centrally planned economies	220	611	707	705	950	1,040	3.4	1.8	2.8
Total	1,902	2,625	3,384	3,536	5,240	6,135	4.5	3.2	4.0
				(percent)					
Natural rubber market share									
World	54.1	37.2	31.8	31.2	28.2	26.1	—	—	—
World, excluding centrally planned economies	59.1	36.4	32.4	33.6	32.2	30.8	—	—	—

— Not applicable.
Source: Actual data, International Rubber Study Group.

Table 5–6. *Isoprenic Rubber Share of Total Rubber Consumption*
Outside the Centrally Planned Economies, 1965, 1970, 1975, and 1976

Item	1965	1970	1975	1976
	(thousands of metric tons)			
Isoprenic rubber consumption	1,952.0	2,466.0	2,852.0	3,051.5
NR	1,882.5	2,317.5	2,652.5	2,837.5
IR	69.5	148.5	199.5	214.0
Total rubber consumption	4,842.5	6,849.5	7,582.5	8,419.0
	(percent)			
Isoprenic rubber share	40.3	36.0	37.6	36.2
NR	38.9	33.8	35.0	33.7
IR	1.4	2.2	2.6	2.5

Note: Isoprenic rubber includes NR and IR.

position of NR outside the centrally planned economies is expected to deteriorate appreciably because of insufficient supply.

In 1976 the market share of isoprenic rubber (NR and IR) outside the centrally planned economies was about 36 percent: NR held roughly 33.5 percent of the market for all elastomers, and IR held the other 2.5 percent of the total. The market share of isoprenic rubbers has remained quite stable since the late 1960s, when the commercial development of synthetic IR began on a sufficiently large scale (Table 5–6).

It has been argued that, on technical grounds, the market share of isoprenic rubber outside the centrally planned economies could be as high as 43 percent.[11] On economic grounds—with natural rubber prices at around 45¢ a pound c.i.f. (in 1977 constant U.S. dollars) and IR prices 5 to 10 percent above that—isoprenic rubbers should at least be able to maintain their share of the total rubber market in the foreseeable future.[12] The analysis in Chapter 4 pointed quite clearly

11. See, P. W. Allen, P. O. Thomas, B. C. Sekhar, *The Techno-Economic Potential of NR in Major End-Uses* (Kuala Lumpur: MRRDB, 1973), p. 34.

12. This is the almost unanimous opinion of rubber analysts. See for example Ruebensaal, *Changing Markets and Manufacturing Patterns in the Synthetic Rubber Industry*, p. 10 and M. J. Rhoad, "Isoprene Worldwide" *Proceedings of the 15th Annual Meeting* (New York: IISRP), p. 9. The latter analyst argues that the share of isoprenic rubber in total world elastomer consumption—including the centrally planned economies—could be as high as 39.2 percent in 1983.

Table 5-7. World Natural Rubber Trade, Actual Averages, Projected, and Growth Rates, 1955 to 1990, Selected Years

Economic region	Actual averages (thousands of metric tons)				Projected (thousands of metric tons)		Growth rates (annual percentage)			
	1955–57	1966–68	1971–73	1975–77	1985	1990	1956–76	1976–85	1985–90	1976–90
Exports										
Developed countries	...	...	...	...	...	...	—	—	—	—
Developing countries	1,794	2,304	2,909	3,058	4,480	5,180	2.7	4.3	2.9	3.8
Centrally planned economies	43	85	33	40	140	160	−0.4	14.9	2.7	10.4
Total	1,837	2,389	2,942	3,098	4,620	5,340	2.6	4.5	2.9	4.0
Imports										
Developed countries	1,518	1,570	2,007	2,097	3,240	3,795	1.6	5.0	3.2	4.3
Developing countries	104	170	261	341	530	635	6.1	5.0	3.7	4.5
Centrally planned economies	235	636	663	687	850	910	5.5	2.4	1.4	2.0
Total	1,857	2,376	2,931	3,125	4,620	5,340	2.6	4.4	2.9	3.9

— Not applicable.
... Zero or negligible.
Sources: Actual data, International Rubber Study Group.

to the conclusion that NR has a strong technical and economic potential to compete successfully with IR within the market for isoprenic rubbers. Assuming that the market for isoprenic rubbers outside the centrally planned economies remains at close to recent levels—36 to 37 percent of the total elastomers market—maintaining a total market share for NR of 34 to 35 percent appears to be quite feasible. To reach this objective, the supply of NR in 1990 should be about 0.5 million metric tons above the levels envisaged in current projections.

The Trade Outlook for Natural Rubber

The balance of supply and demand for NR (Table 5-5) has clear trade implications. Exports of NR from developing countries can be expected to grow 3.8 percent a year between 1976 and 1990. This compares with a historical rate of 2.7 percent a year. Exports are expected to increase at a much faster rate between now and 1985 than during the second half of the 1980s, closely reflecting the expected future natural rubber production patterns. The increases are expected to be 4.5 percent a year during the earlier years, compared with 4.0 percent a year between 1985 and 1990 (Table 5-7).

Imports of NR by developed and developing countries are expected to increase about 4.5 percent a year between 1976 and 1990. Total imports by centrally planned economies are foreseen to grow at a much slower rate, about 2 percent a year. Only China is expected to increase its imports of NR during the next fifteen years, whereas imports by the U.S.S.R. and Eastern Europe are expected to remain virtually unchanged. Even in China, the growth of natural rubber imports is expected to slow down in the 1980s, as more SR becomes available domestically and as indigenous production of NR is expanded.

6

•••

Conclusions and Implications

On the whole, the natural rubber industry is facing favorable prospects for growth. Its market potential is probably greater than at any time in the past twenty years. The quadrupling of the real price of crude oil between 1973 and 1979 has enhanced considerably the competitive position of natural rubber (NR) in the short-term, and its long-term competitiveness appears to have been strengthened even further.

The Future of the Synthetic Rubber and Natural Rubber Industries

Aside from the new kinds of specialty synthetic rubbers (SR)—such as thermoplastic rubber, resin-rubber blends, block-butadiene polymers —and possibly polyisoprene (IR), technological innovations in synthetic rubber production, as well as in economies of scale, seem to have run much of their course. Their future effect on the cost and price of the traditional kinds of SR is likely to be much less strong than in the 1950s and 1960s, although by no means negligible. After twenty-five years of unrestrained expansion, the synthetic rubber industry is reaching a stage where emphasis is likely to be put on rationalization, consolidation, and more planned growth.

Apart from the economic constraint to further rapid growth posed by high and possibly still-rising real energy costs, the synthetic rubber industry will have to face uncertainties concerning the availability and the price of chemical feedstocks, mounting pressures over environmental issues related to the production of chemicals, and some critical questions concerning the potential health hazards of prolonged exposure of workers to certain basic chemicals. Environmental concerns are likely at least to limit the previous freedom of choice of plant location enjoyed by the industry. The concentration of chemical production operations near densely populated areas is likely to heighten existing environmental concerns. Japan and Western Europe are already faced with this situation. The cost of pollution control systems is expected also to increase substantially the unit cost of sr.[1] Finally, the potential health problems related to prolonged exposure to chemicals, such as benzene, are now being investigated in the United States and elsewhere. This will likely increase worker and government concern over the safety of some synthetic rubber production processes, thereby increasing the uncertainties connected with planning new production capacity.

The natural rubber industry, however, although faced with problems connected with its diversity, fragmentation, and location, is just emerging from a period of retrenchment, profound internal transformation, and rationalization. The full benefits of long-term research and development programs pursued tenaciously during the past thirty years, of the spread of technical innovations in production and processing, of the rationalization measures introduced to improve internal and external marketing, and of the efforts made to improve the technical and economic credibility of the product are still to be reaped by the industry. As a natural raw material still competing directly with industrial raw materials, nr can expect another phase of relatively strong growth in demand. The industry can face this new period of expansion starting from a solid technoeconomic base.

Productivity can be increased enormously during the next thirty years by spreading existing tree-breeding and selection technology and by propagating, distributing, and planting locally suitable trees.[2] The use of high-yielding trees would help to bring smallholder yields closer to the levels reached by estates.

During the normal exploitation of existing rubber trees, chemical stimulants also can produce great economic advantages, particularly on trees tapped on first renewed bark. These advantages include significantly increased latex output, reduced labor costs, and an in-

1. See Ralph Stone and Company, "The Impact of Pollution Control on the Production Costs of Selected Natural and Synthetic Material," Reference no. ENV/73/007 (draft final report to unctad) (September 1975; processed).

2. See E. K. Ng and Pee Teck Yew, "Innovations in Natural Rubber Technology: Some Malaysian Lessons," Rubber Research Institute of Malaysia, Kuala Lumpur, 1976; processed.

creased responsiveness to changing price conditions. Stimulation can be used on old, low-yielding trees to at least double their latex output, enhancing the responsiveness of the industry to changing market prices. Alternatively, average yields can be maintained with less labor.

A greater amount of short-term stability in natural rubber prices is now within reach. Partly as a consequence of the greater elasticity of supply that could result from the use of stimulants and partly as the result of efforts initiated by producers to organize the market, short-term fluctuations in prices should be reduced considerably in the future. The first concrete example of the willingness and capability of producers to influence market prices through direct and positive market action occurred in Malaysia at the end of 1974. When natural rubber prices declined to an unacceptably low level as a result of the world economic recession, production and export control measures were implemented quickly and forcefully to arrest the fall in prices during 1975 and to avoid more serious disruptions in the production process.

Since then, the focus of producer efforts has shifted from unilateral to multilateral action aimed at establishing a workable scheme to stabilize rubber prices, protecting the interests of both producers and consumers. Within the framework of the Association of the Natural Rubber Producing Countries (ANRPC),[3] producers agreed on a rubber price stabilization scheme in November 1976.[4] The producers, however, emphasized immediately that the scheme was open to consuming countries as well, and solicited their participation in the agreement.

Consultations between producers and consumers began almost immediately thereafter in conjunction with the UNCTAD (United Nations Conference on Trade and Development) Integrated Program for Commodities. In late 1978 producers and consumers began to negotiate an international agreement on rubber, which would stabilize natural rubber prices at approximately market levels. In October 1978 the negotiations came to fruition, and a new Inter-

---

3. The ANRPC was formed in 1970. Present members are: India, Indonesia, Papua New Guinea, Malaysia, Singapore, Sri Lanka, and Thailand.

4. The Jakarta Agreement was signed by Malaysia, Indonesia, Thailand, Sri Lanka, and Singapore. It envisaged the operation of an internationally controlled buffer stock that would stabilize prices in conjunction with measures to rationalize supply. The size of the buffer stock was fixed at 100,000 metric tons for the first two years of the scheme.

national Natural Rubber Agreement was reached.[5] Producers and consumers agreed to share equally the responsibilities and benefits of the new agreement, which aims to stabilize the market price through an internationally held and financed buffer stock of 550 thousand metric tons of NR. The buffer stock is meant to maintain natural rubber prices above the floor of Malaysian $1.5 per kilogram, but below a ceiling of Malaysian $2.7 per kilogram. There will also be a moving price stabilization band between the established floor and ceiling prices. The stabilization band will be reviewed every eighteen months, whereas the floor and ceiling will be reviewed every thirty months.

It is obviously too early to judge the effect of the new international agreement on natural rubber consumers. The fact that an agreement was reached shows, however, that both producers and consumers of NR want stable market prices. The use of the buffer stock seems adequate to attain this objective. The key to the success of this operation, however, will be the setting of realistic price stabilization bands.

A Strategy for Natural Rubber

There are solid reasons to expect a period of strong expansion in the world natural rubber economy during the next fifteen years. Yet, if the industry is to take full advantage of its market potential, a number of important conditions will have to be fulfilled:

(a) The supply of NR will have to keep pace with the expected growth of demand for isoprenic rubber, and the supply will have to be made secure; this is the only way for NR to maintain its price competitiveness with synthetic polyisoprene (IR) and to prevent a new wave of investment in IR;

(b) Existing production technologies will have to be adopted and spread within and across countries; and

(c) Research and development on production and utilization of NR will have to continue and be intensified.

5. The agreement is scheduled to go into effect on October 1, 1980, following ratification by member governments. For the text of the agreement, see United Nations Conference on Trade and Development (UNCTAD), *International Natural Rubber Agreement, 1979* (Document TD/Rubber/15) (New York, October 17, 1979).

The basic elements of a strategy that will ensure the development of the world natural rubber economy and maximize the potential of NR are quite clear. The implementation of such a strategy, however, will require timely decisions, a considerable degree of cooperation among producers, some international assistance, and continuing dialogue and collaboration between the producers and consumers of NR.

Maintaining the growth of supply of NR in line with the growth of world demand for isoprenic rubber is clearly the most important and urgent problem. The projections presented in Chapter 5 indicate that this growth is likely to continue until the early 1980s. Beyond that, however, the supply of NR will probably grow more slowly than the potential demand. Even with the relatively conservative assumptions made regarding the growth of world demand for all rubbers and the natural rubber requirements of the centrally planned economies, and with the relatively optimistic assumptions concerning the pattern of growth of the natural rubber supply, a potential demand gap of about 0.5 million metric tons appears likely by 1990. If this gap outside the centrally planned economies is not met by increased *Hevea* rubber supplies, it will be filled by synthetic *cis*-IR or another general purpose SR. The possibility of producing NR from alternative sources, such as guayule, on a significant scale before 1990 is unlikely.[6] Despite recent renewed interest in guayule, its economics are quite uncertain, since the production and processing technologies have not been improved and evaluated.[7]

---

6. Except in Brazil, NR is derived today exclusively from the tree, *Hevea brasiliensis*. The guayule shrub, *Parthenium argentatum*, is another possible source. Guayule originated in the upland plateaus of Mexico and Texas, where temperature is subtropical and rainfall is low. Guayule rubber and *Hevea* rubber have identical chemical and physical properties. Guayule rubber was produced briefly in Mexico during the 1910s. Interest in guayule revived during World War II, under the Emergency Rubber Project (ERP) sponsored by the U.S. Government. The ERP was terminated in 1946. Guayule development has continued during the past thirty years only in Mexico. Mexico plans to produce guayule rubber from an estimated 4 million hectares of wild guayule shrubs.

7. A recent report on guayule rubber, issued by the U.S. National Academy of Sciences, emphasizes the potential importance of guayule to the U.S. and Mexican economies and to U.S. security, but expresses doubts about the commercial viability of the plant under existing agricultural techniques and rubber extraction methods. See National Academy of Sciences, *Guayule: An Alternative Source of Natural Rubber* (National Academy of Sciences: Washington, D.C., 1977), pp. 3–10.

To increase the supply of NR in the 1990s, investment decisions will have to be made immediately in the key producing countries. Obviously, the relative economic and social advantages of investments in rubber will have to be evaluated carefully on a country-by-country and on a case-by-case basis. No attempt is made here to examine investment alternatives in rubber producing countries. Such analysis would require in-depth work on each country, and is well beyond the scope of this study.

Investment in replanting and rehabilitation

Within the bounds of country comparative advantages, acceleration of existing plans to replant old trees with new high-yielding varieties seems to be the best way for producers to increase the natural rubber supply. This is even more likely to be the case in countries where yields in the smallholder sector are low because of insufficient replanting in the past.

Thailand, assisted by the World Bank, is currently implementing a large replanting program in the smallholder sector. The economic feasibility of a large-scale replanting and rehabilitation program for the smallholders' sector in Indonesia has been examined recently, and the program will be implemented in the near future, also with World Bank assistance. If this scheme is successful, the possibility of enlarging its scope should be examined as soon as possible. The rehabilitation of the rubber industries of Sri Lanka and Nigeria also offer scope for increasing production in the relatively short term. Similar prospects would be offered by rehabilitating the rubber sectors of Vietnam and Cambodia. India also can expand her production beyond what is presently planned. International assistance to these government programs will probably be needed. The experience accumulated in the Thai replanting program should provide a solid basis for extending similar assistance to other countries.

Governments need to ensure that all of their efforts are concentrated on measures which will require maximum replanting. Insufficient attention to replanting during the 1960s has resulted in a lag of production behind the potential that might have been expected. In many areas this pattern has also continued into the present decade and is, in fact, responsible for the gap which is projected to develop during the 1980s. Given the lag between the time investment decisions are taken and the time the results are achieved, it is essential that governments take a long-range view and ensure that all of the conditions are created which will lead to replanting at the rate required. If not, the potential benefits which might otherwise have accrued to natural rubber producing countries will not be realized.

Attention should also be focused on the possibility of increasing the use of chemical stimulation on existing old trees. The experience of Malaysia in this field could provide a useful basis for programs designed to speed up the introduction of chemical stimulation among smallholders. The programs would have to be specifically designed for this purpose in order to ensure the profitability of this technique in each country.

Once the possibilities for replanting and rehabilitation have been exhausted, increasing the investments in newly planted rubber is another alternative for natural rubber producers. At the expected average c.i.f. prices of 40¢ a pound (in 1977 U.S. dollars), new investments in NR should be financially attractive to both foreign and domestic private capital in many rubber-producing countries. Private capital for expanding rubber production on estates seems to be amply available. It should be used wherever possible, within the development priorities established by the various governments. Serious attention should be given to existing institutional factors (such as the tax structure), which influence the relative profitability of competing estate crops (such as oil palm, coconut, and rubber).

Continuity of supply

Finally, a continuous, adequate supply of NR to respond to market needs will require constant government attention to the internal prices of rubber, particularly to the prices received by smallholders. The amount of short-term price responsiveness to supply that now exists depends to a large extent on the prices received by smallholders. The suitability of existing tax structures (particularly export taxes), the amount of financial and other assistance provided by government agencies to growers, and the efficiency and equity of internal marketing and distribution systems all will have to be critically evaluated, and changed where necessary, if they are to provide full support to the producers of NR.

The security of supply is still a large concern in the minds of natural rubber consumers. Measures to stabilize prices in the short term will go a long way to improve consumer confidence and to overcome the fear of the risks involved in relying on a raw material produced thousands of miles away from its main market outlets.

Stocking operations, such as the one envisaged by the new International Natural Rubber Agreement, should diminish existing fears of market disruptions.

Increased research and development

In the longer term, however, only the ability of the natural rubber industry to meet growing market demand will enable it to realize its full potential. A natural raw material that competes with industrial raw materials for the same market can only survive and prosper if it can share the benefits of modern technologies. Research and development on production and consumption are essential. The experience of the past thirty years has proven this point beyond any doubt. Innovation in natural rubber technology has come so far mostly from the Malaysian industry and government. Other countries and industries have contributed, but the burden has been shouldered largely by Malaysia.

Further support is also required for research work currently going on in the institutes of India, Indonesia, the Ivory Coast, Malaysia, Nigeria, and Sri Lanka. The efforts of the International Rubber Research and Development Board (IRRDB) to coordinate and disseminate the results of the research being carried out in member countries would also be a step in the right direction. It could probably increase the resources available for research and development, ensure a more equitable sharing of the financial burden, and improve the speed of technological transfer. It may also provide for more efficient use of existing resources by avoiding duplication of effort and by providing a more precise focus for national efforts. It could also provide ample grounds for expanding cooperation between producers and consumers, particularly in research on uses for NR, as well as cementing the necessary relation of mutual trust and collaboration between producers and processors.

A greater geographic diversification of the sources of supply would be an additional advantage. International assistance to viable rubber projects in West Africa, Latin America, and small Asian countries, should be intensified. Recent World Bank experience in several West African countries indicates that investments in natural rubber projects in that region are economically attractive and financially sound at the prices expected in the future. Progress in the control of the South American leaf blight disease could make expansion of natural rubber production in Brazil a feasible proposition, but more research is required to ensure the economic viability of such production. Brazil has a large potential for rubber production, because of the available virgin land and the access to development capital. The private and public efforts currently being made there to increase natural rubber production deserve encouragement and assistance.

Appendix A

·•·

Technical and Economic Characteristics of the Main Kinds of Synthetic Rubbers

The many kinds of synthetic rubbers (SR) commercially produced in the world differ not only in their technical attributes, but also in their economic characteristics. The technical attributes depend on the structure of the elastomer; the economic characteristics, on the costs of production, which are in turn tied to the scale of the production operation and to the technologies used in the production process. It would be very difficult, if not impossible, to exhaustively review and compare the main technical and economic characteristics of all SR's. This appendix expands the review of the most important kinds of SR, particularly those which compete with natural rubber (NR).

Styrene-Butadiene Rubber

Styrene-butadiene rubber (SBR) is, in terms of tonnage, by far the single most important kind of rubber in the world. SBR has some important technical advantages over NR, but also some inferior properties. Its resilience and tensile strength are lower than those of NR, whereas its resistance to mechanical, temperature, and environmental factors is roughly comparable to that of NR. SBR, however, can be easily extended with oil, giving it good wear resistance and excellent grip. Its vulcanization behavior is also better than that of NR.

More than 60 percent of all SBR is consumed in tires. Nontire uses include footwear, conveyor belts, cable insulation, hose, battery containers, and adhesives. SBR is used mostly in automobile tire treads, where extension with oil gives it a good wear resistance and excellent grip (low skidding on wet surfaces). SBR, blended with polybutadiene (BR), is the preferred tread rubber for cross-ply, bias-belted, and radial car tires.[1] SBR is also used in automobile tire carcasses and sidewalls, but not as the prevalent compound. In the tire carcass, NR is the prevalent compound, with SBR (or BR) as the subsidiary one.[2] The rubber blend in car tire carcasses depends on the kind of tire; for example, more NR is used in radial than in cross-ply and bias-belted tire carcasses. In the sidewalls of car tires SBR (or a blend of SBR and polybutadiene) is again the prevalent compound for cross-ply and bias-belted tires.[3] In radial tires, however, the performance requirements of sidewalls are more stringent, because the carcass is thinner and because the degree of flexing and heat aging in service are much greater than in cross-ply and bias-belted tires. NR/SBR, NR/BR, or NR/SBR/BR blends must be used. NR is the prevalent compound because of its superior tack and green strength.[4]

1. About one-third of all the rubber used in car tires goes into the tread.

2. About 30 percent of all the rubber used in cross-ply car tires goes into the carcass. In radial car tires, carcasses account for about 20 percent of total rubber use.

3. About 14 percent of all rubber used in cross-ply car tires goes into the sidewall; in radial car tires, more than 20 percent of rubber used in tires goes into the sidewall. In both cross-ply and radial car tires, the remaining 13 to 17 percent of the total rubber used goes into the liners. Inner liners in tubeless tires are often NR/BR blends. Inner tubes are almost always 100 percent BR. For a detailed analysis of rubber tire uses see K. A. Grosh, "Natural Rubber in Tires," *Proceedings of the Natural Rubber Conference, Kuala Lumpur, 1968,* pp. 1–19; and J. G. Anderson, "The Rubber Manufacturer's Choice: Natural or Synthetic Rubber?" *Plastics and Rubber International* (July/August 1977), p. 171, table 1. For some aspects of rubber use in radial tires, see J. J. Leyden, "Radial Tire Compounding," *Rubber Age* (1972), pp. 51–53.

4. More NR is used in radial than in cross-ply and bias-belted car tires. Although rubber compounds for tires can vary quite substantially among manufacturers, all available estimates indicate that the proportion of NR is two to three times greater in radial than in nonradial tires. According to one estimate that refers to the United Kingdom, the overall NR/SR ratio is 10 : 90 percent in cross-ply car tires and 36 : 64 percent in radial car tires. See J. E. Diamond, "Tyres and Natural Rubber," *Proceedings of the NRPRA 3rd Rubber in Engineering Conference,* London, 1973, paper K, p. 3. Another estimate referring to Western Europe that recently has become available broadly confirms Diamond's previous one: in cross-ply car tires the NR/SR ratio is 18 : 72, whereas in radial car tires a 40 : 60 ratio prevails. In absolute amounts a typical cross-ply car tire requires 2.88 kilograms of rubber, whereas a radial tire takes 3.34 kilograms of rubber. See Anderson, "The Rubber Manufacturers' Choice: Natural or Synthetic Rubber?" *Plastics and Rubber International* (July/August 1977), p. 171, table 1.

SBR is produced by polymerization. The monomers, styrene and butadiene, are generally mixed in a proportion of 25:75. Copolymerization of styrene and butadiene is still generally done in emulsion. Solution polymerization has started relatively recently, but it is gaining momentum. Emulsion polymerization had substantial advantages over solution polymerization, because it was technically simpler, and it became the standard method for producing SBR. Emulsion polymerization, however, could not yield a stereo-regular SBR, whereas solution polymerization could.[5] The technical difficulties of solution polymerization now have been overcome, and the solution SBR is gaining in popularity because of its more desirable characteristics as a car tire compound: it has higher abrasion and fatigue resistance than emulsion SBR, while, at the same time, it has lower heat buildup. In 1974 solution SBR accounted for about 6 percent of total SBR consumed outside the centrally planned economies.[6]

The ability to extend the polymer with oil was one of the technical breakthroughs that launched SBR into large-scale production and use (the other being cold polymerization). Oil extension made SBR substantially cheaper to produce, as well as improving its processability and giving it desirable properties for use in car tire treads.[7] Oil extension can be varied over a large range. The most common oil-extended emulsion SBR has 37.5 parts of oil.[8] About 90 percent of all SBR produced in the world is shipped in dry form. Latex SBR, which is used in paper and carpet backing, accounts for the remaining 10 percent.

SBR is the cheapest type of SR available in the market. SBR-1500 (a basic grade not extended with oil) has generally been sold at prices below that of NR. Only in 1971 and 1975 were SBR-1500 prices above the prevailing market prices of NR. SBR-1712 (a basic oil-extended

---

5. Stereoregularity refers to the geometry of the molecules in the polymer. When the geometry of the molecules is precisely defined in three dimension, stereoregularity is achieved. Natural and synthetic isoprene are stereoregular, as are solution SBR and solution BR.

6. IISRP statistics, as reported in *Rubber World* (August 1975), p. 21.

7. High resilient types of rubber, such as NR, have a low skid resistance on wet surfaces. SBR, as observed before, has low resilience, and its resilience is further lowered by oil extension. Its skid resistance is, therefore, higher than that of NR.

8. The classification of the various SBR types is extremely detailed. Generally SBR-1500s are not extended with oil, and SBR-1600s and SBR-1700s are. SBR-1200s are solution-SBR types; they can be extended with oil or not. See IISRP, *Description of Synthetic Rubbers and Latices* (New York: IISRP Inc., 1968).

grade, containing 37.5 percent oil) has generally been priced 25 percent below SBR-1500, and therefore, in addition to a technical advantage, it has enjoyed a substantial price advantage over NR as a tire-tread rubber.

Polybutadiene Rubber

Polybutadiene rubber (BR) is the second most important kind of SR and the third most important kind of rubber in terms of volume. A key characteristic of BR is that it is hardly ever used alone. Normally BR is blended with SBR or NR. Because of its high resilience—higher than that of SBR and NR—high abrasion and cracking resistance, and low heat buildup, BR is used to improve the performance of SBR in car tire treads and sidewalls.[9] Blended with NR, it is also used in the sidewalls and carcasses of car tires and in commercial vehicle tires, where its high abrasion resistance improves tread wear. BR is, therefore, almost exclusively a tire rubber. Nontire uses of BR, which make use of its abrasion resistance, include conveyor belts, golf balls, hoses, shoe soles, and motor mounts.

BR is obtained from the polymerization of butadiene. Solution polymerization is by far the most popular process used to produce BR. Solution polybutadiene dry rubber is produced both with and without oil extenders.[10] The most common kind of oil-extended solution BR contains 37.5 percent oil.

Until the mid-1960s BR was priced above SBR-1500. From the mid-1960s onward, however, BR prices have been quite close to those of SBR. On the whole, therefore, BR (like SBR) has been priced consistently at competitive levels in relation to NR.

Butyl Rubber

Butyl rubber (IIR) is the third most important kind of SR in terms of volume, and, like polychloroprene and SBR, is a "first generation" SR, having been developed before World War II. IIR is obtained from

9. The high resilience of BR makes it difficult to process.
10. Like SBR, BR can accept high loadings of oil.

the copolymerization of isobutylene, with the addition of isoprene. IIR has excellent resistance to weather, oxidation, ozone, and water. It also has one additional and very desirable property: high impermeability to gas. IIR, however, is not compatible with other synthetics and cannot be extended with oil. Its resilience is also poor.

Because of its impermeability to gas, IIR found its major outlet in inner tubes and bags where it substituted for NR. The second largest outlet is in automobile tires, followed by cables and miscellaneous industrial applications. IIR has been traditionally priced at 35 to 40 percent above SBR, and only slightly below EPDM. Its cost depends heavily upon that of isobutylene and to a lesser degree on that of isoprene.

Polychloroprene Rubber

Polychloroprene rubber (CR), also called Neoprene, is, in terms of tonnage, the fourth most important kind of rubber.[11] It is obtained from emulsion polymerization of chloroprene, and its general strength properties are similar to those of NR and SBR. The chlorine content, however, gives CR some special properties: excellent resistance to weather and ozone as well as to fire. CR, moreover, is relatively resistant to oil and chemicals. The main technical drawbacks of CR are its poor properties at low temperatures.

CR finds its major applications in automotive and other mechanical goods, as a bonding agent in nonwoven textiles, in wire and cables, in hoses and belts, and in miscellaneous products requiring good flame resistance. In automotive goods (about 20 percent of total CR consumption in the United States in 1972), CR competes mostly with EPDM. In some mechanical goods, CR competes with NR, but for the most part CR competes with other specialty SR's, particularly NBR.

CR is an expensive rubber. The large capital investments required and the high cost of raw materials and catalysts results in production costs and prices that are almost double those of SBR and at least 25 percent higher than those of EPDM. CR, in addition, has high specific gravity, which adds to its basic relative cost disadvantage.[12]

11. This was the DuPont brand name for CR. DuPont was for a long time the only producer of CR.

12. See footnote 24 in this Appendix.

Polyisoprene Rubber

Polyisoprene rubber (IR), the sixth most important kind of SR in terms of tonnage, is the closest synthetic approximation of the natural elastomer. Both IR and NR are polymers of the isoprene monomer.[13] IR accounted in 1977 for 3.6 percent of all SR's and 2.4 percent of all rubber consumed outside the centrally planned economies. The development of IR in the mid-1950s "represented a major triumph for the polymer synthesists and a landmark in the world of rubber,"[14] and it began to be commercially produced in 1960.[15] Of the two main kinds of IR that were commercially produced, the kind first produced by Shell is about 91 percent cis-1,4, whereas the kind first produced by Goodyear (Natsyn) is about 98 percent cis-1,4.[16] These two kinds of IR have different properties. The 98 percent cis form is easier to process than the 90-to-91 percent cis form; it also has a slightly greater green strength, tensile strength, and heat buildup.[17]

The processing behavior and end-use properties of the 98 percent cis IR and NR are very similar, given the slight differences in the molecular structures of the two rubbers. This kind of IR has a lower tensile strength than NR and a lower tear resistance. In compounding, it also has a lower green strength than NR. However, 98 percent cis IR has a greater elongation than NR and requires little or no breakdown before compounding.[18] This last property gives IR a limited processing cost advantage over NR. The 91 percent cis IR, on the contrary, has

---

13. Natural rubber is cis-1,4-polyisoprene. The cis form refers to the geometry of the molecules; the 1,4 indicates that the isoprene units are joined at each end. The cis-form arrangement of the polyisoprene (natural or synthetic) molecule is stereoregular.

14. P. W. Allen, *Natural Rubber and the Synthetics* (London: Crosby Lockwood, 1972), p. 139.

15. See American Chemical Society, *Chemistry in the Economy* (Washington, D.C.: American Chemical Society, 1973) pp. 132–34.

16. The Shell IR was produced commercially in 1960 using a lithium catalyst; Goodyear's Natsyn was produced commercially in 1962 using a catalyst system of aluminum trietyl and a cocatlyst.

17. G. W. Atkinson, "Polyisoprene—Present Status and Future Prospects," *Proceedings of the IRSG Symposium on the Present Position and Prospects for the Newer Rubbers*, in Sao Paulo, Brazil, October 1967 (London: IRSG, 1968), p. 13.

18. This advantage over NR is also shared by 91 percent cis IR.

substantial disadvantages when compared with NR. It is mostly used as a filler in blends with other rubbers including NR.

IR has been used in areas where NR previously was chosen on the basis of its physical and processing characteristics. Although the claim that IR can replace NR in all uses still constitutes a slight exaggeration on the side of IR manufacturers, it is clear that the development of IR has made the changeover from natural to the synthetic elastomers even easier. Car, truck, and bus tires constitute the largest outlet for IR, about 50 percent of the total. The remainder goes into a variety of nontire uses, such as mechanical goods, pharmaceutical goods, and footwear. In tire uses, IR is usually blended with other kinds of rubber.

IR is produced by the polymerization of isoprene. The process is complex and technically quite difficult. As was mentioned above, the solution of these difficulties has been a major achievement of polymer science and chemical engineering. The basic monomer, isoprene, is produced in various ways. There are at least five commercial processes for the synthesis of isoprene:

(a) Isoamylene extraction and dehydrogenation (used by Shell at Pernis and Goodrich in Texas);
(b) Propylene dimerization, isomerization, and pyrolysis (used by Goodyear in Texas);
(c) Isobutylene-formaldehyde condensation and cracking (used in the U.S.S.R. and by Kuraray in Japan);
(d) Isopentane dehydrogenation (used in the U.S.S.R.); and
(e) Acetone/acetylene condensation and cracking (used by Anic at Ravenna, Italy).

Apart from the five basic synthetic routes and the by-product route to isoprene (recovery by solvent extraction), several variations are being experimented with and commercialized. For example, within the isobutylene-formaldehyde process, a single-step isoprene process has been developed by Sumitono and another by Takeda Chemical Inc., both in Japan. Goodyear has announced recently the commercial operation (at Le Havre in France) of a new method to recover isoprene from C_5 streams by fractional distillation.[19] In the future,

19. See M. J. Rhoad, "Isoprene Worldwide," Proceedings of the 15th Annual Meeting of the International Institute of Synthetic Rubber Producers (New York: IISRP, 1974).

the dominant source is expected to be recovery of isoprene from steam cracking of heavy liquids.[20]

The variety of existing basic routes to isoprene, as well as the number of variations that are being experimented with, illustrates the effort made by the chemical industry to produce isoprene monomer at lower costs. The relatively high cost of isoprene synthesis and isoprene recovery has been one of the most important reasons that the commercial development of IR has evolved relatively slowly. IR—at least the 98 percent *cis* kind—has never become fully cost competitive with NR, and the substitution of NR with IR has proceeded slowly outside the centrally planned economies.

Historically, IR producers have sold their high-quality IR at a slightly higher price than that of NR and their lower-quality IR at a substantially lower price than that of NR. IR price changes have followed, by and large, the trend of those of NR.[21] This behavior is still prevalent today. With only about 2.5 percent of the market for all rubbers, IR producers outside the centrally planned economies are behaving as price takers.

Ethylene-Propylene Rubbers

Ethylene-propylene rubbers (EPM and EPDM) are the fifth largest kind of SR, in terms of volume. EPM is a copolymer of ethylene and propylene. It has desirable properties and is resistant to environmental factors, such as weather, ozone, oxidation, and temperature. It is difficult and costly to vulcanize and to process, however. To overcome the vulcanization problem, one-third (unsaturated) material—usually a diene—is added to the ethylene-propylene combination. The resulting combination of three monomers (EPDM) can be vulcanized by using sulfur in the normal way.

EPDM has some interesting properties. Like EPM, it has excellent resistance to environmental factors (such as weather, ozone, and oxidation), good tensile strength, and high resistance to heat. Its

20. When naphtha or gas-oil is cracked to produce ethylene, several by-products are obtained, since isoprene is a part of the C_5 fraction. Isoprene yields vary from 2 to 5 percent of ethylene production. The development of large ethylene production units has made the recovery of isoprene from the C_5 stream commercially possible.

21. Without the short-term ups and downs of NR prices.

resilience, however, is lower than that of NR and IR. Other desirable properties of EPDM are its ability to accept high oil-black loadings and its ease in processing (mixing, extruding, and molding).[22] When first introduced, EPM was heralded as the next low-cost, general purpose rubber. The low cost of the monomers, the resistance of the copolymer to environment, and its processing ease were thought to be the main strengths of this kind of rubber.[23] The difficulty in vulcanization was its main drawback, and the solution to this problem—the addition of diene, very costly material—took away a good deal of the cost advantage of EPM and prevented EPDM from entering the huge tire market. In other uses, however, the higher cost of EPDM was in part compensated for by the low specific gravity that gives it a substantial advantage over NR, IR, SBR, and BR and an even larger advantage over NRB and CR.[24]

EPDM is mostly used in nontire automotive parts: weather stripping, radiators, heater and exhaust emission-control hoses, brake cups, window and windshield gaskets, windshield washers, seals, and more recently in safety bumpers. In the United States these uses accounted in 1975 for 40 percent of total EPDM consumption. The EPDM tire market is limited to sidewalls, cover strips, and some specialty, off-the-road vehicle tires, which require excellent resistance to ozone deterioration. EPDM is also used in tire tubes (together with IRR). In the United States, EPDM use in tires accounted in 1973 for about 20 percent of total EPDM consumption. The remainder of the EPDM goes into domestic appliances, hoses, wire and cable, coated fabrics, footwear, and rug underlay.

EPDM prices have historically been consistently higher than those of SBR and generally higher than those of NR. Whereas ethylene and propylene are relatively inexpensive feedstocks, the solution polymerization technique and the diene are expensive. The growth of the market for EPDM has so far been based on its weathering and ozone-resistance qualities and has taken place in uses where these qualities are required.

22. See Noble Keck, "EPDM Elastomers," *Rubber Age* (September 1973), pp. 43–45; and C. J. Harrington, "Ethylene Propylene Elastomers," *Proceedings of the IRSG Symposium on the Present Position and Prospects for the Newer Rubbers*, Sao Paulo, Brazil, October 1967 (London: IRSG, 1968).

23. The price of both ethylene and propylene has generally been less than half of that of styrene and butadiene.

24. Specific gravities: EPDM 0.86, NR 0.93, IR 0.94, SBR 0.94, BR 0.94, CR 1.25, and NBR 0.98.

Nitrile Rubber

Nitrile rubber (NBR) is obtained from emulsion copolymerization of acrylonitrile and butadiene. Depending on the proportion of acrylonitrile used in the blend, different types of NBR can be obtained. Generally NBR has high tensile strength and resistance to abrasion. High acrylonitrile content gives NBR excellent resistance to oil and solvent.

NBR is used in products where oil and abrasion resistance are essential: oil hoses, oil seals, gaskets, adhesives, sealants, belts, and tubing. In latex form, NBR is used in paper and nonwoven textile manufacture. Strictly speaking, NBR does not compete directly with most other rubbers. The uses of NBR are generally dictated by properties that NR and other SR cannot meet. The high cost of acrylonitrile makes NBR the highest priced SR (excluding the small-volume specialty rubbers). Its use is only justified on technical grounds.

Other Synthetic Rubbers

Included in this category are a large number of specialty rubbers which meet specific needs of certain manufactured products. According to an authoritative compilation, there are at least 170 distinct kinds of small-volume specialty rubbers that can be classified into twenty major categories.[25] A convenient way of classifying some of these specialty elastomers is to divide them into castable, thermoplastic, and powdered elastomers. Castable elastomers—such as urethanes, silicones, and polysulfides—have favorable processing characteristics: they can be quickly cast at relatively moderate costs into various shapes. Polyurethanes are by far the largest single kind, and are used in coating, footwear, sealants, industrial tires, automotive parts, and flooring. Polysulfides are mostly used as sealants. Thermoplastic elastomers are in many ways a bridge between rubber and plastics: when cold they have the same properties as rubber; when hot they can be processed like plastics. Easy processability is their major advantage. Polyurethanes, styrene/butadiene copolymers,

---

25. See C. F. Ruebensaal, *Changing Markets and Manufacturing Patterns in the Synthetic Rubber Industry* (New York: IISRP, Inc., 1973 to 1977 and 1978 (draft)), pp. 16–17.

styrene copolymers and terpolymers, and ethylene/propylene copolymers are the most important kinds. Thermoplastic rubbers find application in automotive parts, coated fabrics, coatings, hoses and tubing, and footwear. Powdered elastomers also have the potential for substantial cost savings in processing. Their actual use, however, is still limited.[26]

Some of these specialty rubbers have well known special properties. Acrylic rubbers, for example, have excellent resistance to temperature and oil, as well as to ozone and cracking. Silicone rubber is resistant to extreme temperature, as are fluorocarbon rubbers. In general, these specialty elastomers have gained markets because of combinations of desirable properties—oil and solvent resistance, resistance to wide temperature ranges, favorable processing characteristics—which make their use attractive despite their often large price disadvantage in relation to both general-purpose and large-tonnage specialty SR's.

Because of the variety of specialty elastomers and the difficulties in classifying them—for example, in plastics or rubbers—statistics are difficult to find and to compare. According to an authoritative source, total production capacity of these specialty rubbers outside the centrally planned economies is currently around 500,000 metric tons a year, equivalent to about 6 percent of all synthetic rubber capacity.[27]

26. For a detailed account of specialty elastomers and their uses in the United States, see David Dworkin, "Changing Markets and Technology for Specialty Elastomers," *Rubber World* (February 1975), pp. 43–46.

27. Ruebensaal, *Changing Markets and Manufacturing Patterns in the Synthetic Rubber Industry*, p. 17. Ruebensaal's figures exclude chloroprenes, nitriles, and EPDM's from specialty rubbers, since he classifies them as large-volume specialty rubbers.

Appendix B

•‒•

Quantitative Evidence on Natural Rubber Market Shares

Economic analysis of rubber consumption has been difficult. To the usual technical problems connected with single-equation
estimation procedures in the presence of substitute products, researchers have had to face serious practical problems deriving from lack of
reliable data on synthetic rubber prices in the various consuming areas.
Yet the quantification of the effect of price changes on rubber consumption is a necessary first step toward a better understanding of
the dynamics of the competition between natural rubber (NR) and
synthetic rubbers (SR).

Having overcome, at least in part, the most serious difficulties concerning the availability of price data by consuming region, the relation between NR and SR is explored here by concentrating on the
factors that determine the market share of NR. In doing so, it was
assumed that the market share of NR could be considered independent
of all the forces that affect the demand for all elastomers to the same
extent (for example, the level of economic activity).

The Market Share Model

This model assumes that rubber users have a production function
that includes both NR and SR; that NR and SR are close, but not perfect
substitutes; and that changes in the relative prices of these two kinds
of inputs and in technology affect relative use only gradually, given
the uncertainties about the nature of the price change (temporary
or permanent), the time and cost involved in shifting from one input
to the other, and the institutional constraints that limit the process
of adjusting inputs. The rationale for these assumptions stems from
the market analysis presented in Chapter 3.

112

Given the size of the total market for elastomers, the market share for NR (MS_{NR}) is hypothesized to be a function of the price of NR (P_{NR}), the prices of SR (P_{SR}), and technology ($TECH$).

(1) $$MS_{NR} = f(P_{NR}, P_{SR}, TECH)$$

If rubber product manufacturers adjust their utilization patterns gradually in response to changes in relative prices and technology, only a fraction of the expected use of NR in total rubber use can be expected within a certain period. Using a partial adjustment type of model, a reduced form equation of the kind presented below can be derived and used to obtain the statistical estimates.

(2)

$$MS_{NR_t} = \delta\alpha + \delta\beta \left[\frac{P_{NR}}{P_{SR}} \right]_t + (1-\delta) MS_{NR_{t-1}} + \delta\gamma\, TECH_t + Se_t$$

Several problems have to be faced in estimating the model equations: possible multicollinearity in the prices of rubber, serial correlation in the presence of a lagged dependent variable, and, finally, the difficulty of adequately proxying technological change. To reduce the risk of multicollinearity the prices of NR and SR were entered into the equation as a ratio. A three-pass procedure was used in estimating the model equations to deal with serial correlation problems, wherever present.[1] The effect of technological changes in the production of tires on the market share of NR was proxied using, where appropriate, time series of the market penetration of radial tires. To account for the downward historical trend in natural rubber market shares due to the technological changes that have affected the processing and performance characteristics of SR, a time trend variable was also included in the equations.

Application of the Model to North America, Western Europe, and Japan

This model was applied to North America, Western Europe, and Japan. Because of the lack of reliable data on SR prices, other developed consuming countries, developing countries, or centrally planned economies could not be covered. North America, Western

---

1. See K. R. Wallis, "Lagged Dependent Variables and Serially Correlated Errors," *Review of Economics and Statistics* (1967), pp. 555–67.

Table B-1. Determinants of the Natural Rubber Market Share in North America, Western Europe, and Japan, 1957 to 1977, Annual Data

| Equation for economic region | Constant term a_0 | Regression coefficients | | | | Multi-type correlation coefficient $\overline{R}^2$ | Standard error of estimate | Durbin-Watson statistics | ρ |
		$a_1 = \dfrac{P_{NR_t}}{P_{SR_t}}$	$a_2 = MS_{NR_{t-1}}$	$a_3 = TECH$	$a_4 = TIME$				
(1) North America[a] $MS_{NR} = 0.295418$		-0.043582 (-2.64)	$+0.495786$ (3.47)	$+0.153968$ (2.59)	-0.004607 (-3.49)	0.87	0.019	1.89	0.32
(2) Western Europe $MS_{NR} = 0.369206$		-0.045205 (-2.81)	$+0.412521$ (1.95)		-0.001851 (-2.03)	0.75	0.013	2.00	0.74
(3) Japan $MS_{SR} = 0.593611$		-0.074283 (-3.25)	$+0.432375$ (2.37)	$+0.003476$ (2.86)	-0.024097 (-2.76)	0.98	0.014	1.90	0.0

Note: MS_{NR} = Natural rubber share of the rubber market.
P_{NR} = Price of NR (North America, average price of RSS1, spot N.Y., dollars per metric ton; Western Europe, average price of RSS1 and RSS3, c.i.f., London, dollars per metric ton; Japan, wholesale price index of NR).
P_{SR} = Price of SR (North America, average price of SBR, BR, IR, dollars per metric ton; Western Europe, average price of SBR in the United Kingdom, France, and Germany, dollars per metric ton; Japan, wholesale price index of SBR).
$TECH$ = Share of radial tires in total automobile tire market.
$TIME$ = Time trend (1956 = 1).
t values are given in parentheses.
a. Estimated from 1952 to 1977.

Europe, and Japan, however, are the largest consuming areas, accounting together for about 60 percent of total world rubber consumption and for 97 percent of total rubber consumption in developed countries.

Two alternative regression equations were used to estimate the market share of NR in North America, Western Europe, and Japan:

$$(3a) \quad MS_{NR_t} = a_0 + a_1 \ln \left[\frac{P_{NR}}{P_{SR}} \right]_t$$

$$+ a_2 MS_{NR_{t-1}} + a_3 TECH_t + a_4 TIME + u_t$$

$$(3b) \quad \ln MS_{NR_t} = a_0 + a_1 \ln \left[\frac{P_{NR}}{P_{SR}} \right]_t$$

$$+ a_2 \ln MS_{NR_{t-1}} + a_3 TECH_t + a_4 TIME + u_t$$

where a_0 is a constant term; a_1, a_2, a_3, and a_4 are regression coefficients defined in Table B–1; $TIME$ is the time trend ($1956 = 1$); and u_t is the error term.

The regression results are summarized in Table B–1. Since the results from the linear form of the estimating equations were consistently better from the statistical standpoint than those obtained from the log form, the latter are here omitted.

The model results are quite satisfactory from the statistical standpoint. The relative price variable is highly significant in all three equations and so is the $TECH$ variable in equations (1) and (3), clearly showing the positive effect on the market share of NR of the introduction of radial tires.[2] The time variable also has the correct sign and is statistically significant in all three equations. The coefficients of the lagged dependent variables have similar magnitudes: the adjustment process seems to have roughly the same speed in all three major consuming areas. All three equations seem to be relatively free of serial correlation problems. The short and long-term price elasticity of natural rubber market shares implicit in the estimated equations deserve some additional comment. The short-term price

2. Information on radial tire penetration is not available for Western Europe as whole. The process, however, started much earlier in Western Europe than in North America or Japan, and its effects on market shares of NR were slower and more uniformly distributed over time.

elasticities computed at the mean values of the relevant variables and the long-term elasticities (derived from the short-term ones and the adjustment coefficients) are summarized in Table B–2.

It can be seen from Table B–2 that short-term elasticities are, as expected, much smaller in absolute value than long-term elasticities. Relative market prices for the current year influence only slightly the choice of rubber inputs. This is consistent with a priori expectations, given the technical adjustment costs that are involved when a rubber user switches from one kind of input to another. In the longer run, however, the choice of rubber inputs is clearly and more strongly influenced by changes in relative prices.[3] Another interesting finding is that the values of the long-term market share elasticities are higher in Western Europe than in North America and Japan. In Western Europe the tire industry is much less vertically integrated than in North America. This result, therefore, is in line with expectations. Slightly more surprising, on the surface, is the result for Japan, given the apparent similarity of the structure of the rubber industry of that country with that of Western Europe. In Japan, however, informal ties between synthetic rubber producers and tire manufacturers are much stronger than in Western Europe and so are institutional pressures in favor of domestically produced rubber. These factors probably account for the lower long-term elasticity of the natural rubber market share in this country with respect to Western Europe.

Table B–2. *Estimates of the Natural Rubber Market Share Elasticities in North America, Western Europe, and Japan*

Equation for economic region	Rate of adjustment $\delta = 1 - a_2$	Short-term elasticity [a]	Long-term elasticity
North America	0.504	−0.18[b]	−0.36[b]
Western Europe	0.587	−0.13[b]	−0.46[b]
Japan	0.568	−0.14[b]	−0.25[b]

a. Computed at the mean values of the relevant variables.
b. Significant at the 95 percent confidence level.

3. Although much higher than in the short-term, the estimated long-term elasticity coefficients are lower than would have been expected, given the close, competitive relation between NR and SR. The difficulties that are involved in estimating these elasticities, however, still make the confidence bands around them quite large.

Appendix C

Estimate of the Full Supply Price of Newly Planted Natural Rubber in Malaysia

There are many ways to invest in natural rubber (NR): part of existing acreage can be replanted by commercial estates and smallholders, new areas can be brought under rubber, or smallholders can practice "fringe alienation" (that is, occupy small parts of existing uncultivated land and turn it into a rubber holding). Government land-development authorities such as the Federal Land Development Authority (FELDA) can set up new land schemes by developing virgin lands to resettle large numbers of farmers.[1] Other investment structures are possible and each will carry different expenditures for developing new rubber. A major concern of the government of Malaysia in opening up new land is to provide employment for a rapidly growing population and to limit the expansion of urbanization.

Until recently FELDA divided newly opened land among the settlers. Each family head became the owner of from 8 to 12 acres and was responsible for paying off the investment cost on his plot fifteen years after his crop matured. Because of the possible fragmentation of existing land plots after the death of the original owner, the government has begun to consider new forms of land ownership. One

Note: This appendix is based on a paper prepared for The World Bank by Maria 't Hooft-Welvaars, "The Profitability of NR and SBR Investments," *World Bank Staff Commodity Paper* (draft) (Washington, D.C.: The World Bank, 1978).

1. FELDA was established in 1956 as a loan board for state governments undertaking developments of new lands.

possibility is that the newly developed and planted land would remain as one unit and be run as an estate, the new settlers being both workers and shareholders in the estate. Thus, the advantages of estate organization would remain, fragmentation would be prevented, and mobility would be preserved through the right to sell one's share.

Since new investments in rubber sponsored by government agencies are likely to have this or a similar organization, it is appropriate to estimate the expenditure required to establish and exploit such an estate, treating the new settlers as ordinary workers receiving a wage in accordance with the collective wage agreement currently in force. As the workers gradually buy their share of the new estate, they could be required to pay taxes on their earnings. This would mean, in fact, that a new settler starting from scratch would, during the first fifteen years, have less disposable income than an ordinary estate worker, but would end up owning part of an estate.

Given the theoretical nature of these calculations, there are two distinct advantages in assuming this kind of organization: it allows the results to be compared with those reached in a 1970 study by the same author, and both the receipts from workers acquiring their estate shares as well as their expenditures on tax payments can be disregarded in the cash flow calculations.[2] All expenditures will be merely the normal expenditures of an estate not subject to taxation, and all receipts will merely be receipts from selling the rubber produced.

Definition of the Full Supply Price for Natural Rubber

As explained in the text, "full supply price" here indicates the price which, if received over the entire lifetime of the investment, would equate the present value of all expenditures to the present value of all receipts. In calculating present values, three discount rates have been used: 8, 10, and 12 percent. All the calculations were done in real terms (that is, at constant prices). It is assumed that all expenditures over the entire lifetime of the rubber estate are to be at the 1974 price level and that the same would be true for the unit price

---

2. 't Hooft-Welvaars, "The Profitability of New Investments in Rubber Plantings in Malaysia," UNCTAD doc. TD/B/C.1, Geneva, June 1971 (processed), pp. 1–16.

of NR received. If all expenditures and receipts were inflated by the same annual percentage rate over the lifetime of the estate, the nominal discount rates would have to be increased by the same percentage to arrive at the same results. (At an inflation rate of 5 percent for all entries, the nominal discount rates would then be 13, 15, and 17 percent.) In reality, however, the average rate of inflation would not apply equally to all expenditures and receipts, even if it remained constant over the years. Therefore, even if yields from each hectare and all physical inputs into the production process remained the same, the fact that some costs increase more than others would require an updating of the exercise, especially when new planting material and new cultivation methods are taken into account.[3]

Calculating a cost price as a full supply price by using the discounted cash flow method has two additional advantages. It can take into account the change in production capacity over the lifetime of the estate, and, above all, it clearly brings out the importance of interest. Because of the yield profile of rubber trees, production capacity varies over the years, and so do costs and revenues. Moreover, despite the fact that planting and producing NR is a labor intensive operation, the role of capital, and thereby of interest, is nevertheless important, since the plantings take six years to mature. Substantial expenditures are incurred, therefore, before any yields (and revenues) become available. The higher the discount rate is, the higher the supply price will become. This effect is magnified when wages and export levies are not calculated on the basis of an independently given gazetted price, but at the final supply price itself. When the full supply price is defined as a price which, if prevailing over the entire period, would cover all expenditures and leave a desired real rate of return, wages and export duty plus surcharge should be calculated on the basis of this particular price. Using a higher real discount rate (that is, aiming at a higher internal rate of return on capital) will increase especially the investment elements in the supply price. This increase then will influence those elements of expenditure which are related to price, that is, wage cost and export duty plus surcharge. The latter, in turn, increase the supply price. Finally, supply prices, wage cost, and export levies only can be determined together. The discount rate used thus has both a direct and an indirect effect on the supply price. Taking the calculations of the 1974 natural rubber

---

3. A desk update of these calculations was conducted, in fact, for 1976.

supply price (f.o.b. Malaysia) as an example, discount rates of 10 and 12 percent make the supply price, respectively, 21 and 52 percent higher than that calculated at an 8 percent discount rate.[4]

Description of the Estate

The hypothetical estate taken here as a model is assumed to consist of 3,000 hectares. Planting of the first 1,000 hectares is assumed to start in year 1, with the second and third 1,000 hectares planted in years 2 and 3, respectively. Immaturity is assumed to last six years. The calculations cover twenty-eight years from the first clearing of land; by then the last 1,000 hectares of area planted would have been in production for twenty years. The actual lifetime of an estate is likely to be longer than twenty-eight years, but under a discounting system with high interest rates, the later years would not carry much weight. The rubber latex from the estate is supposed to be processed into crumb rubber in a factory built as part of the new plantation. Staff and workers are assumed to be living on the estate.

Costs and Supply Prices for the Estate and Factory

Table C–1 shows both total yields during the twenty-eight-year lifetime of the estate and the expenditure for various items during these years, at 1974 prices. The present value was calculated for all categories at discount rates of 8, 10, and 12 percent.

Wages on rubber plantations in Malaysia include bonus payments depending on the gazetted natural rubber price. These payments were entered in Table C–1 at a value corresponding to a gazetted price of M¢60–65 per pound.[5] They have, however, been calculated for all relevant price ranges, in order to enter wage costs commensurate with the final supply price.

After twenty-eight years an estate still has a residual value: trees are still tappable, buildings are still in operation, and so forth. Since

---

4. In the 1970 paper, the indirect effect of the rate of interest on the supply price was not considered, since the gazetted price (M¢55 to M¢60 per pound) was assumed to be given independently. The 1970 and 1974 figures, therefore, compare best at the lowest discount rate used (8 percent).

5. A gazetted price of M¢60 to M¢65 per pound is equivalent to an export price (including duties) of M¢156 to M¢167 per kilogram.

total investment in field establishment, estate buildings, housing, and premium (for land) amounts to M$14 million for this model estate, it is assumed that the residual value after twenty-eight years will be 10 percent: that is, M$1.4 million. The present value of this residual was also calculated to discount rates of 8, 10, and 12 percent, and was subtracted from the present value of total expenditure.

Table C–2 gives the sum of all values for yields and for various expenditure items, as well as their present values at discount rates of 8, 10, and 12 percent.[6] Dividing expenditures by yields (taking present values for both) results in the supply price: that is, the price that would be required to cover all expenditures and to earn an interest of 8, 10, and 12 percent on all capital engaged over the lifetime of the estate.

Table C–2 shows that the rubber supply price for this estate would be M¢96.5 per kilogram at 8 percent discount, M¢112.6 per kilogram at 10 percent discount, and M¢132.0 per kilogram at 12 percent discount. The breakdown of these cost prices, which shows the heavy influence of interest on the investment items (field establishment, estate buildings, and housing) also is shown in Table C–2. The direct influence of interest on the investment items (field establishment, estate buildings, and housing) as well as its indirect influence on tapping costs, through the increase in the supply price, also can be gauged from Table C–2.

Assuming that 70 percent of the annual production capacity of the estate would consist of SMR-5-CV rubber and 30 percent of SMR-20 rubber, the total cost of crumb rubber production will be M¢19.6 per kilogram at 8 percent discount, M¢20.0 per kilogram at 10 percent discount, and M¢20.6 per kilogram at 12 percent discount.

Correction for the Time Lag between Expenditures and Receipts

The implicit assumption in the calculation so far—that expenditures and receipts would occur at the end of each year—is an over-simplification; expenditures, in fact, occur over the entire year, and so do receipts. There is, moreover, an average time lag of three months between the time when rubber is produced and when payments from

---

6. In the case of tapping costs, the figures given in Table C–2 are related to the final f.o.b. supply price at different discount rates. They are not, therefore, the figures used in Table C–1 as tapping costs.

Table C–1. *Yields and Expenditures for an Estate of 3,000 Hectares*
(thousands of Malaysian dollars (1974), unless otherwise noted)

Year from planting	Yield (thousands of kilograms)	Field establishment	Estate buildings and installations, including upkeep	Estate staff housing, including upkeep	Workers' quarters, including upkeep
1	0	1,458	0	262.5	1,100
2	0	1,977	383.6	115.5	11
3	0	2,397	48.9	100.0	11
4	0	1,334	37.5	10.0	11
5	0	1,173	57.6	10.0	11
6	0	1,087	38.1	28.0	286
7	818	692	28.2	10.0	564
8	1,979	334	28.2	10.0	514
9	3,466	0	28.2	10.0	24
10	4,335	0	28.2	10.0	24
11	4,845	0	28.2	10.0	24
12	5,181	0	28.2	10.0	24
13	5,461	0	28.2	10.0	24
14	5,725	0	28.2	10.0	24
15	5,817	0	28.2	10.0	24
16	5,686	0	28.2	10.0	24
17	5,934	0	28.2	10.0	24
18	6,336	0	28.2	10.0	24
19	6,770	0	28.2	10.0	24
20	6,770	0	28.2	10.0	24
21	6,558	0	28.2	10.0	24
22	6,580	0	28.2	10.0	24
23	6,739	0	28.2	10.0	24
24	6,892	0	28.2	10.0	24
25	6,780	0	28.2	10.0	24
26	6,583	0	28.2	10.0	24
27	6,425	0	28.2	10.0	24
28	6,345	0	28.2	10.0	24
Total	122,025	10,452	1,186.1	746.0	2,988

Field upkeep, including stimulation	Material costs of field collection	Tapping costs	Estate staff salaries	Premium, quit rent, and insurance	Total estate expenditure
0	0	0	129.6	466	3,416.1
0	0	0	175.4	25	2,688.5
0	0	0	205.2	29	2,791.1
0	0	0	205.2	32	1,629.7
0	0	0	205.2	109	1,565.8
0	201.7	0	205.2	114	1,960.0
217	232.6	502.7	212.4	114	2,572.9
430	223.6	1,019.4	212.4	114	2,885.6
635	115.0	1,605.8	212.4	114	2,744.4
626	59.6	1,724.0	212.4	114	2,798.2
629	82.2	1,828.2	212.4	114	2,928.0
634	117.3	1,883.4	212.4	114	3,023.3
631	117.1	1,923.9	212.4	114	3,060.6
623	88.4	1,957.9	212.4	114	3,057.9
655	66.8	1,971.2	212.4	114	3,081.6
683	156.9	1,951.4	212.4	114	3,179.9
739	139.6	2,000.3	212.4	114	3,267.5
750	197.2	2,074.7	212.4	114	3,410.5
768	109.7	2,148.9	212.4	114	3,415.2
753	88.1	2,147.4	212.4	114	3,377.1
734	90.8	2,106.9	212.4	114	3,320.3
734	44.8	2,099.7	212.4	114	3,267.1
701	51.7	2,111.1	212.4	114	3,252.4
675	109.4	2,122.9	212.4	114	3,295.9
637	109.4	2,095.8	212.4	114	3,230.8
625	125.3	2,062.1	212.4	114	3,201.0
611	70.8	2,010.0	212.4	114	3,080.4
602	69.9	1,975.7	212.4	114	3,036.2
14,092	2,667.9	41,323.4	5,977.6	3,283	82,538.0

Table C–2. *Yields and Expenditures for an Estate,*
at Real Discount Rates of 8, 10, and 12 Percent
(1974 prices, unless otherwise noted)

| | Real discount rate (percent) | | | | | |
	8	10	12	8	10	12
Yields (thousands of kilograms)	31.252	23.234	17.540			
Item	Discounted values (thousands of Malaysian dollars)			Supply prices (Malaysian cents per kilogram)		
Field establishment	7,996	7,524	7,096	25.6	32.4	40.5
Estate buildings and installations	640	576	526	2.0	2.5	3.0
Estate staff housing	518	488	463	1.7	2.1	2.6
Workers' quarters	1,967	1,818	1,692	6.3	7.8	9.6
Field upkeep, including stimulation	3,895	2,952	2,270	12.5	12.7	12.9
Material cost of field collection	924	742	605	3.0	3.2	3.5
Estate staff salaries	2,219	1,853	1,576	7.1	8.0	9.0
Premium, quit rent, and insurance	1,378	1,184	1,038	4.4	5.1	5.9
Estate expenditure other than tapping cost	19,537	17,137	15,266	62.5	73.7	87.0
Tapping cost	10,773	9,134	7,948	34.5	39.3	45.3
Total estate expenditure	30,310	26,271	23,214	97.0	113.0	132.3
Residual value	162	97	59	0.5	0.4	0.3
Total estate cost	30,148	26,174	23,155	96.5	112.6	132.0

its sales are received. To correct the above oversimplification it was assumed that expenditures would be incurred at mid-year, whereas receipts (supply price times total yields) would occur three months later. This requires that the present value of expenditures be multiplied by $(1 + r)^{1/2}$, and the discounted yields by $(1 + r)^{1/4}$. Since the supply price is obtained by dividing the present value of expenditures by the discounted yields, the adjustment can be made by multiplying the total supply prices for the estate and factory by $(1 + r)^{1/4}$ or $1 + (1/4 r)$. As shown in the 1974 section of Table C–3, the ex-factory supply prices then become M¢118.4, M¢135.9, and M¢159.2 at real discount rates of 8, 10, and 12 percent, respectively.

Total Supply Prices F.o.b. and C.i.f.

In Table C–3 f.o.b. charges, a research tax, and export duty plus surcharge are added to the corrected ex-factory supply price, to arrive at the supply price f.o.b. Malaysia. F.o.b. charges include transport to port, shipping charges, and selling commission. It has been assumed that the replanting tax, which is levied on exported rubber, will be refunded.

Export duty plus surcharge increases steeply at higher discount rates. At the f.o.b. supply price of M¢130.3 per kilogram, which corresponds to the 8 percent discount rate calculation, these export levies amount to M¢5.2 per kilogram: that is, only 4 percent of the f.o.b. price. At a discount rate of 10 percent, these export levies amount to 9.6 percent. At a discount rate of 12 percent, the export duty plus surcharge amount to 17.3 percent. Adding the average freight rates in 1974 to the f.o.b. Malaysia supply price then gives the supply prices c.i.f. Western Europe and New York in Malaysian cents per kilogram.[7]

Updating the 1974 Supply Price Calculations

Since 1974, when the field research for these calculations was conducted, a new wage agreement for rubber estate workers has come into effect. The Rubber Research Institute of Malaysia (RRIM) also published a new *Rubber Owners' Manual*, which contains a wealth of new information on input cost and production economics.[8] It was felt, therefore, that the cost calculations could and should be updated in light of the changes in wage structures that occurred in 1976 and the valuable new information that became available through the *Rubber Owners' Manual*. Since labor cost—the major input in natural rubber production—did not change by much in 1977 (the Malaysian rate of inflation from 1976 to 1977 was only 5 percent), the updating of the 1974 supply prices is assumed to be representative of the situation both in 1976 and in 1977.

---

7. The 1974 supply prices were converted from Malaysian dollars to U.S. dollars at the exchange rate of US$1 = M$2.50.

8. Pee Teck Yew and Ani bin Arope, *Rubber Owners' Manual* (Kuala Lumpur: RRIM, 1976).

Table C-3. *Natural Rubber Supply Prices F.o.b. and C.i.f. in 1974 and 1976/77, at Real Discount Rates of 8, 10, and 12 Percent*

	Real discount rate (percent)								
	1974			1976/77					
				8		10		12	
Item	8	10	12	Low	High	Low	High	Low	High
Malaysian cents per kilogram									
Total estate cost	96.5	112.6	132.0	95.1	107.3	111.0	125.2	129.4	142.9
Production cost of crumb rubber	19.6	20.0	20.6	19.3	19.3	19.9	19.9	20.6	20.6
Total ex-factory supply price	116.1	132.6	152.6	114.4	126.6	130.9	145.1	150.0	163.5
Corrected ex-factory supply price	118.4	135.9	157.2	116.7	129.1	134.2	148.7	154.5	168.4
f.o.b. charges	4.5	4.5	4.5	6.0	6.0	6.0	6.0	6.0	6.0
Research tax	2.2	2.2	2.2	2.2	2.2	2.2	2.2	2.2	2.2
Export duty and surcharge	5.2	15.1	34.4	5.2	13.1	15.0	26.1	33.0	50.4
f.o.b. supply price Malaysia	130.3	157.7	198.3	130.1	150.4	157.4	183.0	195.7	227.0

Freight to Western Europe								
17.0	17.0	17.0	17.8	17.8	17.8	17.8	17.8	17.8
Freight to New York								
21.0	21.0	21.0	17.5	17.5	17.5	17.5	17.5	17.5
c.i.f. supply price Western Europe								
147.3	174.7	215.3	147.9	168.2	175.2	200.8	213.5	244.8
c.i.f. supply price New York								
151.3	178.7	219.3	147.6	167.9	174.9	200.5	213.2	244.5
Malaysian cents per pound								
f.o.b. supply price Malaysia								
59.1	71.5	89.9	59.0	68.2	71.4	83.0	88.8	103.0
c.i.f. supply price Western Europe								
66.8	79.2	97.7	67.1	76.3	79.5	91.1	96.8	111.0
c.i.f. supply price New York								
68.6	81.0	99.5	67.0	76.2	79.3	90.9	96.7	110.9
U.S. cents per kilogram[a]								
f.o.b. supply price Malaysia								
52.1	63.1	79.3	52.0	60.2	63.0	73.2	78.3	90.8
c.i.f. supply price Western Europe								
58.9	69.9	86.1	59.2	67.3	70.1	80.3	85.4	97.9
c.i.f. supply price New York								
60.5	71.5	87.7	59.0	67.2	70.0	80.2	85.3	97.8
U.S. cents per pound[a]								
f.o.b. supply price Malaysia								
23.6	28.6	36.0	23.6	27.3	28.5	33.2	35.5	41.2
c.i.f. supply price Western Europe								
26.7	31.7	39.1	26.8	30.5	31.8	36.4	38.7	44.4
c.i.f. supply price New York								
27.4	32.4	39.8	26.8	30.5	31.7	36.4	38.7	44.4

a. U.S.$1 = M$2.50.

Table C–4. *Estate Supply Prices in 1974 and 1976/77, at Real Discount Rates of 8, 10, and 12 Percent*
(Malaysian cents per kilogram)

Item	Real discount rate (percent)								
	1974			1976/77					
				8		10		12	
	8	10	12	Low	High	Low	High	Low	High
Field establishment	25.6	32.4	40.5	22.2	27.7	28.1	35.1	35.1	43.9
Estate buildings and installations, including upkeep	2.0	2.5	3.0	2.5	2.5	3.0	3.0	3.6	3.6
Estate staff housing, including upkeep	1.7	2.1	2.6	1.5	1.5	1.9	1.9	2.4	2.4
Workers' quarters, including upkeep	6.3	7.8	9.6	6.3	6.3	7.8	7.8	9.7	9.7
Field upkeep, including stimulation	12.5	12.7	12.9	8.8	12.5	9.0	12.7	9.1	12.9
Material cost of field collection	3.0	3.2	3.5	3.2	3.2	3.5	3.5	3.8	3.8
Estate staff salaries	7.1	8.0	9.0	9.0	9.0	10.1	10.1	11.4	11.4
Premium, quit rent, and insurance	4.4	5.1	5.9	4.4	4.4	5.1	5.1	5.9	5.9
Estate expenditure other than tapping cost	62.5	73.7	87.0	57.9	67.1	68.5	79.2	81.0	93.6
Tapping cost	34.5	39.3	45.3	37.7	39.4	41.2	44.7	46.9	49.6
Total estate expenditure	97.0	113.0	132.3	95.6	106.5	109.7	123.9	127.9	143.2
Residual value	0.5	0.4	0.3	0.5	0.5	0.4	0.4	0.3	0.3
Total estate cost	96.5	112.6	132.0	95.1	106.0	109.3	123.5	127.6	142.9

Table C–4 gives the breakdown of supply prices for NR in Malaysian cents per kilogram, at various real discount rates, in 1974 and 1976/77. The cost of some items actually decreased between 1974 and 1976/77, in part, because 1974 was a year of extreme scarcities and correspondingly of high prices for inputs such as fertilizers and other chemicals. The *Rubber Owners' Manual*, moreover, gives lower average cost figures in 1976 for some items than those used for our 1974 estimates. Wherever this was the case, a lower and higher price are shown, with prices from the *Rubber Owners' Manual* as the low price, and our updated estimates as the high price. As a result, a low and a high supply price are shown at each real discount rate for 1976/77, instead of a single estimate, as for the 1974 calculations.

As with the 1974 calculations, it was assumed that the gazetted price (on the basis of which wages, export duty, and surcharge have to be calculated) would equal the final supply price. This, again, required calculating the tapping cost for the entire relevant range of supply prices. To illustrate the effect of the new wage agreement on tapping cost, a comparison is made between 1974 and 1976/77 supply prices and their tapping cost components, both at 10 percent discount rate, and in Malaysian cents per kilogram. Although the estimate of the low 1976/77 supply price is practically equal to that of 1974, tapping costs have increased from M¢39.3 to M¢41.2 per kilogram, or by nearly five percent.

		1976/77	
Item	*1974*	*Low*	*High*
Supply price, f.o.b. Malaysia	157.7	157.4	183.0
Tapping cost	39.3	41.2	44.7

Factory expenditures taken into account in the estimates were based on the actual accounts of MRDC factories in 1974.[9] Since these factories were then still at their early stages of operation and also were used for training purposes, they were considerably overstaffed and showed higher than normal costs. Table C–3 also indicates that, despite the increase in investment expenditure between 1974 and 1976/77, the increased efficiency in these factories since 1974 slightly lowered the production cost of crumb rubber.

9. The freight rates used were valid until September 1977.

Table C–3 shows the various natural rubber supply prices in 1974 and 1976/77 at the three real discount rates, both f.o.b. Malaysia and c.i.f. Western Europe and the United States.[10] Comparison of the f.o.b. supply prices in 1974 with the high estimate for 1976/77 shows that between 1974 and 1976/77 the supply price of NR in Malaysia is estimated to have increased by 15 percent. The actual increase was probably smaller than 15 percent, since the 1976/77 high estimate tends to overstate cost. Finally, it is shown again that expenditures related to price, such as tapping costs and export levies, have an important effect on the final supply price.

10. In 1975 rubber prices were low, whereas in 1977 they were high.

Appendix D

•◦•

Estimate of the Full Supply Prices of Butadiene, Styrene, and SBR in Western Europe

Creating new capacity for producing styrene-butadiene rubber (SBR) involves either extending the production capacity of existing facilities to the maximum (debottlenecking) or setting up new production plants. The latter alternative can mean either establishing SBR polymerization plants that depend on styrene and butadiene monomers produced elsewhere, or setting up integrated operations that include the production of the monomers as well as their polymerization. Only the establishment of a new SBR production facility as part of an integrated chemical operation is considered here, since this alternative probably involves the least cost for producers and, therefore, is the most representative one.

It has been assumed that SBR-1500 is made from butadiene and styrene by the well-established process of SBR emulsion, in which the two base materials react in an aqueous medium at low temperature (5° to 10° C) using an emulsifier such as Dresinate. Unconverted butadiene and styrene are stripped from the resulting latex, and the rubber is then coagulated, dewatered, dried, baled, and packed.

It has also been assumed that the butadiene, styrene, and SBR plants are all part of a large petrochemical complex, with a naphtha cracker as its base. Butadiene is obtained by recovering the C_4 stream

Note: This appendix is based on a paper prepared for The World Bank by Maria 't Hooft-Welvaars, "The Profitability of NR and SBR Investments," *World Bank Staff Commodity Paper* (draft) (Washington, D.C.: The World Bank, 1978).

of the naphtha cracker; styrene is made by reacting benzene with ethylene from the cracker to produce ethylbenzene, followed by catalytic dehydrogenation.

Definition of the Full Supply Price for SBR

As in the case of natural rubber (NR), the full supply price of SBR is defined as the price which, if received over the entire lifetime of the plant, would equate the present value of all expenditures to the present value of all receipts. For SBR, however, a supply price range expressed in terms of oil prices, labor, and capital costs is determined first for butadiene. A supply price is also calculated for styrene, taking ethylene and benzene as given.[1] An SBR supply price is then derived from the styrene and butadiene prices. To facilitate the comparisons of these results with those obtained for NR, the same three real discount rates—8, 10, and 12 percent—were used to calculate the present values of expenditures and receipts for SBR.

Collection of Investment Data

Calculating a full supply price by the discounted cash flow method requires that all expenditures and receipts be entered in the year in which they occur. This in turn requires data on: (a) total requirements of investment capital; (b) phasing of plant construction; (c) time profile of production buildup after the plant has come onstream (including stockbuilding requirements); (d) requirements of physical input (feedstocks, utilities, labor) and their prices; (e) plant maintenance and overhead; (f) expenditures for selling and for research and development; and (g) tax payments.

To collect the necessary data a number of Western European and American firms were interviewed, including chemical producers, SBR producers, and engineering firms. Technical literature also was con-

---

1. The supply prices of ethylene and benzene were not calculated using a discounted cash flow method. Instead, a formula relating the value of these chemicals to the prices of crude oil, naphtha, and fuel oil and to some capital and labor costs was used to simplify the calculations.

sulted. The information was cross-checked and extensive use was made of published reference data to ensure consistency.

Since SBR production is a capital-intensive operation, a major cost element in its supply price is, of course, investment capital. Accurate capital cost estimates are crucial to the calculations of the full supply price.

A serious impediment to making these estimates was the heterogeneous mixture of investment data for Western Europe. Investment figures often referred to plants of different sizes located in different countries. Figures were also sometimes available for comparable size plants, but for different years. An additional problem was the exact specification of investment costs: inside battery limits or full costs.[2] The main cause of these difficulties was that few investments were actually carried out between 1972 and 1976 and that, to a large extent, only engineering estimates were available. Finally, it was difficult to compare investment data between countries because of the relatively large changes in exchange rates that occurred in this period. National investment figures for 1973 were converted into U.S. dollars, therefore, averaged, and set as the base for cost indexes that were updated using the *Engineering News Record* index of capital costs. Despite the fact that this cost index refers to the United States, the derived U.S. dollar estimates for subsequent years checked rather well against available estimates for specific years, expressed in U.S. dollars.[3]

Labor costs are another component of the SBR supply price. They, again, vary from country to country. An average cost figure ($21,500 a year for a chemical operator) was taken as representative for 1973.[4] This figure includes direct wages, benefits, and social premiums, as well as the cost of supervision. A labor cost index expressed in U.S. dollars that represents an amalgam of wage indexes in the petrochemical industries of the key Western European countries was used to update labor costs to 1977.

The costs of raw materials and utilities that go into the production

---

2. An inside battery limits investment is one that becomes part of an ongoing production operation and, therefore, benefits from the presence of the operation in terms of cost.

3. This result is caused, in part, by the nature of the goods in question. Capital investment goods are internationally traded, and their prices in different markets are closely related.

4. This figure includes labor benefits, social premiums, and supervision costs.

of sbr are related to the price of oil. Utilities are produced with fuel oil, and raw materials are based on naphtha, whose cost, in turn, depends on oil. Table D–1 shows the average c.i.f. prices of crude oil, naphtha, and fuel oil that were calculated for the major Western European countries on the basis of *Platt's Oilgram* monthly quotations. It also shows the capital and labor cost indexes used to calculate sbr supply prices.

Tax payments, which vary from country to country, also had to be expressed in an approximate common denominator. The average effective tax rate on profits was assumed to be 45 percent. This rate probably understates slightly the nominal tax on profits in Western Europe, but often rebates that are linked to investment are granted to producers by national governments, so that the effective average tax rate is probably not too different from the one assumed here. Taxable profits were defined as the total value of sales (adjusted for stocks) in a given year; minus the value of base materials and utilities used in production; minus labor, maintenance, and overhead costs; and minus capital depreciation.

Table D–1. *Basic Price Data and Indexes Used to Calculate* sbr *Supply Price*
(*U.S. dollars per metric ton*)

Item	1973[a]	1974	1975	1976	1977[a]
Crude	23.5	78.5	87.5	92.5	98.0
Naphtha	43.0	123.0	110.0	131.0	130.0
Fuel oil, 3 ½ percent sulfur	17.5	69.5	62.5	67.5	75.0
Fuel oil, 0 percent sulfur	28.0	76.0	72.0	76.0	82.5
Relations					
Naphtha/crude	1.83	1.57	1.26	1.42	1.33
Fuel oil, 3 ½ percent sulfur/crude	0.74	0.89	0.71	0.73	0.77
Fuel oil, 0 percent sulfur/crude	1.19	0.97	0.82	0.82	0.84
Capital and labor cost indexes (mid-year; 1973 = 100)					
Capital cost[b]	100	112.4	127.0	137.1	152.8
Labor cost[c]	100	118.0	135.0	147.8	162.6

a. Average for the first half of the year, except for capital and labor cost indexes.

b. Derived from *Engineering News Record*. The index is lagged one year, and its values refer to the first quarter.

c. Average of the major Western European countries.

Assumptions and Estimates for Butadiene Production

It was estimated that a butadiene plant having an annual capacity of 60,000 metric tons would have cost US$8 million in 1973.[5] Such a plant would take about three years to begin production. In year 0 plant costs consist exclusively of site preparation and general planning. The direct plant investment outlays were, therefore, phased over three years at, respectively, 15, 40, and 45 percent of the total. The production buildup was assumed as follows: 25 percent of capacity in year 2, 70 percent in year 3, 85 percent in year 4, and 100 percent from year 5 onward. Stocks were taken as one-sixth of annual production. Depreciation, which has to be calculated only for tax purposes, was assumed to be linear for ten years, starting in year 3. The life of the plant was considered to be twelve years and its scrap value 20 percent of the initial investment value. It was also assumed that an average two-month credit would be extended to all customers by the producers.

The valuation of the butadiene feedstocks presented a major problem. The C_4 stream—the input into butadiene production—is difficult to cost, since its value depends more on the market price of butadiene than vice versa. To circumvent this problem low and high values of the C_4 feed were taken: the former assumes a market surplus situation, whereas the latter assumes buoyant demand conditions for the butadiene monomer. Between 1973 and 1975 the only way to dispose of surplus C_4 was to use it as fuel. At times of high demand, surplus C_4 can, instead, be cracked as naphtha. The minimum refinery value of C_4 appears, therefore, to have gone from the lower fuel value to the higher naphtha value. Yet even between 1973 and 1975, the market values of C_4 were never even remotely near those of fuel. Entering the naphtha value as the lower limit of the C_4 stream costs in all years from 1973 to 1977 does not, therefore, introduce any severe bias in the calculations. Again, based on the observation that from 1974 onward, the actual values of C_4 fluctuated between 1.7 and 2.4 times those of naphtha, the high value for C_4 used in the calculations was twice that of naphtha.

---

5. Capacity is defined throughout this appendix as the annual production of a plant that is technically feasible, allowing for normal maintenance and repair.

Assumptions and Estimates for Styrene Production

A styrene plant having an annual capacity of 250,000 metric tons was estimated to have cost US$50 million in 1973. Total expenditure was assumed to be phased over four years: 10 percent of the total in year 0, 30 percent in year 1, 40 percent in year 2, and 20 percent in year 3. Production buildup was taken as follows: 25 percent of capacity in year 3, 70 percent in year 4, 85 percent in year 5, and 100 percent from year 6 onward. Stocks were taken at one-sixth of an annual production. Depreciation was assumed to be linear over ten years. The life of the plant was put at thirteen years. Its liquidation value was taken at 20 percent of the initial investment value. Again, an average two-month credit to all customers was assumed.

To value the ethylene and benzene feedstocks that go into styrene production, formulas were used that relate the value of these chemicals to the price of crude oil, naphtha, and fuel oil and to some elements of cost for capital and labor.

Assumptions and Estimates for SBR Production

The cost of an SBR plant having an annual capacity of 60,000 metric tons was estimated at US$22 million in 1973. This total expenditure was assumed to be phased over three years: 15 percent of the total in year 0, 40 percent in year 1, 45 percent in year 2. The production buildup was taken as follows: 25 percent of capacity in year 2, 70 percent in year 3, 85 percent in year 4, and 100 percent from year 5 onward. Stocks were taken at one-sixth of annual production, and depreciation was assumed to be linear over ten years. The plant was assumed to operate for twelve years and to have a scrap value of 20 percent of the initial investment value. Two-month credit to all clients was again postulated.

The calculations of the supply price for butadiene and styrene (at different real discount rates) formed the basis of the SBR feedstock valuation. Low and high butadiene prices used in the calculations yielded corresponding low and high estimates of SBR supply prices. Transport costs for styrene and butadiene also entered the calculations of SBR supply prices, as well as packing costs (a packing worker was assumed to have cost the producer $15,000 a year in 1973). Packing costs were naturally entered in the calculation proportionally to the assumed production buildup.

Most synthetic rubber producers in Western Europe are not tire manufacturers. They, therefore, incur selling costs when marketing their products. Selling costs, together with expenditure for research and development, were assumed to be at 10 percent of the full supply price. This overstates the SBR supply price for the tire manufacturers that produce their own rubber. This type of producer, however, is not often integrated with a petrochemical company; he usually has to buy the butadiene and styrene monomers. In such cases, selling costs should be added to the full supply price of styrene and butadiene, and some expenditures on research and development would also be required. The full supply price of SBR for a tire manufacturer producing his own SBR is, therefore, likely to be less than 10 percent below the full supply price that includes selling and full research and development costs.

Differentiation of Expenditures

In the more detailed background paper on supply prices of NR and SR, the various elements of expenditure for producing butadiene, styrene, and SBR-1500 are split up into three categories containing oil-related input costs, labor cost, and capital cost.

For example, the price of utilities per ton is defined as:

$$FS_P = P(x) + C(y) + L(z)$$

where: FS_P = price relation between fuel oil ($3\frac{1}{2}$ percent sulfur) and crude oil; P = price of crude oil; C = unit capital cost (in 1973, therefore, $C = \$1.0$, in 1974, $\$1.124$, etc.); L = unit labor cost (in 1973, $L = \$1.0$, in 1974, $\$1.180$, etc.)[6]; and x, y, and z are coefficients. This differentiation of expenditure categories has several advantages. First, it makes it possible to analyze the sensitivity of SBR supply prices to changes in crude oil prices or to changes in capital and labor costs.[7] Second, it allows country-specific information concerning labor and capital investment costs to be incorporated quickly and efficiently and the corresponding SBR supply prices to be formulated

---

6. See indexes in Table D–1.

7. To examine the sensitivity of SBR supply prices to changes in crude oil price, a relation between crude oil, naphtha, and fuel oil prices has to be established. Where this is done, the sensitivity analysis becomes straightforward. The results of this exercise can be found in Table 4–5.

Table D–2. *Full Supply Prices of Butadiene, Styrene, and* SBR-1500 *in Western Europe, at Real Discount Rates of 8, 10, and 12 Percent*

				Real discount rate (percent)					
	1973			1975			1977		
Item	8	10	12	8	10	12	8	10	12
U.S. dollars per metric ton									
Butadiene									
Low	99.93	105.15	110.50	203.68	211.03	218.52	242.85	251.67	260.66
High	146.13	151.76	157.51	322.11	330.54	339.05	382.86	392.95	403.16
Styrene	218.06	227.42	237.12	400.65	413.68	427.09	478.86	494.51	510.62
SBR-1500									
Low	428.78	453.66	479.28	699.02	733.28	768.38	838.92	880.10	922.29
High	467.86	493.49	519.82	799.22	835.39	872.33	957.39	1,000.82	1,045.18
U.S. cents per pound									
Butadiene									
Low	4.61	4.85	5.10	9.24	9.57	9.91	11.02	11.42	11.82
High	6.71	6.97	7.23	14.61	14.99	15.38	17.37	17.82	18.29
Styrene	10.05	10.47	10.92	18.17	18.76	19.37	21.72	22.43	23.16
SBR-1500									
Low	20.42	21.57	22.75	31.71	33.26	34.85	38.05	39.92	41.83
High	22.19	23.37	24.58	36.25	37.89	39.57	43.43	45.40	47.41

without having to go through the whole discounting exercise item by item.[8]

Estimates of the Full Supply Price of SBR

Table D–2 shows the supply prices of butadiene, styrene, and SBR-1500 at the three real discount rates chosen for the calculations; the high and low butadiene supply prices correspond to the high and low SBR-1500 supply prices. The supply price of SBR-1500 appears to have increased by from 60 to 70 percent between 1973 and 1975 and by another 20 percent between 1975 and 1977. Between 1973 and 1977 the supply price of SBR-1500 is estimated to have almost doubled.

The data in Table D–2 also show that the oil price increase that occurred between 1973 and 1977 had the strongest effect on the price of butadiene, whose prices are closest to those of naphtha. The effect is lower for styrene, which is further removed from naphtha, and, of course, is even lower for SBR-1500. This illustrates well the process of passing through costs which is characteristic of the petrochemical industry.

The supply price of SBR-1500 is broken down by major items in Tables D–3 and D–4. A similar breakdown for styrene, butadiene, and SBR-1500, but with a single rate of discount (10 percent) is given in Table D–5. Tables D–3 and D–4 illustrate quite clearly the influence of the desired rate of return (the real discount rate) on the various cost elements. The items that are influenced heavily by the real discount rate are, naturally, investment costs and taxes. The other cost elements on which a difference in discount rates bears heavily are stockbuilding and credit, whereas base materials, utilities, labor, and other costs are relatively less affected.

---

8. This way it was possible to correct the labor component in the 1973 SBR supply price. It was clearly too high when computed in terms of U.S. dollars, because of the exchange rate changes during that year.

Table D–3. *Low and High* SBR-1500 *Supply Prices in Western Europe,*
at Real Discount Rates of 8, 10, and 12 Percent
(U.S. dollars per metric ton)

Item	Real discount rate (percent)								
	1973			1975			1977		
	8	10	12	8	10	12	8	10	12
SBR-1500, low									
Investment	59.14	65.50	72.24	75.10	83.19	91.75	90.36	100.89	110.39
Base materials and utilities	231.34	237.31	243.44	410.48	418.84	427.39	491.95	501.99	512.26
Labor, maintenance, and overhead	76.85	77.74	78.65	114.23	115.55	116.90	137.55	139.13	140.75
Taxes	13.90	19.59	25.22	19.96	27.70	35.32	23.98	33.28	42.45
Stockbuilding	5.29	6.87	8.56	8.63	11.11	13.72	10.36	13.33	16.47
Debtors	5.17	6.70	8.33	8.43	10.83	13.36	10.12	13.00	16.03
Selling and research and development	41.88	44.24	46.66	68.28	71.50	74.80	81.94	85.82	89.78
Total per ton	433.58	457.95	483.10	705.11	738.42	773.24	846.26	886.65	928.14
Liquidation value of plant	4.80	4.29	3.82	6.09	5.44	4.86	7.33	6.55	5.84
Supply price (per ton)	428.78	453.66	479.28	699.02	733.28	768.38	838.92	880.10	922.29
SBR-1500, high									
Investment	59.13	65.50	72.24	75.10	83.19	91.75	90.36	100.09	110.39
Base materials and utilities	274.36	280.66	287.12	496.94	506.08	515.38	594.16	605.13	616.28
Labor, maintenance, and overhead	86.07	87.07	88.08	114.23	115.55	116.90	137.55	139.13	140.75
Taxes	14.80	20.69	26.51	21.48	29.56	37.50	25.78	35.48	45.03
Stockbuilding	6.04	7.81	9.68	9.87	12.66	15.58	11.82	15.16	18.66
Debtors	5.90	7.61	9.42	9.64	12.34	15.16	11.54	14.79	18.17
Selling and research and development	47.79	50.25	52.76	78.06	81.46	84.92	93.51	97.59	101.74
Total per ton	494.10	519.58	545.81	805.32	840.84	877.19	964.72	1,007.37	1,051.03
Liquidation value of plant	4.80	4.29	3.82	6.09	5.44	4.86	7.33	6.55	5.84
Supply price (per ton)	489.30	515.30	541.99	799.02	835.39	872.33	957.39	1,000.82	1,045.18

Table D–4. *Low and High* SBR-1500 *Supply Prices in Western Europe, at Real Discount Rates of 8, 10, and 12 Percent* (U.S. cents per pound)

	Real discount rate (percent)								
	1973			1975			1977		
Item	8	10	12	8	10	12	8	10	12
SBR-1500, low									
Investment	2.68	2.97	3.28	3.41	3.77	4.16	4.10	4.54	5.01
Base materials and utilities	10.49	10.76	11.04	18.62	19.00	19.39	22.31	22.77	23.24
Labor, maintenance, and overhead	3.49	3.53	3.57	5.18	5.24	5.30	6.24	6.31	6.38
Taxes	0.63	0.89	1.14	0.91	1.26	1.60	1.09	1.51	1.93
Stockbuilding	0.24	0.31	0.39	0.39	0.50	0.62	0.47	0.60	0.75
Debtors	0.23	0.30	0.38	0.38	0.49	0.61	0.46	0.59	0.73
Selling and research and development	1.90	2.01	2.12	3.10	3.24	3.39	3.72	3.89	4.07
Total per pound	19.67	20.77	21.91	31.98	33.51	35.07	38.39	40.22	42.10
Liquidation value of plant	0.22	0.19	0.17	0.28	0.25	0.22	0.33	0.30	0.27
Supply price per ton	19.45	20.58	21.74	31.71	33.26	34.85	38.05	39.92	41.83
SBR-1500, high									
Investment	2.68	2.97	3.28	3.41	3.77	4.16	4.10	4.54	5.01
Base materials and utilities	12.44	12.73	13.32	22.54	22.96	23.38	26.95	27.45	27.95
Labor, maintenance, and overhead	3.90	3.95	4.00	5.18	5.24	5.30	6.24	6.31	6.38
Taxes	0.67	0.94	1.20	0.97	1.34	1.70	1.17	1.61	2.04
Stockbuilding	0.27	0.35	0.44	0.45	0.57	0.71	0.54	0.69	0.85
Debtors	0.27	0.35	0.43	0.44	0.56	0.69	0.52	0.67	0.82
Selling and research and development	2.17	2.28	2.39	3.54	3.70	3.85	4.24	4.43	4.62
Total per pound	22.41	23.57	24.76	36.53	38.14	39.79	43.76	45.69	47.67
Liquidation value of plant	0.22	0.19	0.17	0.28	0.25	0.22	0.33	0.30	0.27
Supply price per ton	22.19	23.37	24.58	36.25	37.89	39.57	43.43	45.40	47.41

Table D-5. *Full Supply Prices of Butadiene, Styrene, and* sbr-1500 *in Western Europe, at a Real Discount Rate of 10 Percent*
(U.S. dollars per metric ton)

Item	Butadiene, low 1973	Butadiene, low 1975	Butadiene, high 1973	Butadiene, high 1975	Styrene 1973	Styrene 1975	sbr-1500, low 1973	sbr-1500, low 1975	sbr-1500, high 1973	sbr-1500, high 1975
U.S. dollars per ton										
Investment	23.82	30.25	23.82	30.25	37.88	48.11	65.50	83.19	65.50	83.19
Base materials and utilities	60.57	148.37	104.86	261.93	160.51	321.44	237.31	418.84	271.33	506.08
Labor, maintenance, and overhead	12.93	18.61	12.93	18.61	12.36	16.75	77.74	115.55	77.74	115.55
Taxes	6.25	9.46	7.17	11.84	12.19	17.97	19.59	27.70	20.31	29.56
Stockbuilding	1.59	3.20	2.30	5.01	3.44	6.27	6.87	11.11	7.47	12.66
Debtors	1.55	3.12	2.24	4.88	3.36	6.11	6.70	10.83	7.29	12.34
Selling and research and development	—	—	—	—	—	—	44.24	71.50	48.12	81.46
Total per ton	106.70	213.01	153.32	332.52	229.76	416.65	457.95	738.72	497.77	840.84
Liquidation value of plant	1.56	1.98	1.56	1.98	2.33	2.97	4.29	5.44	4.29	5.44
Supply price per ton	105.15	211.03	151.76	330.54	227.42	413.68	453.66	733.28	493.49	835.39
U.S. cents per pound										
Investment	1.08	1.37	1.08	1.37	1.72	2.18	2.97	3.77	2.97	3.77
Base materials and utilities	2.75	6.73	4.76	11.88	7.28	14.58	10.76	19.00	12.31	22.96
Labor, maintenance, and overhead	0.59	0.84	0.59	0.84	0.56	0.76	3.53	5.24	3.53	5.24
Taxes	0.28	0.43	0.33	0.54	0.55	0.82	0.89	1.26	0.92	1.34
Stockbuilding	0.07	0.15	0.10	0.23	0.16	0.28	0.31	0.50	0.34	0.57
Debtors	0.07	0.14	0.10	0.22	0.15	0.28	0.30	0.49	0.33	0.56
Selling and research and development	—	—	—	—	—	—	2.01	3.24	2.18	3.70
Total per pound	4.84	9.66	6.95	15.08	10.42	18.90	20.77	33.51	22.58	38.14
Liquidation value of plant	0.07	0.99	0.07	0.09	0.11	0.13	0.19	0.25	0.19	0.25
Supply price per pound	4.77	9.57	6.88	14.99	10.32	18.76	20.58	33.26	22.38	37.89

Appendix E

•⊕•

Forecasting Frameworks and Demand Estimates for Rubber to 1985 and 1990

The demand for rubber is a derived demand. The automotive industry is the most important consumer of rubber products, and more than 65 percent of all elastomers produced in the world are used in tires and other automotive products. Most of the remaining 35 percent is used in fabricating industrial goods. Since the production and use of motor vehicles are very sensitive to changes in economic conditions, rubber demand also closely follows these changes. In the past twenty-five years, the relation between gross national product (GNP), motor vehicle production (or motor vehicle use), and rubber consumption was so strong and stable that, in forecasting future rubber demand, it actually mattered little whether the link between growth of GNP and growth of motor vehicle production (or the motor vehicle park) and rubber demand was estimated or whether the elasticity of rubber demand with respect to GNP was estimated directly.[1]

The Traditional Forecasting Approach

Time-series analysis of rubber demand during the past twenty-five years clearly shows that a strong and stable statistical relation existed between total elastomer consumption and growth of GNP (or in-

---

1. Use of existing vehicles, which affects the replacement rate of the vehicles in use as well as the rate at which tires and other rubber automotive parts are worn out, is also closely related to GNP.

dustrial production) in all major consuming areas. Almost all past demand forecasts published by international organizations, rubber companies, and individual researchers were based on this direct approach. Coefficients of income elasticities of demand for rubber were computed on the basis of time-series (or cross-section) analysis, and rubber demand was estimated directly, using projections of future GNP growth. Interestingly enough, despite the fact that the chosen income elasticity coefficients were broadly similar and were taken as constant over time (which turned out to be a correct assumption for the 1950s and 1960s) most past forecasts of rubber demand erred greatly on the conservative side, since projected GNP growth rates were invariably lower than the realized ones.

Shortcomings of the traditional framework

Whether this forecasting framework is still useful is questionable. Apart from the estimation problems that have to be overcome, there are several reasons to doubt that the more serious shortcomings of the direct approach to forecasting future rubber demand through income elasticity coefficients could be remedied. First, the degree of motor vehicle use in most developed countries has increased so much and so rapidly that declining growth rates can be expected over the next ten to fifteen years. Second, the intensity of motor vehicle use, particularly for private automobiles, can also be expected to grow less rapidly than in the past as a consequence of physical crowding and higher costs of vehicle maintenance and use. These factors— whose importance has been heightened first by the increasing awareness of the economic drawbacks resulting from the current widespread reliance on private means of transport, and more recently by the sharp increases in fuel prices—will not only negatively affect the "direct" demand for rubber, resulting in a decreased rate of growth of demand for new vehicles, but also will affect the "replacement" demand for rubber, since decreased use of vehicles leads to decreased growth of demand for replacement rubber products. Third, fuel conservation policies that governments in most oil-importing countries are bound to implement (or to toughen over time), will also mean that in some major rubber-consuming areas (notably, North America) smaller and lighter cars will be produced, thereby reducing both the rubber demand per vehicle produced and possibly the rate of wear of tires.

The above considerations—which are by no means exhaustive— clearly point to the fact that for at least a major portion of the rubber market—the tire market—the historical relation between growth of GNP and growth of demand is likely to undergo substantial changes. To capture these as well as other changes in the structure of rubber demand, a more disaggregated forecasting approach seems to be necessary. In trying to disaggregate demand into its main components, however, the conceptual and practical difficulties encountered, particularly on the data side, become very serious. The natural tendency for the forecaster is, therefore, to try to salvage the traditional framework and adapt it, somewhat mechanically, to the expected changes in the structure of rubber demand.

Adapting the traditional framework to the expected changes

One way of doing this is to scale down over the forecasting period the historical coefficients of income elasticity of rubber demand to try to capture some of the expected structural changes, making the implicit assumption that the structure of demand is likely to change relatively smoothly. In effect, because the historical relation between GNP and elastomer consumption is expected to continue in developing countries and centrally planned economies where rubber use is still relatively low, it becomes necessary to make a priori adjustments in the income elasticity coefficients only for developed countries.[2] If this approach is followed, demand forecasts can be derived straightforwardly from the assumptions regarding the growth of the shift variables (GNP/GDP and population).

The estimation of the income elasticity coefficients is not, however, trouble-free. Although it would be theoretically preferable to estimate the elasticity coefficients from a relation between per capita consumption and per capita income, this is in practice difficult, since the consumption statistics that are available refer only to direct domestic use of rubber in manufacturing and do not reflect the trade balances in finished rubber products. This makes it impossible to disaggregate consumption beyond broad economic regions (developed countries, developing countries, and centrally planned economies) and prevents, in effect, the use of cross-section analysis of individual

---

2. Another way of achieving the same result would be to use in estimating the historical relation between rubber demand and income functions that allow for an automatic decline of income elasticity over time. The problem here is that for the developed countries as a group the historical relation is best represented by a log-log function (semi-log or inverse function do not fit the data nearly as well).

country data. Aggregation of statistics on (country) domestic use by economic regions helps to deal with the problem of regional trade in finished products (which is the largest portion of total trade), but still does not solve the difficulties caused by inter-regional trade.[3]

Although both Eastern Europe with the U.S.S.R. and China are practically self-sufficient in rubber products, developed countries are net exporters of rubber manufactures (especially tires), and developing countries are net importers. The available statistics of total rubber use thus overstate the quantity of rubber actually consumed in developed countries and understate it in developing countries. The consequence is that the regional income elasticity of demand coefficients estimated on the basis of these statistics are probably biased upward for the developed countries and downward for the developing countries.[4] The lack of uniformity and incompleteness of the available trade data series for rubber products make it impossible to factor in trade balances and to arrive at reasonably accurate estimates of actual consumption even for broad groups of countries.[5]

Projections based on adjusted coefficients of income elasticity

Subject to these qualifications, the historical coefficients of income elasticity for rubber demand estimated from time-series analysis of annual data (using the estimated equations in Table E–1) range from 1.3 to 1.4 for the developed countries, 1.6 to 2.0 for the developing countries, and 1.4 to 1.6 for the centrally planned economies. The 1978 working assumptions of the World Bank concerning GDP and population growth to 1990 by major economic regions are summarized in Table E–2. On the basis of these assumptions and the chosen coefficients of income elasticity, projections of future elastomer consumption can be derived. The projections presented here are based on scaled-down coefficients of income elasticity for

3. Because of the large regional trade in rubber manufactures, for most of the individual countries, per capita consumption data that are derived by dividing direct domestic use of rubber by population are virtually meaningless.

4. Implicit is the assumption that rubber imports of developing countries have increased more rapidly than total utilization of rubber products.

5. Trade in several rubber products is only recorded in value terms. When quantities of products, such as tires, are available, the weights refer to the actual weight of the product and not to its rubber content. The country coverage also lacks uniformity.

1976–80 and on declining coefficients of income elasticity for 1980–90. This adjustment is particularly important for developed countries, where (as discussed above) substantial changes are expected in the historical relation between income and rubber consumption, and the use of functions that would allow for an automatic decline in the elasticity coefficients over time series runs into serious difficulties.[6] Coefficients of per capita income elasticities of 1.2, 1.1, and 1.0 were used in making the forecasts for 1976–80, 1980–85, and 1985–90, respectively. They compare with the values of 1.42 and 1.39 estimated for 1955–75 and 1960–75.

Similar, if smaller, adjustments were made in the per capita coefficients of income elasticity of the developing countries and the centrally planned economies. For the developing countries the historical coefficient (1.98) was scaled down to 1.8 for 1976–80, 1.6 for 1980–85, and 1.4 for 1985–90. Eastern Europe and U.S.S.R., however, were differentiated from China. Income-elasticity values of 1.4, 1.3, and 1.2—which compare with the historical 1.6—were used in the projections for Eastern Europe and the U.S.S.R. as a group over the three times intervals, whereas a constant coefficient of 1.4 was used for China. The projections for China, moreover, were worked out on the basis of the relation between total consumption and total income. China was treated differently because consumption levels there are so low that the use of rubber is expected to continue to increase in some fixed relation to industrial production or income and because the relation between per capita consumption and per capita income is not very relevant, since private consumption of rubber products is more strictly restricted there than in any other country.

The projections indicate that even under conservative assumptions regarding the values of income elasticities and long-term economic growth in industrialized countries (Table E–2), world rubber con-

---

6. In the past the relation between rubber consumption and income in developed countries was clearly linear in logs. The use of other functions in the estimation of the historical relation yields either poor statistical fits (such as semi-log functions) or untenable results (such as inverse or log-inverse functions). The latter problem is well exemplified by equations (1.5) and (1.6) in Table E–1. The inverse function yields a saturation level of 35.5 pounds per capita that is 20 percent higher than the current U.S. level and does not represent a feasible level of per capita consumption for the whole of the developed countries. The log-inverse function yields a saturation level of 60 pounds per capita, which is definitely out of reach for any single country let alone the whole of the developed countries.

Table E–1. *Relation between Total Elastomer Consumption and Real Income (GDP) in Major Consuming Areas: Time Series Regression Results*

Economic region	Constant term a_0	Regression coefficients $a_1 = \ln GDP$	$a_1 = \ln GDP/N$	$a_1 = \dfrac{1}{GDP/N}$	Multiple correlation coefficient $\bar{R}^2$	Standard error of estimate	Durbin-Watson statistics	Time period for annual data
Developed countries								
(1.1)	$\ln CE = -3.7088$	$+1.3264$ (38.4)			0.99	0.0349	1.60	1955–75
(1.2)	$\ln CE = -3.1506$	$+1.2877$ (15.5)			0.95	0.0343	1.51	1960–75
(1.3)	$\ln CE/N = -2.3603$		$+1.4272$ (33.8)		0.98	0.0336	1.61	1955–75
(1.4)	$\ln CE/N = -2.0325$		$+1.3856$ (14.1)		0.94	0.0339	1.50	1960–75
(1.5)	$CE/N = 16101.5$			$-.22731 \cdot 10^{-8}$ (−8.5)	0.81	0.277	1.50	1955–75
(1.6)	$\ln CE/N = 10.218$			-3477.4 (−22.7)	0.97	0.0344	1.59	1955–75

				R^2			
Developing countries							
(2.1)	$\ln CE = -7.734$	$+1.592$ (23.3)		0.98	0.043	1.86	1960–75
(2.2)	$\ln CE/N = 5.623$		$+1.980$ (11.7)	0.91	0.047	2.10	1960–75
Centrally planned economies U.S.S.R. and Eastern Europe							
(3.1)	$\ln CE = -6.942$	$+1.565$ (7.6)		0.83	0.031	2.37	1960–75
(3.2)	$\ln CE/N = -3.737$		$+1.600$ (5.5)	0.72	0.032	2.35	1960–75
China							
(4.1)	$\ln CE = -4.415$	$+1.361$ (9.0)		0.85	0.136	0.38	1960–75
(4.2)	$\ln CE/N = -2.585$		$+1.458$ (6.2)	0.73	0.144	0.38	1960–75

Note: The Cochrane-Orcut procedure was used to correct for autocorrelation in all regressions except for China. OLS were used throughout. CE = total elastomer consumption, GDP = gross domestic product (at constant U.S. dollar and exchange rates), N = population, and CE/N = kilograms per 1,000 people; t values are in parentheses.

149

Table E–2. *Forecasts of GDP and Population Growth for Major Economic Regions, 1980, 1985, and 1990*
(annual percent)

Item	1976–80	1980–85	1985–90
GDP (constant U.S. dollars)			
Developed countries	4.1	4.2	4.2
Developing countries	6.0	6.5	6.5
Centrally planned economies			
Eastern Europe, U.S.S.R.[a]	5.5	5.5	5.0
China	5.0	5.5	6.0
Population			
Developed countries	0.9	0.9	0.8
Developing countries	2.7	2.7	2.6
Centrally planned economies			
Eastern Europe, U.S.S.R.	0.7	0.9	0.8
China	1.6	1.4	1.2

a. Net material product.
Sources: World Bank, Economic Analysis and Projections Department; UN Secretariat, Population Division.

sumption can be expected to continue to grow about 5.4 percent a year during the next ten years: that is, about 1.0 percent below the historical rate experienced between 1948 and 1973 or about 1.8 percent a year below the growth rate realized between 1956 and 1976 (Table E–3). Alternative projections worked out on the basis of the relation between total elastomer consumption and income growth for all country groups using scaled-down elasticity coefficients yielded similar results.

An Alternative Forecasting Approach

Any attempt to forecast future rubber demand on the basis of its uses necessarily has to start with a broad division between the rubber that is used in automotive uses and the rubber that goes into other uses. Given the variety of nonautomotive uses, this broad breakdown is the only feasible one, at least from the standpoint of long-term forecasting on a world basis.[7] Yet even this rather broad differentiation presents serious problems to the forecaster. Reliable data on total rubber use in the centrally planned economies and in the developing

7. See Chapter 3.

Table E–3. World Demand for Elastomers, Actual Averages, Projected, and Growth Rates, 1955 to 1990, Selected Years

Economic region	Actual averages (thousands of metric tons)				Projected (thousands of metric tons)		Growth rates (annual percentage)			
	1955–57	1966–68	1972–74	1975–77	1985	1990	1956–73	1976–85	1985–90	1976–90
Developed countries	2,640	4,895	7,121	7,084	10,900	13,000	6.0	4.9	3.6	4.4
Developing countries	207	599	1,147	1,339	2,800	4,000	10.4	8.6	7.4	8.1
Centrally planned economies	673	1,517	2,367	2,883	5,300	7,000	7.7	7.0	5.7	6.5
U.S.S.R. and Eastern Europe	(617)	(1,310)	(2,100)	(2,573)	(4,700)	(6,200)	(7.5)	(6.9)	(5.7)	(7.1)
China	(56)	(207)	(267)	(310)	(600)	(800)	(9.6)	(7.6)	(5.9)	(11.1)
Total	3,520	7,011	10,635	11,327	19,000	24,000	6.7	5.9	4.8	5.4

Source: Actual data, International Rubber Study Group.

countries as a group are not available, and it is even difficult to find reliable data series on total rubber use in the automotive industry of developed countries. Only a breakdown of rubber consumption into that for tires and that for nontire uses is available for the main countries and can be reconstructed for the rest. This less-than-satisfactory division has to be used for lack of any more precise and detailed information.

Starting from this basic division of rubber used in tires and rubber in nontire uses in developed countries, an attempt was made to forecast these two major components of elastomer demand for North America, Western Europe, Japan, and other developed countries. This at least would cover a major portion (70 percent) of world rubber demand and would be a check on the demand forecasts obtained using the traditional approach. Since the most serious doubts about the reliability of the direct forecasting method are harbored in the developed countries, this limited application of the disaggregated approach has the obvious advantage of focusing on the most troublesome area of forecasting future rubber demand.

A disaggregated model for forecasting demand

The forecasting model used for the developed countries is summarized below.

TIRE AND NONTIRE USES

$$(1) \qquad CR = CRT + CRNT,$$

where CR = total consumption of rubber, CRT = total consumption of rubber in tires, and $CRNT$ = total consumption of rubber in nontire uses. All relations are summed over the four geographic areas: North America, Western Europe, Japan, and other developed countries; the summation signs are omitted throughout for economy of exposition.

TIRE SECTOR

$$(2) \qquad CRT = CRTA + CRTCV,$$

where $CRTA$ = consumption in automobile tires, and $CRTCV$ = consumption in commercial vehicle tires.

Consumption in automobile tires:

(2.1) $CRTA = k(TA_{oe}) + k(TA_{rp}) + k(\overline{TA_x}).$

Consumption in commercial vehicle tires:

(2.2) $CRTCV = v(TCV_{oe}) + v(TCV_{rp}) + v(\overline{TCV_x}),$

where TA_{oe}, TCV_{oe} = original equipment tires (number), TA_{rp}, TCV_{rp} = replacement tires (number), $\overline{TA_x}$, $\overline{TCV_x}$ = tire exports (exogenous), k = average elastomer weight of automobile tires, and v = average elastomer weight of commercial vehicle tires.

(2.3) $TA_{oe} = f(O_a{}^+),$

where O_a = production of automobiles (including exports).[8]

(2.4) $TCV_{oe} = f(O_{cv}{}^+),$

where O_{cv} = production of commercial vehicles (including exports).

(2.5) $TA_{rp} = f(AP^+, AU^+, PMAT^-, TH),$

where AP = automobile park, AU = automobile use (average miles driven a year), $PMAT$ = potential mileage of automobile tires (proxied by the market share of radial tires), and TH = other technical shift factors (such as snow tires).

(2.6) $TCV_{rp} = f(CVP^+, CVU^+, PMCV^-, TH),$

where CVP = commercial vehicle park, CVU = commercial vehicle use (average miles driven a year), $PMCV$ = potential mileage of commercial vehicle tires, and TH = other technical shift factors (such as size composition of CVP).

(2.5.1) $AU = f(Y^+, G_p{}^-, A/N^-, Z),$

---

8. + and − indicate the expected sign of the relation between the dependent and independent variable.

where Y = personal real disposable income, G_p = real price of gasoline, A/N = number of cars per household, and Z = other car maintenance costs (such as insurance and repair costs).

$$(2.6.1) \qquad CVU = f(IIP^+, \frac{AMCCV^-}{AMCOT}, F),$$

where IIP = industrial production, $AMCCV/AMCOT$ = relative average mile cost of commercial vehicle transport, and F = structural factors (such as highway versus rail system development).

NONTIRE SECTOR

$$(3) \qquad CRNT = f(GNP^+),$$

where GNP = real gross national product.

The specification of this demand model involves some important simplifications, and its statistical estimation also runs into difficulties because of the incomplete availability of data. Tire exports are treated exogenously, and so are the most important technical factors: potential mileage of tires, sizes of vehicle parks, and average weights of tires (which depend on the former). The effect of government policies (such as taxation, developments of specific kinds of transport infrastructures) and regulations (such as maximum allowable tire tread wear and other safety measures) are only indirectly taken into account in determining the values of the exogenous variable over the projection periods. Another important simplification is the treatment of nontire demand, which is simply taken as a function of GNP. Data difficulties, however, prevent the same specification from being tested uniformly for all equations in all four consuming areas, and a few adjustments had to be made on that ground.

Finally, important components of this demand model—the estimation of rubber consumption in original equipment tires and the influence of the size of the vehicle park on demand for rubber in replacement tires—depend critically on assumptions about motor vehicle production and use. It was, therefore, necessary to develop a submodel of the motor vehicle industries in the four consuming areas considered in the main model. The demand projections for motor vehicles to 1985 and 1990 were based on a submodel that is summarized below.

A submodel of motor vehicle demand

(4) $$APK = f(GNP^+),$$

where APK = automobile park, and GNP = real gross national product.[9]

(5) $$CVPK = f(GNP^+),$$

where $CVPK$ = commercial vehicle park.

(4.1) $$NDA = \Delta APK,$$

where NDA = new demand for automobiles.

(4.2) $$RDA = z(APK),$$

where RDA = replacement demand for automobiles, and z = automobile scrap rate.

(4.3) $$ATDA = NDA + RDA,$$

where $ATDA$ = apparent total demand for automobiles.

(4.4) $$O_a = ATDA + \overline{AX},$$

where O_a = production of automobiles, and $\overline{AX}$ = exports of automobiles (exogenously determined).

(5.1) $$NDCV = \Delta CVPK,$$

where $NDCV$ = new demand for commercial vehicles.

(5.2) $$RDCV = g(CVPK),$$

9. This equation was actually specified using car per capita as the dependent variable and GNP per capita as the independent variable, taking population projections as exogenous. The results were then checked against those derived from a long term logistic trend of cars per capita.

where $RDCV$ = replacement demand for commercial vehicles, and g = commercial vehicle scrap rate.

(5.3) $ATDCV = NDCV + RDCV,$

where $ATDCV$ = apparent total demand for commercial vehicles.

(5.4) $O_{cv} = ATDCV + \overline{CVX},$

where O_{cv} = production of commercial vehicles, and $\overline{CVX}$ = exports of commercial vehicles (exogenously determined).

It is apparent that this model of motor vehicle demand is quite simplistic. Apart from income and population, several other economic, demographic, and technical factors influence motor vehicle demand. Government policies and changes in consumer preferences are additional important determinants of demand. There is no lack of sophisticated models used to project vehicle demand (particularly automobile demand) that incorporate a large number of economic, demographic, and technical factors. In terms of specifications, most automobile demand models have evolved from the basic Chow and Nerlove stock adjustment models, in which the derived stock of vehicles is made to depend on economic and demographic variables, and the speed at which the actual stock adjusts to the desired stock is a linear function of their difference.[10] Subsequent models, beginning with Suits, have emphasized other factors (such as credit conditions) as determinants of new car demand.[11] More recent models for the United States have tried to capture the influence of cyclical economic variables such as unemployment[12] and "consumer senti-

10. G. Chow, *Demand for Automobiles in the United States: A Study in Consumer Durables* (Amsterdam: North Holland Publishing Co., 1957), and M. Nerlove, "A Note on Long Run Automobile Demand," *Journal of Marketing* (July 1957), pp. 57–64. Using the 1921–53 data, Chow found that the income elasticity of demand for cars in the United States is between 1.14 and 2.03, and the price elasticity is between −0.74 and −1.56. Nerlove's estimates are −1.2 for the long-run price elasticity and 3.8 for the income elasticity. Both estimates have been criticized on various grounds.

11. D. B. Suits, "The Demand for New Automobiles," *Review of Economics and Statistics* (August 1958), pp. 273–80.

12. M. Evans, *Macroeconomic Forecasting* (New York: Harper and Row, 1969).

ment" using the indexes worked out by the University of Michigan Survey Research Center.[13]

Most of these models attempt to forecast automobile demand in the short terms. The poor forecasting track record shown by most of these models reflects the objective difficulty encountered in incorporating consumer expectations in short-term forecasting models. But, if car sales have proved to be elusive to predict in the short term even with the help of sophisticated demand models, the long-term forecasting record of much simpler models has been more satisfactory. Whenever the effect of cyclical variables was disregarded and the trend in sales was the aim of the forecasts, models of car demand have produced acceptable results.

It is precisely because the objective of this submodel is to predict long-term trends in car ownership and production that a simple model based on income and population was chosen. For the same reason replacement demand in this model is derived from scrap rates that aim to approximate the average lives of vehicles. The model, therefore, disregards the short-term effect of changes in the prices of new and secondhand vehicles, changes in fiscal and credit policies, and consumer expectations on replacement demand. It is based on the premise that levels of ownership and physical durability of vehicles determine the long-run demand trend.

Projections based on the disaggregated model

The projections of the vehicle park that are the cornerstone of the vehicle production projections were made on the basis of the relation between per capita car ownership and per capita real GNP. Since in most developed countries car ownership per person has already reached high levels, the projections were made using functions that specifically incorporate the notion that after a period of rapid growth in per capita car ownership induced by income growth, a point is reached after which, despite further income growth, the growth of per capita car ownership decelerates and converges to a saturation level. Inverse and log-inverse functions were, therefore, used. They performed well for Japan, Western Europe, and Australia, but less

13. S. Hymans, "Consumer Durable Spending: Explanation and Prediction," *Brookings Papers on Economic Activity*, vol. 2 (1970) and F. T. Juster and P. Wachtel, "Anticipatory and Objective Models of Durable Goods Demand," *Exploration and Economic Research*, MBER, vol. 1 (1974).

well for the United States and Canada, where the historical relation between per capita car ownership and per capita GNP is clearly linear in terms of logs. Yet inverse functions were used to make the projections even for the United States and Canada (Table E–4) on the notion that the historical relation is bound to stop during the projection periods. To test the long-run projections, logistic trends were estimated for all the four consuming areas and were extended to 1990.

The commercial park projections, on the contrary, were made on the basis of the historical relation between the vehicle park and industrial projection. Double-log and semi-log functions were estimated for all major consuming areas (Table E–5), and the statistical results were satisfactory in most cases. The automobile and commercial-vehicle park projections are summarized in Tables E–6 and E–7. They clearly indicate a notable slowdown in the historical growth of the vehicle park and vehicle production in all areas.

From the projections of vehicle production, demand for original-equipment tires and rubber demand for both automobiles and commercial vehicles were derived using estimates of the number of tires per vehicle and rubber content of tires.[14] Replacement rates were estimated statistically and the projected rates were applied to the vehicle projections to derive tire demand for replacement (Table E–8).[15] Rubber demand was then calculated on the basis of the same estimates of the rubber content of tires used to calculate original-equipment tire demand. Demand for tire exports was projected on the basis of historical trend.

Nontire demand was estimated using the historical relation of nontire rubber consumption and real GDP growth (Table E–9). The aggregate demand projections to 1980, 1985, and 1990 for the three major developed consuming areas (North America, Western Europe, and Japan) plus estimated demand for Australia, New Zealand, and other developed countries are contained in Table E–10.[16]

14. In estimating the future number of tires per vehicle produced, production of "knocked" vehicles for exports (that is: vehicles to be shipped unassembled) and the possible introduction in the 1980s of puncture-resistant tires that would eliminate the need for spare tires were taken into account.

15. The replacement functions for Japan could not be estimated because of lack of data. Rates projected by MITI were used to make these forecasts.

16. Lack of data on replacement tires has so far prevented the estimation of future demand for rubber in Australia and New Zealand on the basis of vehicle production and use.

The detailed projections for North America, Western Europe, and Japan are contained in Tables E–11, E–12, and E–13.

These projections show that total elastomer consumption in developed countries will grow at about 4 percent a year between 1976 and 1990, roughly 1 percent a year below the historical rate. The slowdown in the expansion of elastomer demand is expected to be particularly pronounced in the second half of the 1980s. These projection results parallel those of the motor-vehicle park and production; the expected slowdown of the process of motor vehicle use in developed countries, coupled with the less intensive use of existing vehicles (particularly automobiles) is shown to negatively affect rubber consumption in tires. Japan and Western Europe—the two areas where rubber consumption expanded at the fastest rate in the 1960s—are expected to experience the most marked slowdown in the rate of growth of elastomer demand in the 1980s. The projections also show quite clearly that the overall level of future expansion of rubber demand will be mainly sustained by the growth of nontire uses.

These projections of uses produce overall results that are broadly consistent with those obtained for developed countries using the modified framework for forecasting income elasticity. The results are, therefore, quite encouraging from the forecasting standpoint. Clearly, the methodology needs to be refined and more research must be done on the assumed technical coefficients. Yet, the results of the use projections provide strong support for the notion that rubber demand will continue to grow at a healthy rate even in developed countries where the effect of the energy crisis will be felt more severely than elsewhere and where rubber consumption has already reached high levels.

Table E–4. Relation between per Capita Automobile Ownership and per Capita Real Income (GDP) in the Developed Countries: Time Series Regression Results

Developed country or region	Constant term a_0	Regression coefficients $a_1 = \dfrac{1}{GDP/N}$	$a_1 = \ln \dfrac{1}{GDP/N}$	$a_3 = GDP/N$	Multiple correlation coefficient $\overline{R}^2$	Standard error of estimate	Durbin-Watson statistics	Time period for annual data
United States (1.1)	CAR/N = 0.7575	−603.181 (−5.5)			0.56	0.0034	2.18	1950–76
(1.2)	CAR/N = 1.7312		−9.24918 (−5.4)		0.56	0.0034	2.12	1950–76
Canada (2.1)	ln CAR/N = −1.5253			+0.000129 (6.4)	0.63	0.01312	1.40	1950–76
Western Europe (3.1)	CAR/N = 0.4821	−627.471 (−12.5)			0.89	0.00259	1.44	1954–76
(3.2)	CAR/N = 2.5587		−18.1822 (−15.5)		0.92	0.0054	1.66	1954–76
Japan (4.1)	CAR/N = 1.6637		−11.8310 (−7.2)		0.81	0.0077	1.01	1962–72
Australia (5.1)	CAR/N = 0.6646	−965.968 (−17.9)			0.94	0.0084	1.66	1954–76

Note: The Cochrane-Orcut procedure was used to correct for autocorrelation in all regressions. OLS were used throughout. CAR/N = car per capita, and GDP/N = per capita GDP (at constant U.S. dollars and exchange rates); t values are in parentheses.

Table E–5. *Relation between Commercial Vehicle Park and Industrial Production in the Developed Countries: Time Series Regression Results*

Developed country or region	Constant term a_0	Regression coefficients $a_1 = \ln IIP$	Regression coefficients $a_2 = GDP$	Multiple correlation coefficient $\bar{R}^2$	Standard error of estimate	Durbin-Watson statistics	Time period for annual data
United States							
(1.1)	$\ln CVPARK = 5.3578$	+0.98032 (15.7)		0.91	0.0819	0.41	1958–75
(1.2)	$CVPARK = -56715.6$	+16617.1 (9.3)		0.84	1920.6	0.30	1858–75
Canada							
(2.1)	$\ln CVPARK = 5.7339$	+0.30320 (10.8)		0.90	0.0113	2.27	1958–75
(2.2)	$CVPARK = -329.07$	+345.14 (5.6)		0.67	25.34	2.23	1958–75
Western Europe							
(3.1)	$\ln CVPARK = 5.4163$	+0.80601 (23.8)		0.98	0.0213	1.47	1958–75
(3.2)	$CVPARK = -19579.1$	+6249.7 (31.8)		0.99	149.1	1.50	1958–75
Japan							
(4.1)	$\ln CVPARK = 7.9267$	+0.29375 (5.0)		0.69	0.0171	1.05	1962–75
(4.2)	$CVPARK = -23266.9$	+6960.9 (43.4)		0.99	290.5	1.52	1962–75
Australia							
(5.1)	$\ln CVPARK = 6.3119$		0.01687 (7.8)	0.81	0.0213	1.50	1958–75

Note: The Cochrane-Orcut procedure was used to correct for autocorrelation in all regressions except for (1.1) and (1.2). OLS were used throughout. CVPARK = commercial vehicle park (total registration), IPP = index of industrial production, and GDP = gross domestic product (at constant U.S. dollars and exchange rates); *t* values are in parentheses.

Table E.-6. *Motor Vehicle Park in the Developed Countries, Actual Averages, Projected, and Growth Rates, 1958 to 1990, Selected Years*

Item	Actual averages (million units)				Projected (million units)		Growth rates (annual percentage)			
	1958–60	1964–66	1971–73	1974–76	1985	1990	1958–60 to 1964–66	1964–66 to 1971–73	1974–76 to 1985	1985 to 1990
Automobiles										
North America	63.24	80.40	104.68	107.01	141.7	154.9	4.1	3.8	2.8	1.8
Western Europe	20.25	43.03	74.56	87.14	118.0	132.5	13.4	8.6	3.1	2.4
Japan	0.35	2.22	12.52	17.19	29.4	35.5	36.0	30.0	5.5	3.9
Oceania	2.40	3.64	5.24	6.20	8.8	10.3	7.2	5.3	3.6	3.2
Total	86.24	129.29	197.00	217.54	297.9	333.2	7.0	6.2	3.2	2.3
Commercial vehicles										
North America	12.90	16.32	23.58	28.48	43.7	52.5	4.0	5.4	4.4	3.7
Western Europe	5.50	7.54	9.56	10.35	13.9	15.3	5.4	3.5	3.0	2.1
Japan[a]	0.72	4.18	9.90	11.12	15.6	18.2	28.0	13.1	3.4	3.1
Oceania	0.94	1.12	1.31	1.48	1.8	2.0	3.0	2.3	2.0	2.2
Total	20.06	29.16	44.35	51.43	75.0	88.0	5.5	6.2	3.8	3.3

a. Including light trucks.
Source: Actual data, U.S. Motor Vehicle Manufacturers Association, *World Motor Vehicle Data* (1977).

Table E-7. Motor Vehicle Production in the Developed Countries, Actual Averages, Projected, and Growth Rates, 1958 to 1990, Selected Years

Item	Actual averages (million units)				Projected (million units)		Growth rates (annual percentage)			
	1958–60	1964–66	1971–73	1974–76	1985	1990	1958–60 to 1964–66	1964–66 to 1971–73	1974–76 to 1985	1985 to 1990
Automobiles										
North America	6.02	9.21	10.17	8.64	12.00	13.80	7.3	1.4	3.3	2.8
Western Europe	4.55	7.85	11.52	10.59	14.10	15.85	9.5	5.6	2.9	2.4
Japan	0.10	0.72	4.07	4.51	6.75	7.90	39.0	28.0	4.1	3.2
Oceania	0.13	0.28	0.37	0.38	0.60	0.70	13.6	4.1	4.7	3.1
Total	10.80	18.06	26.13	24.12	33.45	37.65	9.0	5.4	3.3	2.4
Commercial vehicles										
North America	1.13	1.87	2.84	3.09	4.30	5.10	8.8	6.1	3.4	3.5
Western Europe	0.84	1.08	1.38	1.43	2.00	2.40	4.3	3.6	3.4	3.8
Japan[a]	0.21	1.24	2.32	2.60	3.70	4.45	35.0	9.4	3.6	3.8
Oceania	0.04	0.05	0.08	0.09	0.14	0.17	3.8	6.9	4.5	4.0
Total	2.22	4.24	6.62	7.21	10.14	12.20	11.3	6.6	3.5	3.7

a. Including light trucks.
Source: Actual data, U.S. Motor Vehicle Manufacturers Association, World Motor Vehicle Data (1977).

Table E–8. Replacement Rates for Passenger Car and Commercial Vehicle Tires in Western Europe and in the United States

Kind of motor vehicle	Constant term a_0	Regression coefficients					Number of observations	Multiple correlation coefficient $\bar{R}^2$	Standard error of estimate	Durbin-Watson statistics
		a_1 = MVY	a_2 = RAD	a_3 = SCP	a_4 = RH	Form				
Passenger cars										
PCRR$_{WE}$ = −0.3342		+0.1191 (6.4)	−0.0020 (−1.6)	+0.0085 (3.0)		Linear	15	0.92	0.1056	1.80
PCRR$_{NA}$ = −0.4691		+0.0002 (3.1)	−0.0117 (−8.7)	+0.0171 (10.3)		Linear	20	0.92	0.0486	1.37
Commercial vehicles										
CVRR$_{WE}$ = 2.7690			−0.0970 (−2.7)		+0.0850 (4.6)	Linear	28	0.57	0.5773	1.19
CVRR$_{NA}$ = 0.5313			−0.0048 (−4.9)		+0.00094 (7.1)	Linear	20	0.75	0.0369	1.68

Note: PCRR$_{WE}$ = annual replacement rate for passenger cars in Western Europe (percent), PCRR$_{NA}$ = annual replacement rate for passenger cars in North America (percent), CVRR$_{WE}$ = annual replacement rate for commercial vehicles in Western Europe (percent), CVRR$_{NA}$ = annual replacement rate for commercial vehicles in North America (percent), MVY = mileage driven per vehicle per year (actual mileage), RAD = degree of radialization in total market (DE + REP, in percent), SCP = size composition of car park, and RH = Eurofinance road haulage index for Western Europe (tons/kilometer/per vehicle) and intercity motor truck freight index for the United States (tons/mile/per vehicle); t values are in parentheses.

164

Table E-9. *Relation between Total Elastomer Consumption in Nontire Uses and Real Income (GDP) in Major Developed Consuming Areas: Time Series Regression Results*

Developed country or region	Constant term a_1	Regression coefficient $a_2 = \ln GDP$	Multiple correlation coefficient $\bar{R}^2$	Standard error of estimate	Durbin-Watson statistics	Time period for annual data
North America						
(1.1)	$\ln CENT = 1.4161$	$+1.00910$ (24.3)	0.97	0.0495	1.89	1955–76
(1.2)	$CENT = -3539.9$	$+904.49$ (17.2)	0.94	57.8	1.42	1955–76
Western Europe						
(2.1)	$\ln CENT = -0.7768$	$+1.4664$ (37.4)	0.99	0.0393	1.64	1958–76
(2.2)	$CENT = -4122.9$	$+971.06$ (14.5)	0.93	36.7	1.99	1958–76
Japan						
(3.1)	$\ln CENT = 0.5115$	$+0.9376$ (4.9)	0.62	0.0832	1.65	1959–76
(3.2)	$CENT = -1019.0$	$+243.91$ (11.1)	0.90	28.5	1.95	1959–76

Note: The Cochrane-Orcut procedure was used to correct for autocorrelation in all regressions except for (1.1). CENT = total elastomer consumption in nontire uses, and GDP = gross domestic product (at constant U.S. dollars and exchange rates); *t* values are in parentheses.

Table E-10. Elastomer Demand in the Developed Countries, by Major Uses, Estimated, Projected, and Growth Rates, 1965 to 1990, Selected Years

Item	Estimated (thousands of metric tons)			Projected (thousands of metric tons)		Growth rates (annual percentage)			
	1965	1970	1976	1985	1990	1965–76	1976–85	1985–90	1976–90
North America									
Tire uses	1,427.0	1,747.5	1,921.0	2,526.0	2,770.0	2.7	3.1	1.9	2.6
Nontire uses	801.0	955.0	1,285.0	2,000.0	2,500.0	4.4	5.0	4.6	4.9
Total	2,228.0	2,702.5	3,206.0	4,526.0	5,270.0	3.4	3.9	3.1	3.6
Western Europe									
Tire uses	815.5	1,159.0	1,320.0	1,883.0	2,215.0	4.5	4.0	3.3	3.8
Nontire uses	767.0	1,198.0	1,425.0	2,110.0	2,600.0	5.8	4.5	4.3	4.4
Total	1,582.5	2,357.0	2,745.0	3,993.0	4,815.0	5.1	4.3	3.8	4.1
Japan									
Tire uses	182.7	399.0	574.5	856.0	989.0	11.0	4.5	2.9	4.0
Nontire uses	194.3	380.0	385.0	705.0	910.0	6.4	7.0	5.3	6.3
Total	377.0	779.0	959.5	1,561.0	1,899.0	8.9	5.6	4.0	5.0
Other developed									
Total	157.5	189.0	265.0	390.0	485.0	4.8	4.4	4.5	4.4
Total rubber demand	4,345.0	6,027.5	7,175.0	10,470.0	12,469.0	4.7	4.3	3.6	4.0

Table E–11. Elastomer Demand in North America, by Major Uses, Estimated, Projected, and Growth Rates, 1965 to 1990, Selected Years

Developed country or region	Estimated (thousands of metric tons)			Projected (thousands of metric tons)		Growth rates (annual percentage)			
	1965	1970	1974–76	1985	1990	1965–70	1970–75a	1975a–85	1985–90
Tire uses									
Original equipment tires	393.0	380.0	482.0	640.0	720.0	−0.7	4.9	2.9	2.4
Automobiles[b]	243.0	198.0	251.0	310.0	340.0	−4.0	4.9	2.1	1.9
Commercial vehicles[c]	150.0	192.0	231.0	330.0	380.0	5.1	3.8	3.6	2.9
Replacement tires	734.0	1,092.0	1,166.5	1,550.0	1,670.0	8.3	1.3	2.9	1.5
Automobiles[b]	452.0	704.0	708.5	820.0	850.0	9.2	0.2	1.5	0.7
Commercial vehicles[c]	282.0	391.0	458.0	730.0	820.0	6.8	3.2	4.8	2.4
Other tires[d]	90.5	119.0	136.0	200.0	240.0	5.6	2.7	3.9	3.7
Exports of loose tires	26.5	20.5	53.0	51.0	60.0	−5.0	21.0	−0.3	3.3
Automobiles	10.3	8.3	32.0	18.0	20.0	−4.2	31.0	−5.2	3.2
Commercial vehicles	12.0	7.0	15.0	25.0	30.0	−10.2	16.5	5.3	3.7
All others	4.2	5.2	6.0	8.0	10.0	4.4	2.9	2.9	4.6
Other tire uses	183.0	136.0	114.0	85.0	80.0	−5.7	−3.5	−2.9	−1.2
Total	1,427.0	1,747.5	1,951.0	2,526.0	2,770.0	4.1	2.2	2.6	1.9
Nontire uses									
Total	801.0	955.0	1,229.5	2,000.0	2,500.0	3.6	5.2	5.0	4.6
Total rubber demand	2,228.0	2,702.5	3,180.5	4,526.0	5,270.0	3.9	3.3	3.6	3.1

a. 1974–76 average.
b. Including snow tires.
c. Including light trucks.
d. Farm, aircraft, and industrial tires.

Table E–12. *Elastomer Demand in Western Europe, by Major Uses, Estimated, Projected, and Growth Rates, 1965 to 1990, Selected Years*

	Estimated (thousands of metric tons)			Projected (thousands of metric tons)		Growth rates (annual percentage)			
	1965	1970	1975	1985	1990	1965–70	1970–75	1975–85	1985–90
Tire uses[a]									
Original equipment tires	208.2	294.4	273.6	481.0	574.0	7.2	–1.5	5.8	3.6
Automobiles	105.8	149.0	136.9	200.0	219.0	7.1	–1.7	3.9	1.8
Commercial vehicles	103.4	145.4	139.4	281.0	355.0	7.1	–0.8	7.2	4.8
Replacement tires	573.0	801.5	899.0	1,203.0	1,333.0	6.9	2.3	3.0	2.1
Automobiles	178.9	289.4	345.3	498.0	539.0	10.1	3.6	3.7	1.6
Commercial vehicles	394.1	512.1	553.7	705.0	794.0	5.4	1.6	2.4	2.4
Export of loose tires	34.3	63.1	82.4	199.0	308.5	13.0	5.5	9.2	9.2
Automobiles	12.2	27.2	35.3	100.0	168.5	17.4	5.4	11.0	11.0
Commercial vehicles	22.1	35.9	47.1	99.0	140.0	10.2	5.6	7.7	7.2
Total	815.5	1,159.0	1,255.0	1,883.0	2,215.0	7.3	1.6	4.2	3.3
Nontire uses									
Total	767.0	1,198.0	1,247.0	2,110.0	2,600.0	9.3	0.8	5.4	4.3
Total rubber demand	1,582.5	2,357.0	2,502.0	3,993.0	4,815.0	8.3	1.2	4.8	3.8

a. Excluding inner tubes and tires for bicycles, motorcycles, farm equipment, and off-the-road vehicles.

Table E–13. Elastomer Demand in Japan, by Major Uses, Estimated, Projected, and Growth Rates, 1965 to 1990, Selected Years

	Estimated (thousands of metric tons)			Projected (thousands of metric tons)		Growth rates (annual percentage)			
	1965	1970	1975	1985	1990	1965–70	1970–75	1975–85	1985–90
Tire uses									
Original equipment	60.5	146.8	181.7	281.0	330.0	19.4	4.4	4.5	3.3
Automobiles	13.8	53.7	78.7	107.0	120.0	31.3	7.9	3.1	2.3
Commercial vehicles	46.7	93.1	103.0	174.0	210.0	14.8	2.0	5.4	3.8
Replacement tires	47.9	110.6	140.7	263.0	297.0	18.2	4.9	6.5	2.5
Automobiles	11.9	43.1	76.7	105.0	115.0	29.5	12.2	3.2	1.8
Commercial vehicles	36.0	67.5	64.0	158.0	182.0	13.4	–1.1	9.5	2.9
Other tires	11.6	27.2	31.0	45.0	53.0	18.6	2.7	3.8	3.3
Exports of loose tires	36.2	77.7	144.2	212.5	248.0	16.5	13.2	4.0	3.1
Automobiles	7.9	18.6	19.2	37.5	49.0	18.7	0.6	6.9	5.5
Commercial vehicles	23.7	44.3	92.5	125.0	140.0	13.3	15.9	4.2	2.3
All others	4.6	14.8	32.5	50.0	59.0	26.4	17.0	4.4	3.4
Other tire uses	26.5	36.7	42.4	55.0	61.0	6.7	2.9	2.5	2.1
Total	182.7	399.0	540.0	856.5	989.0	16.9	6.2	4.7	2.9
Nontire uses									
Total	194.3	380.0	330.0	705.0	910.0	14.4	–2.8	7.9	5.2
Total rubber demand	377.0	779.0	870.0	1,561.0	1,899.0	15.6	2.2	6.0	4.0

169

Appendix F

•-•--•

Projections Framework and Production Estimates for Natural Rubber to 1985 and 1990

Natural rubber is a perennial crop. The lag between planting and first harvesting is about six years, and the economic life of the tree lasts for twenty-five to thirty years. The yield, moreover, follows a fairly uniform pattern, increasing rapidly for about ten years after maturity (roughly sixteen years after planting) and then beginning to decline.[1] Rubber planting is based on economic considerations (expected relative profitability of rubber), but in several countries government policies play a key role. Government investments in infrastructure, subsidization of basic inputs, credit, and tax incentives are important determinants of the investment decision. Once the area under rubber is determined, however, rubber production depends basically on agronomic factors.[2]

Projections Framework and Aggregate Results

During most of the projection period—1976 to 1990—the world rubber supply is to a large extent predetermined. It depends on the acreage and yield profiles of the trees that have already been planted.

1. Rubber yields, after peaking at fifteen to sixteen years after planting, exhibit another temporary peak around the twenty-first year. The decline in yields after the fifteenth or sixteenth year can now be stemmed by using chemical stimulants.
2. In the very short term the decision to tap is clearly influenced by the prevailing market prices.

Trees planted during the first half of the 1970s started to bear toward the end of the 1970s and will reach a maximum yield toward the end of the 1980s. Any planting and replanting done during the last part of the 1970s will have only a limited effect on production during the second half of the 1980s. Its full effect will be felt in the 1990s.[3]

Because price changes still have only a limited effect on output in the short term, production trends have not been projected on the basis of specific price assumptions; they simply assume that natural rubber prices will remain high enough to insure continuous tapping and a moderate use of Ethrel-type stimulation during the last years of the economic life of the tree.[4] Depending on the price trend, both the intensity of tapping and the use of chemical stimulants can be changed and the output trend can correspondingly deviate from the projected norm, but the deviation would not be very great.

The production norm was derived for all the major producing countries (except for Indonesia) using the best information available on areas under rubber, age distribution of trees, and yield profiles. Assumptions were made about rates of new planting and replanting and about the use of chemical stimulants. The assumptions used and the actual methodologies adopted—which vary slightly from country to country depending on the data available—are described below. In Indonesia and in eight smaller producing countries, the production was projected on the basis of expert judgement, considering past trends, national plans (whenever available), and country-specific information available to FAO and the World Bank.

The projections of production summarized in Table F–1 show that world rubber output is likely to increase relatively quickly until the mid-1980s (4.8 percent a year during 1977–85), but that growth will decelerate during the second half of the 1980s to about 3.2 percent a year, reflecting the decline in the rate of new planting and replanting in most major countries during the 1970s. Between 1977 and 1990 rubber production is projected to grow at above historical rates in

3. Although the immaturity period of the rubber tree has been reduced to three-and-a-half years after planting, it is assumed that the inevitable lags in spreading this new technique will prevent it from having a significant effect on production until 1990.

4. At a price for RSS1, c.i.f. New York, of about 40¢ per pound (1977 dollars), these assumptions can probably be fulfilled.

Table F-1. World Natural Rubber Production, Actual, Projected, and Growth Rates, 1955 to 1990, Selected Years

Economic region and country	Actual (thousands of metric tons)					Projected (thousands of metric tons)		Growth rates (annual percentage)			
	1955	1960	1970	1976	1977	1985	1990	1955–77	1977–85	1985–90	1977–90
Developing countries	1,857	1,883	2,902	3,492	3,511	5,035	5,875	2.9	4.6	3.1	4.0
Malaysia	708	765	1,269	1,640	1,613	2,400	2,700	3.8	5.1	2.4	4.0
Indonesia	750	620	815	847	835	1,010	1,100	0.5	2.4	1.7	2.1
Thailand	133	171	287	392	425	785	1,140	5.4	8.0	7.7	7.9
Sri Lanka	95	99	159	152	146	185	195	2.0	3.0	1.1	2.3
India	23	25	90	148	152	200	220	9.0	3.5	1.9	2.9
Others	148	203	282	313	340	455	520	3.8	3.7	2.7	3.3
Centrally planned economies	93	114	42	78	80	210	260	−0.7	12.8	4.4	9.5
Vietnam	66	77	29	33	35	100	120	−2.8	14.0	3.7	9.9
Cambodia	27	37	13	20	15	35	40	−2.7	11.2	2.7	7.8
China	—	—	—	25	30	75	100	—	12.2	5.9	9.7
World total[a]	1,950	2,035	3,102	3,565	3,600	5,245	6,135	2.8	4.8	3.2	4.2

a. For 1955, 1960, 1970, 1976, and 1977 the world total is not the sum of the totals. The differences are the statistical discrepancies shown in IRSG data.
Source: Actual data, International Rubber Study Group.

Thailand, the smaller producing countries, and possibly Indonesia. On the whole the trend for growth of world production is expected to be higher than that between 1955 and 1977: 4.2 percent a year in 1977–90, compared with 2.9 percent a year in 1955–77.

Production Estimates, by Country

Future natural rubber production has been estimated for the five major producing countries and eight minor producing countries.

Malaysia

Malaysia is the largest producer of natural rubber (NR), accounting in 1977 for 45 percent of the total world output and 50 percent of total world exports. Over 50 percent of the country's production originates in the smallholding sector, which comprises all holdings of 40 hectares and less, averaging about 2.6 hectares. Within the estate sector, over half of the acreage is owned by transnational companies which have larger, more modern holdings than the locally owned small estates. Between 1970 and 1975 total output expanded 4.0 percent a year. Growth is expected to continue until 1985 at a comparable rate, but it is projected to decline sharply during the second half of the 1980s as a result of the decline in the expansion of acreage and in the rate of replanting during 1965–75, compared with the second half of 1955–65 (see Table F–1).

The production of the estate and smallholding sectors has been projected separately, although rough estimates have had to be made for much of the basic data relating to the smallholdings. The basic parameters and assumptions used in the projections are given below.

The average annual rate of replanting on estates has fallen over the past two decades as shown below:[5]

Year	Hectares planted per year
1955–59	27,900
1960–64	26,300
1965–69	11,300
1970–74	11,300

5. All area figures were converted from acres to hectares (1 hectare = 2.47 acres) and rounded off.

This decline—a reduction in the rate from the maximum of 5 percent of the mature area in the early 1960s to less than 2 percent in 1972–73, has been due primarily to the decreasing proportion of old rubber on estates as a result of earlier replanting and to the widely followed policy of diversifying estate holdings to 50 percent oil palm and 50 percent rubber. For the future, a replanting rate of 16,200 hectares, or 3 percent a year, has been assumed. This implies that about 80 percent of all trees thirty years old will be replanted every year.

Replanting began in the smallholder sector on a large scale in 1953, when the first of what proved to be five replanting schemes was begun. The rate of replanting reached its peak in the early 1960s as follows:

Year	Hectares replanted per year
1953–59	17,800
1960–64	32,800
1965–69	25,100
1970–74	24,300

It was assumed that replanting would accelerate to an average 28,000 hectares a year during 1975–80, 32,400 hectares a year during 1980–85, and 40,500 hectares a year during 1985–90.

During the past two decades new planting (as opposed to re-planting) on estates also has fallen off sharply (from 5,300 hectares a year in 1960–64 to 2,000 a year in 1970–74), and together with the conversion of land to other crops, has resulted in a decrease in the total estate area under rubber from 0.77 million hectares in 1960 to 0.61 million hectares in 1974. For the future, new planting is assumed to continue at the low rate of 2,000 hectares a year under the constraints of the investment policies of the plantation companies, the inadequate rate of return on investment in rubber relative to other faster-yielding crops, and a shortage of available land.

Information on new smallholder plantings is incomplete. It is estimated that new plantings in this sector averaged 14,500 hectares a year during 1950–74 under the schemes run by FELDA, RISDA, FELCRA, and the various state development agencies. It is assumed that new planting during 1977–90 will average 20,200 hectares a year.

Between 1960 and 1970 average yields are estimated to have increased at the rapid rate of 4.6 percent a year on estates and 5.6 percent a year on smallholdings, reflecting the increase in the area under high-yielding material at the expense of unselected seedlings and mixed materials.[6] During 1977–90 better management practices and the use of progressively higher-yielding clones are expected to increase yields further, although the rate of expansion is unlikely to be as rapid as that during 1960–70. During 1985–90 the average yield on smallholdings may actually be somewhat lower than in the immediately preceding years, because of the relatively large proportion of newly tapped area in the total, which will follow from the acceleration of replanting that is planned for the second half of the 1970s. The development of yields during 1960–70 and the assumed levels for the future are indicated to be:

Year	Estates (kilograms per hectare)	Smallholdings (kilograms per hectare)
1960	758	436
1970	1,189	751
1985	1,588	1,116
1990	1,597	1,108

No accurate data are available on the acreage under Ethrel stimulation in Malaysia. In the smallholding sector stimulation is not widely practiced, and in the estate sector 170,000 hectares were estimated to be under Ethrel stimulation in 1973 before the government ban on its use.[7]

In estimating the production increase which is likely to result from the wider use of chemical stimulation during 1980–90, two assumptions must be made. The first relates to the area which will come under stimulation and the second to the average yield response. For the purpose of this projection, it is assumed that:

(a) Chemical stimulants will be applied on trees more than fifteen years old (according to the RRIM recommendation);

(b) On smallholdings, 25 percent of the area more than fifteen

---

6. Unselected seedlings and mixed material are estimated to yield half that of high-yielding material in 1970.

7. This ban, which was imposed in late 1974, was lifted toward the end of 1975 when natural rubber prices recovered from the low level of the previous two years.

years old will be stimulated in 1980, and 65 percent in both 1985 and 1990;

(c) On estates, 50 percent of the area more than fifteen years old will be stimulated in 1980 and 1985, and 100 percent in 1990; and

(d) Yields from trees under stimulation will increase 50 percent on smallholdings and 60 percent on estates.

The effect of the foregoing assumptions on average annual increases in yields and on total production will depend to a large extent on the practice followed in regard to tapping patterns. Many estates now use chemical stimulants to reduce tapping intensity and hence production costs, rather than to obtain an increase in yields. To the extent that this policy is followed, the average increases in yields will tend to be below the potential indicated above.

Indonesia

Indonesia is the second largest rubber-producing country, accounting in 1977 for 23 percent of total world output and 25 percent of total world exports. Over two-thirds of the total production is estimated to come from smallholdings, most of which are less than 3 hectares in size.

The lack of comprehensive data on replanting rate, age distribution of acreage, average yields, and so forth, makes it impossible to make a detailed projection of rubber production. A general assessment indicates, however, that despite the efforts made within the framework of the First and Second Indonesian Development Plans, which have included numerous projects for new planting and replanting, progress so far has been extremely limited. It would thus appear unlikely that production will expand faster than the trend of 1.8 percent a year of 1960–62 to 1974–76. It is expected, however, that there will be some acceleration over the extremely low rate (0.7 percent a year) of the first part of the 1970s (see Table F–1).

Thailand

Thailand accounts for 12 percent of world production and 13 percent of world exports of NR in 1977. The bulk of the output comes from smallholdings, which account for almost 90 percent of the area under rubber. Output expanded extremely rapidly during 1960–70, largely as a result of the expansion in the area under rubber, and is expected to increase even faster in the future under the effect of the acceleration in replantings during the 1960s and early 1970s (see Table F–1).

The rate of replanting in Thailand has accelerated steadily since the early 1960s, rising from 3,900 hectares in 1961 to more than 20,000 hectares a year in the early 1970s. In 1972, 347,000 out of the 1.4 million hectares under rubber were estimated to require replanting.

For the future it is assumed that the replanting rate of 3 percent a year planned under the Accelerated Rubber Replanting Project of the Rubber Replanting Aid Fund will be achieved and that replanting should reach 50,000 hectares a year by 1980 and should continue at that rate. A considerable amount of unrecorded new planting is taking place, particularly in Southeast Thailand, but no estimate is available of the area involved. Official settlement schemes project 40,000 hectares of new rubber by 1980, and, although this target may prove overambitious, the area under rubber should nevertheless continue to increase above its present level of about 1.6 million hectares, given the large amount of smallholder replanting.

At present 347,000 hectares are estimated to be under unselected seedlings, which give peak yields of only 400 kilograms per hectare compared with 2,000 kilograms per hectare on replanted areas. This large expanse of low-yielding area is responsible for a national average yield of about 300 kilograms per hectare, about one-sixth of the yield that can be expected under modern methods of cultivation.

The Accelerated Rubber Replanting Project assumes that the replanting would be carried out with material which would give the following yields:

Year	Kilograms per hectare	Year	Kilograms per hectare
7	500	14	1,800
8	800	15–26	1,800
9	1,050	27	2,250
10	1,300	28	2,250
11	1,500	29	2,250
12	1,600	30	2,050
13	1,700	31	2,050

This assumes that fertilizer will be applied during maturity and that chemical stimulation will be used on 60 percent of all trees more than twenty-six years old.

Sri Lanka

Sri Lanka accounted for some 4 percent of world rubber output and exports in 1977. Of the total 217,700 hectares under rubber in 1973, only 202,000 were considered to be suitable for rubber. The remainder is land with poor soil conditions, high elevation, steep gradient, low rainfall, or water-logging.

Rubber production expanded rapidly in Sri Lanka during 1960–70, but has since been consistently below the 1970 level. This decline was caused by the inadequate rate of replanting from 1963 onward, and by a deterioration in management due to the change in political conditions in recent years. Although rubber production should resume an upward trend in future years, programs to revitalize the rubber sector will not have a substantial effect until after 1990 (see Table F–1).

Total area under rubber is expected to be maintained at 202,000 hectares, which is the area that is presently under good rubber. A replanting rate of 6,000 hectares a year will be necessary to maintain this area, but given the low achievement of recent years (see below), it is unlikely that this target can be reached before 1986.

Year	Hectares replanted per year	Year	Hectares replanted per year
1953–58	7,690	1971	3,430
1959–63	6,880	1972	3,540
1964–68	4,860	1973	2,945
1969	4,890	1975	3,230
1970	4,145	1986 onward	6,000

Current yields are estimated at 392 kilograms per hectare from areas planted before 1953, and 1,166 kilograms per hectare from areas planted in the years following. For the future, it is assumed that yields from newly planted areas can be raised to a peak of 1,400 kilograms per hectare on holdings of over 40 hectares and to 1,230 kilograms per hectare on holdings of less than 40 hectares. It is expected that Ethrel may increase total output by about 10 percent in 1985 and 1990.

India

In India, the rate of growth of production has been extremely rapid over the past two decades, changing the country from a significant importer to self-sufficiency. Having ceased to be a net importer in 1974, India has since exported small quantities of rubber, primarily when domestic demand has been weak and stocks have accumulated. For the future, the rate of expansion is likely to slow down because of the growing scarcity of suitable land for expansion (see Table F-1).

The rate of replanting has declined from 3,500 hectares in 1965 to 1,800 hectares in 1974, and was 2,000 hectares in 1975. The target for the Fifth Plan Period is 25,000 hectares at the rate of 5,000 hectares a year, which would appear to be slow given the total 1976 acreage of approximately 227,000 hectares.

Beginning in 1975 the rate of subsidy for replanting was increased substantially in order to increase the rate to the target level 5,000 hectares per year in 1978, and above that in the years following. The projections made here assume that this scheme will be successful and that the rate of replantings will accelerate as follows:

Year	Hectares replanted per year
1976	3,000
1977	5,000
1978	5,000
1979	6,000
1980	6,000
1981	7,000
1982	7,000
1983	7,000

The target for the expansion of the area under rubber during the Fifth Plan Period (1974–75 to 1978–79) is 25,000 hectares, at the rate of 5,000 hectares a year. Against this, the area planted during 1974 and 1975 would be about 2,000 hectares a year. A realistic estimate from 1976 would be about 2,000 hectares a year, although this may prove to be conservative over the longer run if the experimental plantings in Tripura, Assam, and other states in the northeast region prove successful on a larger scale.

It is assumed that yields in the new areas (and in the old areas planted with budded and clonal varieties) will reach a peak of 1,250 kilograms per hectare and that yields of unselected seedlings will average 400 kilograms per hectare. Some 7,500 hectares were estimated to have been under Ethrel stimulation in 1974. For the future, it is assumed that the coverage could be expanded giving an addition to total production of roughly 10 percent.

Minor producing countries

Over 88 percent of the world output comes from the five major producing countries discussed above, and an additional 8 percent comes from the countries shown in Table F–2. The total production increased by only 10 percent (that is, at 0.7 percent a year) between 1960 and 1976, largely because of the sharp declines in output in Cambodia and Vietnam, but also because of stagnation in other countries. For the future, it would appear that production could rise rapidly from its current growth rate of about 5 percent. This could be achieved easily, considering the currently low base of many of the countries and the good start that Vietnam has made on its reconstruction program.

The information on which the projections for these countries has been made is uneven. For some such as Liberia, where 75 percent of rubber is produced on foreign-owned concessions, the data base is relatively good. More than 50 percent of the total output in this country comes from the Firestone plantations, 25 percent from the other concessions, and 25 percent from farms owned by Liberians.

Table F–2. *Natural Rubber Projections in Minor Producing Countries, Actual and Projected, 1960 to 1990, Selected Years*
(thousands of metric tons)

Country	Actual				Projected	
	1960	1970	1976	1977	1985	1990
Liberia	48.4	83.4	82.4	80.0	135.5	154.5
Nigeria	59.5	65.3	52.5	59.3	80.0	105.0
Zaïre	35.6	40.0	29.3	30.0	40.0	40.0
Brazil	23.5	25.0	20.3	22.6	35.0	40.0
Vietnam	76.6	28.5	32.5	35.0	100.0	120.0
Cambodia	37.1	12.8	20.0	15.0	35.0	40.0
Philippines	—	20.1	60.0	65.0	80.0	85.0
Ivory Coast	—	10.9	17.5	17.3	25.0	40.0
Total	280.7	286.0	314.5	324.2	530.5	624.5

Source: Actual data, International Rubber Study Group.

The average yield on the concession estates is about 1,200 kilograms per hectare compared with 400 to 600 kilograms per hectare on Liberian-owned farms. Most of the areas replanted by the concessions with high-yielding clones reached maturity by the middle of the 1970s, except for Firestone's. As a consequence, the number of trees tapped by the former group will not rise substantially in the future, and output will increase only as yields rise to maximum levels in the early 1980s. The output of Firestone is expected to fall until the replantings made during the early 1970s begin to bear toward the end of the decade. The output of Liberian farm rubber is likely to rise steadily until 1980, and the increase is expected to accelerate thereafter as acreage planted in the late 1970s with higher-yielding materials comes into production. The projections assume that no major programs of new planting will be implemented before 1985.

In Nigeria there has been little replanting in the smallholder sector, which is estimated to have provided more than 60 percent of total output in 1963. By contrast, the government and private estates have stepped up replantings in recent years. Total output is expected to increase only slowly during the next decade, mainly as a result of the absence of a vigorous smallholder sector. Some 80,000 to 120,000 hectares out of the total 185,000 hectares under rubber require replanting. A feasible program might be to replant 8,000 to 12,000 hectares a year over ten to twelve years. Assuming that such a program is gradually implemented, a substantive increase in output could be expected only after 1985.

In Vietnam, the post-war reconstruction appears to be proceeding rapidly. The current five year plan calls for rehabilitating and replanting the existing 100,000 hectares (40 percent of which is estimated to be over 40 years old) and for raising the total area to 400,000 hectares by 1980. Under the component one-year programs, priority in 1976 was given to clearing the undergrowth in the ten-to-twenty-five year blocks with the ambitious goal of raising yields from 800–900 kilograms per hectare to 1,500–2,000 kilograms per hectare by applying fertilizers and stimulants. The 1977 program envisaged the rehabilitation of the 25-to-40 year blocks on which yields were to be increased from 600 kilograms per hectare to 1,000–2,000 kilograms per hectare. In 1978 slaughter tapping of the older trees was to have begun in preparation for subsequent felling and replanting. For this projection, it has been assumed that the target of rehabilitation and replanting 100,000 hectares could be attained, but that the maximum yields would be no higher than 1,000 kilograms per hectare.

In Zaïre, output of rubber from old trees constitutes the bulk of the planted material, and yields appear to have passed peak levels. At the same time, the higher yields on the small replanted areas will not appear until 1980–85. Unless there has been considerable replanting—which seems unlikely—the new supply may merely replace the declining output of ageing trees.

Statistical Appendix

Table SA–1. *World Natural Rubber Production,*
by Main Producing Country and Producing Sector, 1950 to 1977
(thousands of metric tons)

	Malaysia				
Year	Estates	Small-holders	Total, west	Total, east	Total
1950	382	326	708	77	785
1951	333	284	617	62	679
1952	346	247	593	50	643
1953	346	233	579	44	623
1954	350	242	592	43	635
1955	358	290	648	60	708
1956	357	259	616	62	678
1957	373	254	627	62	689
1958	395	252	647	60	707
1959	413	266	679	67	746
1960	420	276	696	74	770
1961	435	283	718	72	790
1962	445	281	726	67	793
1963	466	299	765	67	832
1964	484	319	803	68	871
1965	499	353	852	65	917
1966	522	393	915	57	972
1967	534	404	938	53	991
1968	572	479	1,051	49	1,100
1969	603	596	1,199	69	1,268
1970	621	595	1,216	53	1,269
1971	661	609	1,270	48	1,318
1972	659	599	1,258	46	1,304
1973	673	792	1,465	77	1,542
1974	660	801	1,460	64	1,525
1975	599	818	1,417	61	1,478
1976	679	885	1,564	76	1,640
1977	653	884	1,537	76	1,613

n.a. Not available.
a. Including statistical discrepancies.
Source: International Rubber Study Group, *Rubber Statistical Bulletin* (monthly), various issues.

	Indonesia					
Estates	Small-holders	Total	Thailand	Sri Lanka	Others[a]	Total
n.a.	n.a.	708	115	115	165	1,888
n.a.	n.a.	827	111	107	191	1,915
n.a.	n.a.	763	100	98	214	1,818
309	397	706	98	100	231	1,758
288	468	756	112	95	235	1,833
266	483	749	133	95	265	1,950
257	441	698	136	97	313	1,922
243	453	696	133	100	317	1,935
224	472	696	141	102	327	1,973
215	490	705	174	93	355	2,073
215	405	620	171	99	375	2,035
223	459	682	186	98	357	2,113
209	472	681	195	104	395	2,168
208	374	582	190	105	461	2,170
223	425	648	232	112	500	2,353
219	498	717	216	118	385	2,353
209	528	737	207	131	346	2,393
201	500	701	216	143	472	2,523
233	561	794	259	149	383	2,685
230	550	880	283	151	413	2,995
237	578	815	287	159	572	3,102
239	581	819	316	141	491	3,085
214	559	773	337	140	566	3,120
223	663	886	382	155	540	3,505
248	607	855	379	132	554	3,445
244	578	822	349	149	517	3,315
247	600	847	392	152	534	3,565
249	586	835	425	146	581	3,600

Table SA–2. *Natural Rubber Consumption in Developed Countries, 1950 to 1977*
(thousands of metric tons)

Year	United States	Canada	Western Europe	Australia	Japan	New Zealand[a]	South Africa[a]	Israel[a]	Total
1950	731.8	46.9	530.0	34.7	61.0	5.2	21.9	0.3	1,431.8
1951	461.3	45.1	600.0	36.5	58.2	8.0	27.3	0.6	1,237.0
1952	461.1	34.0	560.0	29.0	65.6	3.3	19.1	0.3	1,172.4
1953	562.4	38.1	615.0	36.6	88.7	6.6	26.2	1.8	1,375.4
1954	605.9	42.2	697.5	45.9	89.6	8.4	29.8	2.0	1,521.3
1955	645.0	45.0	727.5	48.8	87.4	8.6	27.6	1.0	1,590.9
1956	571.0	43.7	660.0	39.7	110.7	6.0	22.5	1.3	1,454.9
1957	547.4	41.5	660.0	35.6	130.3	6.5	25.1	2.8	1,449.2
1958	492.3	37.7	650.0	37.5	129.9	6.7	20.6	4.0	1,378.7
1959	564.0	45.0	670.0	38.6	161.1	5.8	20.2	4.9	1,509.6
1960	486.7	35.7	677.5	37.0	168.4	6.6	19.2	4.3	1,435.4
1961	434.2	32.2	660.0	31.9	178.8	5.6	17.7	4.3	1,364.7
1962	470.2	35.3	677.5	32.3	193.0	5.3	18.0	5.5	1,437.1
1963	464.6	36.6	702.5	37.1	195.5	6.4	21.1	5.8	1,469.6
1964	489.2	40.9	720.0	40.0	206.0	6.1	30.3	5.8	1,539.3
1965	523.0	43.5	737.5	39.0	201.5	7.6	29.3	7.0	1,588.4
1966	554.4	47.3	750.0	37.6	216.0	6.8	21.4	6.4	1,639.9
1967	496.7	46.1	732.5	37.3	243.0	6.6	26.5	5.6	1,594.3
1968	591.2	45.5	795.0	43.9	255.0	7.4	28.2	7.9	1,774.1
1969	607.9	49.7	847.5	42.1	268.0	9.1	27.0	6.9	1,858.2
1970	568.3	50.6	895.0	40.1	283.0	8.4	31.8	10.0	1,887.2
1971	587.1	52.0	915.0	40.5	295.0	8.4	29.0	9.0	1,936.0
1972	650.9	60.4	902.5	46.3	312.0	7.8	34.6	6.6	2,021.2
1973	712.0	60.4	935.0	52.1	335.0	8.4	39.5	5.5	2,147.9
1974	738.4	63.3	930.0	59.4	312.0	10.3	48.1	8.7	2,170.2
1975	666.0	72.3	907.5	49.9	285.2	8.0	39.3	8.3	1,969.9
1976	686.7	84.7	917.5	50.0	302.0	9.1	42.5	8.5	2,101.6
1977	803.5	90.4	934.0	41.4	320.0	10.3	38.4	9.5	2,247.5

a. Net imports.
Source: International Rubber Study Group, *Rubber Statistical Bulletin* (monthly), various issues.

Table SA–3. *Natural Rubber Net Imports by Developed Countries, 1950 to 1977* (thousands of metric tons)

Year	United States	Canada	Western Europe	Australia	Japan	New Zealand	South Africa	Israel	Total
1950	803.3	45.3	540.8	36.5	57.7	5.2	21.9	0.3	1,511.0
1951	742.2	46.9	681.6	57.2	61.5	8.0	27.3	0.6	1,625.3
1952	815.4	33.9	561.9	24.5	69.0	3.3	19.1	0.3	1,527.4
1953	649.5	40.7	618.2	36.7	93.5	6.6	26.2	1.8	1,473.2
1954	599.2	40.8	692.7	47.0	84.7	8.4	29.8	2.0	1,504.6
1955	637.0	47.2	755.6	48.1	92.0	8.6	27.6	1.0	1,617.1
1956	577.0	44.0	635.1	38.4	112.9	6.0	22.5	1.3	1,437.2
1957	551.6	43.3	701.4	35.7	132.6	6.5	25.1	2.8	1,499.0
1958	465.0	38.0	615.5	37.0	131.5	6.7	20.6	4.0	1,318.3
1959	566.1	46.0	632.8	38.5	160.2	5.8	20.2	4.9	1,474.5
1960	404.7	35.3	636.8	36.8	172.5	6.6	19.2	4.3	1,316.2
1961	391.0	32.0	641.2	31.2	185.7	5.6	17.7	4.3	1,308.7
1962	419.6	37.8	654.6	33.4	193.0	5.3	18.0	5.5	1,367.2
1963	367.5	35.9	690.4	38.1	187.9	6.4	21.1	5.8	1,353.1
1964	419.4	43.0	738.4	41.0	214.9	6.1	30.3	6.8	1,499.9
1965	416.3	45.4	749.9	40.2	207.3	7.6	29.3	7.0	1,503.0
1966	389.3	49.7	750.2	35.2	229.1	6.8	21.4	6.4	1,488.1
1967	418.4	44.6	744.1	38.7	243.0	6.6	26.5	5.6	1,527.5
1968	508.0	46.9	795.2	42.7	257.7	7.4	28.2	7.9	1,694.0
1969	572.2	50.1	875.8	42.6	280.9	9.1	27.0	6.9	1,864.6
1970	543.2	52.5	921.8	39.5	292.2	8.4	31.8	10.0	1,899.4
1971	599.0	52.7	923.6	40.0	315.9	8.4	29.0	9.0	1,997.6
1972	592.6	60.7	905.0	45.4	292.0	7.8	34.6	6.6	1,944.1
1973	627.7	66.7	932.7	53.9	365.8	8.4	39.5	5.5	2,100.1
1974	667.2	58.1	934.1	59.7	307.7	10.3	48.1	8.7	2,093.9
1975	639.4	64.8	862.7	48.2	299.1	8.1	39.3	8.3	1,969.9
1976	696.6	86.3	923.2	50.7	292.7	9.1	42.5	8.5	2,109.6
1977	781.2	92.9	934.0	41.7	304.9	10.3	38.4	9.5	2,212.9

Source: International Rubber Study Group, *Rubber Statistical Bulletin* (monthly), various issues.

Table SA–4. Natural Rubber Net Imports by Centrally Planned Economies, 1950 to 1977
(thousands of metric tons)

Year	Bulgaria	Czecho-slovakia	Germany, Democratic Republic of	Hungary	Poland	Romania	Eastern Europe, total	U.S.S.R.	China	Total
1950	1.6	22.9	2.0	3.7	5.5	0.6	36.3	87.2	71.0	194.5
1951	0.3	11.2	1.9	4.6	13.0	0.6	31.6	127.2	74.5	233.3
1952	0.6	20.3	2.3	3.5	11.3	2.8	40.8	148.0	24.0	212.8
1953	0.8	17.3	3.7	6.1	16.1	0.2	44.2	70.0	61.0	175.2
1954	0.3	22.7	5.7	8.4	17.2	0.2	54.5	20.6	63.0	138.1
1955	2.1	30.0	9.5	5.2	19.1	0.9	66.8	25.4	49.0	141.2
1956	3.3	38.4	9.7	7.3	23.5	0.2	82.4	117.5	77.0	276.9
1957	5.0	43.8	16.5	8.9	32.2	2.0	108.4	119.4	58.0	285.8
1958	5.8	48.6	17.0	10.6	32.0	5.3	119.3	241.6	99.0	459.9
1959	6.0	42.4	15.5	9.0	29.9	6.3	109.1	224.7	110.5	444.3
1960	6.1	62.4	23.0	10.1	32.7	9.3	143.6	173.4	121.7	438.7
1961	6.1	57.4	23.9	10.7	35.4	11.5	145.0	334.9	83.8	563.7
1962	7.8	27.0	23.5	13.4	36.2	13.8	121.7	338.2	108.5	568.4
1963	8.0	52.9	24.1	14.9	33.1	19.2	152.2	275.5	109.2	536.9
1964	10.9	45.8	30.1	15.6	39.6	22.3	164.3	162.3	144.2	470.8
1965	9.4	45.7	28.8	16.0	35.8	19.2	154.9	248.1	139.8	542.8
1966	9.6	45.7	29.9	16.2	41.3	24.9	167.6	283.1	172.5	623.2
1967	6.7	43.5	26.0	16.9	39.4	26.7	159.2	253.1	159.8	572.1
1968	14.3	45.0	26.5	17.5	42.9	30.5	176.7	325.9	211.8	714.4
1969	9.8	42.5	26.5	16.7	49.8	36.8	182.1	295.0	275.0	752.1
1970	15.0	53.8	31.0	17.7	50.8	37.1	205.4	3t6.5	181.8	703.7
1971	8.7	53.1	31.0	21.5	56.2	26.9	197.4	246.1	165.2	608.7
1972	18.1	50.0	28.9	20.1	53.4	47.5	218.0	231.1	187.5	636.6
1973	13.5	46.2	29.9	15.8	59.2	54.1	218.7	260.2	265.0	743.9
1974	12.4	53.0	33.3	22.6	61.2	50.4	232.9	314.6	191.0	738.5
1975	15.0	53.7	35.9	19.3	67.1	41.3	232.3	234.6	239.5	706.4
1976	12.0	53.0	40.1	15.7	63.4	68.2	252.5	216.3	222.5	691.3
1977	11.5	52.9	40.0	16.1	58.0	38.0	216.5	198.3	247.0	661.8

Source: International Rubber Study Group, *Rubber Statistical Bulletin* (monthly), various issues.

(thousands of metric tons)

Year	United States	Canada	Western Europe	Australia	Japan	New Zealand	South Africa[a]	Israel[a]	Total
1950	546.9	22.9	20.0	0.2	0.1	...	0.1	...	590.2
1951	771.1	26.9	27.5	0.2	0.3	...	0.2	...	826.2
1952	820.0	34.1	40.0	0.3	0.8	...	0.8	...	896.0
1953	797.4	36.5	45.0	0.4	1.7	...	1.2	...	882.2
1954	646.9	30.6	62.5	0.5	2.1	...	2.8	...	745.4
1955	909.3	40.8	100.0	1.2	4.3	0.4	8.0	0.6	1,064.6
1956	888.4	49.2	152.5	9.5	9.0	0.9	10.4	0.5	1,119.9
1957	940.7	48.3	212.5	15.5	12.9	1.5	13.4	0.4	1,245.2
1958	894.0	47.5	240.0	17.0	16.8	2.1	10.4	0.8	1,228.6
1959	1,089.9	58.1	315.0	20.0	35.0	1.4	13.8	1.0	1,534.2
1960	1,096.6	56.8	455.0	24.3	61.6	2.3	14.8	1.7	1,713.1
1961	1,119.9	63.7	500.0	22.5	85.2	2.6	15.1	1.4	1,810.4
1962	1,276.1	74.2	560.0	28.8	106.0	5.0	17.5	3.0	2,070.6
1963	1,327.8	85.1	640.0	35.1	127.5	5.5	18.8	3.5	2,243.3
1964	1,474.8	92.3	750.0	39.1	162.1	5.0	26.7	4.5	2,554.5
1965	1,564.8	97.7	845.0	40.6	175.5	5.6	22.5	4.9	2,756.6
1966	1,692.8	108.9	935.0	39.0	222.0	5.5	22.6	5.3	3,031.1
1967	1,654.4	110.4	975.0	43.0	273.0	5.3	31.1	5.3	3,097.5
1968	1,926.6	106.2	1,107.5	53.4	348.0	7.7	30.2	9.6	3,589.2
1969	2,056.5	129.1	1,297.5	50.9	426.0	8.4	31.3	8.9	4,008.6
1970	1,948.6	135.5	1,452.5	53.7	496.0	9.8	32.7	11.6	4,140.4
1971	2,126.7	158.3	1,530.0	59.9	525.0	10.5	40.1	10.9	4,461.4
1972	2,328.3	172.8	1,605.0	57.9	588.0	11.8	36.9	11.3	4,812.2
1973	2,440.2	186.2	1,830.0	65.8	710.0	15.0	37.4	12.7	5,297.3
1974	2,210.1	181.3	1,765.0	64.4	615.0	18.8	43.7	16.1	4,914.4
1975	1,963.7	179.3	1,610.0	50.0	584.8	9.2	42.5	18.0	4,457.5
1976	2,172.2	203.9	1,835.0	57.1	658.0	15.0	47.6	18.0	5,007.0
1977	2,480.9	207.1	1,894.0	53.0	690.0	17.0	40.5	20.0	5,402.5

. . . Zero or negligible.
a. Production plus exports and imports.
Source: International Rubber Study Group, *Rubber Statistical Bulletin* (monthly), various issues.

Table SA–6. *Natural and Synthetic Rubber Consumption,*
by Major Country Groups, and Natural Rubber Share
of Total Elastomer Consumption, 1950 to 1977
(thousands of metric tons, unless otherwise noted)

| Year | Developed countries | | | | Centrally planned economies | |
	NR consumption	SR consumption	Total elastomer consumption	NR share (percent)	NR consumption	SR consumption
1950	1,431.8	590.2	2,022.0	70.8	165.0	245.0
1951	1,237.0	826.2	2,163.2	57.2	190.0	275.0
1952	1,172.4	896.0	2,068.4	56.7	217.5	300.0
1953	1,375.4	882.2	2,257.6	60.9	195.0	350.0
1954	1,521.3	745.4	2,266.7	67.1	147.5	425.0
1955	1,590.9	1,064.6	2,655.5	59.9	150.0	450.0
1956	1,454.9	1,119.9	2,574.8	56.5	230.0	450.0
1957	1,449.2	1,245.2	2,694.4	53.8	280.0	460.0
1958	1,378.7	1,228.6	2,607.3	52.9	360.0	465.0
1959	1,509.6	1,534.2	3,043.8	49.6	402.5	487.5
1960	1,435.4	1,713.1	3,148.5	45.6	447.5	532.5
1961	1,364.7	1,810.4	3,175.1	43.0	502.5	565.0
1962	1,437.1	2,070.6	3,507.7	41.0	527.5	572.5
1963	1,469.6	2,243.3	3,712.9	39.6	555.0	627.5
1964	1,539.3	2,554.5	4,093.8	37.6	550.0	702.5
1965	1,588.4	2,756.6	4,345.0	36.6	565.0	780.0
1966	1,639.9	3,031.1	4,671.0	35.1	585.0	855.0
1967	1,594.3	3,097.5	4,691.8	34.0	610.0	905.0
1968	1,774.1	3,589.2	5,363.3	33.1	640.0	955.0
1969	1,858.2	4,008.6	5,866.8	31.7	660.0	1,010.0
1970	1,887.2	4,140.4	6,027.6	31.3	672.5	1,102.5
1971	1,936.0	4,461.4	6,397.4	30.3	685.0	1,275.5
1972	2,021.2	4,812.0	6,833.2	29.6	695.0	1,465.0
1973	2,147.9	5,297.3	7,445.2	28.8	707.5	1,662.5
1974	2,170.2	4,914.4	7,084.6	30.6	717.5	1,852.5
1975	2,036.5	4,457.5	6,494.0	31.4	700.0	2,055.0
1976	2,101.0	5,007.0	7,108.0	29.6	700.0	2,160.0
1977	2,247.5	5,402.5	7,650.0	29.4	715.0	2,320.0

a. Including the residual due to statistical discrepancies.
Source: International Rubber Study Group, *Rubber Statistical Bulletin* (monthly), various issues.

Centrally planned economies		Developing countries[a]			
Total elastomer consumption	NR share (percent)	NR consumption	SR consumption	Total elastomer consumption	NR share (percent)
410.0	40.2	110.7	—	110.7	100.0
465.0	40.9	123.0	1.2	124.2	99.0
517.5	42.0	115.1	1.5	116.6	98.7
545.0	35.8	137.1	5.3	142.4	96.3
572.5	25.8	173.7	4.6	178.3	97.4
600.0	25.0	186.6	7.9	194.5	95.9
680.0	33.8	175.1	22.6	197.7	88.6
740.0	37.8	190.8	27.3	218.1	87.5
825.0	43.6	211.3	33.9	245.2	86.2
890.0	45.2	200.4	48.3	248.7	80.6
980.0	45.7	232.1	101.9	334.0	69.5
1,067.5	47.1	232.8	122.1	354.9	65.6
1,100.0	48.0	245.4	134.4	379.8	64.6
1,182.5	47.0	247.9	154.2	402.1	61.7
1,252.5	43.9	290.7	188.0	478.7	60.8
1,345.0	42.0	294.1	203.4	497.5	59.1
1,440.0	40.6	317.6	253.9	571.5	56.1
1,515.0	40.3	330.7	272.5	603.2	54.8
1,595.0	40.1	365.9	333.3	699.2	52.3
1,670.0	39.5	391.8	351.4	743.2	52.7
1,775.0	37.8	430.3	392.0	822.3	52.3
1,960.0	34.9	471.5	448.6	920.1	51.2
2,160.0	32.2	513.8	453.0	966.8	53.1
2,370.0	29.9	547.1	615.2	1,162.3	47.1
2,570.0	27.9	629.8	683.1	1,312.9	48.0
2,755.0	25.4	631.0	515.0	1,146.0	55.1
2,860.0	24.5	749.0	685.0	1,434.0	52.2
3,035.0	23.6	727.5	710.0	1,437.5	50.6

Table SA–7. *Natural Rubber Exports (Technically Specified or Block) by Producing Countries, 1966 to 1977*
(thousands of metric tons)

Year	Malaysia	Singapore	Indonesia	Thailand	Sri Lanka	India[a]	Ivory Coast[a]	Cameroon	Total[b]	Percentage of total world NR exports[b]
1966	8.7	...	...	...	...	...	...	...	8.7	0.4
1967	23.9	...	...	...	...	...	...	...	23.9	1.0
1968	82.8	...	...	...	...	...	...	...	82.8	3.2
1969	100.7	40.2	8.4	...	...	...	...	...	149.3	5.2
1970	156.1	71.7	32.5	0.3	...	...	10.0	...	270.6	9.7
1971	222.0	97.4	126.2	1.6	...	...	12.0	2.8	462.0	16.3
1972	280.1	87.0	291.7	1.8	0.8	...	13.1	3.8	678.3	24.1
1973	376.1	105.4	360.7	2.0	0.8	...	13.3	6.5	864.8	27.2
1974	404.9	76.8	364.1	7.0	0.5	0.4	15.0	7.3	876.0	28.2
1975	433.0	89.9	401.3	32.5	1.3	1.3	14.4	7.5	981.2	33.7
1976	518.7	98.8	467.5	47.8	2.1	2.9	15.9	8.5	1,162.1	36.7
1977	541.9	102.1	521.4	61.9	1.8	3.3	16.0	9.8	1,258.2	39.2

... Zero or negligible.
a. Refers to production.
b. Does not include Nigeria or Liberia, for which data are not available.
Source: International Rubber Study Group, *Rubber Statistical Bulletin* (monthly), various issues.

Table SA–8. Natural and Synthetic Rubber Consumption in the Tire Sector in Western Europe, the United States, and Japan, 1960 to 1977 (thousands of metric tons, unless otherwise noted)

	Western Europe[a]			United States			Japan		
Year	Rubber consumption in the tire sector	Total rubber consumption	Tire sector share (percent)	Rubber consumption in the tire sector	Total rubber consumption	Tire sector share (percent)	Rubber consumption in the tire sector	Total rubber consumption	Tire sector share (percent)
1960	494.7	909.2	54.4	1,010.8	1,583.3	63.8	99.0	230.0	43.0
1961	508.4	923.3	55.1	972.9	1,554.1	62.6	120.9	264.0	45.8
1962	532.2	971.6	54.8	1,083.5	1,746.3	62.0	136.9	299.0	45.8
1963	576.8	1,048.3	55.0	1,098.0	1,792.3	61.3	158.8	323.0	49.2
1964	618.7	1,138.9	54.3	1,217.4	1,964.0	62.0	178.8	368.1	48.6
1965	672.0	1,212.8	55.4	1,327.3	2,087.8	63.6	182.8	377.0	48.5
1966	695.1	1,277.2	54.4	1,434.4	2,247.2	63.8	204.0	438.0	46.6
1967	711.2	1,316.6	54.0	1,346.9	2,151.1	62.6	251.0	516.0	48.6
1968	772.4	1,446.5	53.4	1,632.1	2,517.8	64.8	300.2	603.0	49.8
1969	873.2	1,633.9	53.4	1,749.2	2,664.4	65.6	351.5	694.0	50.6
1970	938.8	1,760.7	53.3	1,602.9	2,516.9	63.7	399.0	779.0	51.2
1971	968.0	1,797.2	53.9	1,799.7	2,713.8	66.3	424.1	820.0	51.7
1972	969.0	1,803.6	53.7	1,949.1	2,979.1	65.4	481.3	900.0	53.5
1973	974.3	1,992.3	48.9	2,022.3	3,152.2	64.2	562.4	1,045.0	53.8
1974	975.7	1,895.4	51.5	1,965.7	2,948.5	66.7	545.1	927.0	58.8
1975	921.9	1,765.7	52.2	1,643.8	2,629.7	62.5	540.1	870.0	62.1
1976	987.5	1,977.2	49.9	1,712.8	2,858.8	59.9	574.8	960.0	59.9
1977	1,009.6	7,989.5	50.7	2,086.7	3,284.4	63.5	616.3	1,010.0	61.0

a. United Kingdom, France, Federal Republic of Germany, and Italy.
Source: International Rubber Study Group, Rubber Statistical Bulletin (monthly), various issues.

Table SA–9. *Crude Oil Prices in Major Consuming Areas,*
1970 to 1978
(U.S. dollars per barrel)

Year	Western Europe[a] (c.i.f. unit values)	Japan (c.i.f. unit values)	United States Average price at well	United States Refiner acquisition cost
1970	2.25	1.80	3.18	n.a.
1971	2.77	2.18	3.39	n.a.
1972	2.90	2.50	3.39	n.a.
1973	3.96	3.29	3.89	n.a.
1974	11.04	10.78	6.87[b]	9.07
1975	12.00	11.86	7.67	10.38
1976	12.80	12.59	8.18	10.89
1977	13.84	13.41	8.57	11.95
1978	14.04	13.68	9.00	12.46

n.a. Not available.

a. Average of the United Kingdom, France, Germany, Italy, and the Netherlands.

b. From 1974 the figures are averages of "old" and "new" oil. Since September 1976 the average includes "stripper oil." Since July 1977 the average also includes Alaskan North Slope oil.

Source: Federal Energy Administration, *Monthly Energy Review,* various issues; Energy Economics Research Ltd., *International Crude Oil and Product Prices,* various issues.

Table SA–10. *Major Chemical Feedstock Unit Sale Values in the United States, 1960 to 1978*
(U.S. cents per pound)

Year	Styrene	Benzene	Ethyl- ene	Propyl- ene	Buta- diene	Iso- prene
1960	11.0	4.2	5.0	3.9	12.9	n.a.
1961	11.0	4.4	5.0	2.4	11.7	n.a.
1962	10.0	3.4	4.7	2.0	11.3	n.a.
1963	9.0	3.1	4.5	2.4	10.7	n.a.
1964	8.0	3.1	4.7	2.2	10.4	n.a.
1965	8.0	3.3	4.0	2.2	10.3	n.a.
1966	8.0	3.3	4.1	2.1	10.0	n.a.
1967	8.0	3.3	4.0	2.0	9.5	14.1
1968	7.0	2.8	3.4	2.3	8.8	n.a.
1969	6.0	3.0	3.3	2.5	8.4	n.a.
1970	6.0	3.0	3.1	2.7	8.4	10.2
1971	6.0	2.7	3.0	2.7	8.3	7.7
1972	6.0	2.8	3.0	2.9	7.8	n.a.
1973	7.0	4.0	3.3	2.8	8.1	6.3
1974	17.2	9.0	7.5	6.9	14.6	9.7
1975	19.0	9.6	8.8	7.0	16.5	10.5
1976	19.7	10.6	11.2	7.4	17.6	11.7
1977	18.6	10.4	12.0	9.5	17.8	13.7
1978	17.4	10.1	12.5	9.3	19.4	15.6

n.a. Not available.
Source: United States International Trade Commission, *Synthetic Organic Chemicals: United States Production and Sales* (annual), various issues.

Table SA–11. *Synthetic Rubber Unit Sale Values
in the United States, 1954 to 1978*
(U.S. cents per pound)

Year	SBR[a]	SBR[b]	BR	EPM-EPDM	IR	NBR	*Weighted average of all rubbers*[c]
1954	24	n.a.	n.a.	n.a.	n.a.	50	29
1955	24	n.a.	n.a.	n.a.	n.a.	51	29
1956	24	n.a.	n.a.	n.a.	n.a.	49	27
1957	24	n.a.	n.a.	n.a.	n.a.	49	27
1958	23	n.a.	n.a.	n.a.	n.a.	48	27
1959	23	n.a.	n.a.	n.a.	n.a.	49	27
1960	24	n.a.	n.a.	n.a.	n.a.	48	27
1961	24	n.a.	n.a.	n.a.	n.a.	49	28
1962	23	n.a.	n.a.	n.a.	n.a.	51	28
1963	22	n.a.	n.a.	n.a.	n.a.	48	27
1964	23	n.a.	23	n.a.	n.a.	48	27
1965	23	n.a.	22	n.a.	n.a.	47	28
1966	21	n.a.	20	n.a.	n.a.	45	27
1967	22	n.a.	19	n.a.	n.a.	46	27
1968	23	n.a.	19	n.a.	n.a.	46	27
1969	23	n.a.	18	27	n.a.	47	27
1970	23	n.a.	17	29	21	47	27
1971	20	n.a.	17	26	19	46	26
1972	20	n.a.	19	26	18	44	26
1973	20	16	19	27	22	44	28
1974	(28)	24	27	34	n.a.	50	35
1975	(31)	27	29	41	n.a.	57	39
1976	(31)	27	34	45	n.a.	61	n.a.
1977	n.a.	33	30	50	n.a.	65	n.a.
1978	n.a.	28	37	55	n.a.	68	n.a.

Note: Estimated values are in parentheses.
n.a. Not available.
a. Elastomer content basis.
b. Elastomer weight basis.
c. Including polyurethane silicone and butyl.
Source: United States International Trade Commission, *Synthetic Organic Chemicals: United States Production and Sales* (annual), various issues.

Table SA–12. *Synthetic Rubber Unit Export Values in the United States, 1950 to 1978*
(U.S. cents per pound)

Year	SBR[a]	SBR[b]	BR	EPM-EPDM	IR	NBR	IIR	*Weighted average*
1950	25.8	n.a.	n.a.	n.a.	n.a.	46.1	17.3	—
1951	27.4	n.a.	n.a.	n.a.	n.a.	51.5	20.8	—
1952	25.8	n.a.	n.a.	n.a.	n.a.	52.1	22.4	—
1953	26.8	n.a.	n.a.	n.a.	n.a.	51.5	23.3	—
1954	25.6	n.a.	n.a.	n.a.	n.a.	51.4	23.5	—
1955	24.2	n.a.	n.a.	n.a.	n.a.	50.5	23.6	25.7
1956	24.7	n.a.	n.a.	n.a.	n.a.	51.7	23.5	25.9
1957	22.5	n.a.	n.a.	n.a.	n.a.	49.8	22.9	23.5
1958	29.8	21.6	n.a.	n.a.	n.a.	48.0	22.4	23.0
1959	31.8	21.3	n.a.	n.a.	n.a.	49.8	22.7	22.7
1960	31.0	21.5	38.3	n.a.	n.a.	46.5	23.0	22.7
1961	29.7	20.7	38.3	n.a.	n.a.	47.2	23.2	22.2
1962	26.0	19.4	35.9	n.a.	25.7	45.5	22.5	21.1
1963	26.4	18.5	33.5	n.a.	22.9	46.8	24.7	20.7
1964	24.5	17.9	29.9	n.a.	22.9	44.6	25.8	20.4
1965	25.1	18.1	27.5	n.a.	22.9	45.6	24.9	20.5
1966	24.5	17.5	25.1	n.a.	23.8	44.9	25.6	20.3
1967	23.1	17.1	23.9	n.a.	22.0	41.2	25.7	20.0
1968	24.2	17.3	21.6	n.a.	21.1	39.2	25.7	21.6
1969	21.2	18.2	20.4	n.a.	22.0	38.3	25.2	21.6
1970	19.7	17.8	18.7	32.8	19.4	37.8	25.6	21.2
1971	20.5	17.5	19.9	26.3	18.9	36.4	24.7	21.3
1972	17.9	17.5	19.7	28.6	20.2	37.1	24.3	21.3
1973	18.5	19.0	19.3	30.7	22.8	36.3	27.3	23.5
1974	28.5	27.4	32.6	35.3	37.8	42.3	30.7	31.7
1975	29.8	28.3	30.2	45.0	37.3	43.2	38.5	33.9
1976	31.0	30.7	32.0	59.7	48.4	44.6	42.6	38.0
1977	36.4	36.4	31.1	51.3	46.4	56.3	45.3	41.3
1978	37.7	37.0	39.8	56.5	50.4	62.0	47.1	44.4

n.a. Not available.
— Not significant.
a. Excluding latex.
b. Total SBR.
Source: United States Department of Commerce, *U.S. Exports, Commodity by Country*, Schedule B (annual), various issues.

197

Table SA–13. Natural Rubber Prices, 1947 to 1978

Year	New York (U.S. dollars per metric ton)		London (pounds per metric ton)		Kuala Lumpur (Malaysian dollars per metric ton)					Singapore (Singapore dollars per metric ton)	Colombo (rupees per metric ton)
	RSS1 spot	RSS3 spot	RSS1 c.i.f.	RSS3 c.i.f.	RSS1 spot	RSS3 spot	SMR5L	SMR10	SMR20	RSS1 spot	RSS1 spot
1947	462.3	410.5	103.6	n.a.	823	788	n.q.	n.q.	n.q.	823	n.a.
1948	485.2	446.4	115.8	n.a.	929	852	n.q.	n.q.	n.q.	929	n.a.
1949	387.1	355.4	105.2	n.a.	842	765	n.q.	n.q.	n.q.	842	n.a.
1950	906.1	887.4	290.7	278.2	2,385	2,300	n.q.	n.q.	n.q.	2,385	n.a.
1951	1,302.3	1,293.9	448.0	416.2	3,738	3,458	n.q.	n.q.	n.q.	3,738	n.a.
1952	850.3	794.3	256.3	237.1	2,118	1,949	n.q.	n.q.	n.q.	2,118	n.a.
1953	534.2	494.9	181.0	169.5	1,487	1,380	n.q.	n.q.	n.q.	1,487	n.a.
1954	521.2	514.1	182.0	178.2	1,484	1,448	n.q.	n.q.	n.q.	1,484	n.a.
1955	862.9	846.5	302.0	289.0	2,517	2,390	n.q.	n.q.	n.q.	2,517	n.a.
1956	753.3	737.8	257.9	249.3	2,133	2,062	n.q.	n.q.	n.q.	2,133	n.a.
1957	686.7	673.6	238.0	231.3	1,957	1,923	n.q.	n.q.	n.q.	1,957	2,550
1958	618.8	581.5	215.0	200.1	1,769	1,638	n.q.	n.q.	n.q.	1,769	2,061
1959	805.8	789.8	270.0	265.8	2,239	2,191	n.q.	n.q.	n.q.	2,239	2,782

1960	841.2	829.8	288.8	281.1	2,383	2,313	n.q.	n.q.	n.q.	2,383	2,727
1961	653.1	645.1	224.8	220.2	1,842	1,804	n.q.	n.q.	n.q.	1,842	2,213
1962	629.6	615.6	211.7	205.5	1,724	1,672	n.q.	n.q.	n.q.	1,724	2,156
1963	578.9	565.3	196.7	192.0	1,597	1,556	n.q.	n.q.	n.q.	1,597	2,043
1964	556.5	549.3	185.9	182.7	1,502	1,481	n.q.	n.q.	n.q.	1,502	1,973
1965	566.4	556.3	190.7	186.3	1,544	1,512	n.q.	n.q.	n.q.	1,544	2,015
1966	520.8	514.3	179.0	174.8	1,441	1,407	n.q.	n.q.	n.q.	1,441	1,964
1967	438.8	429.8	151.6	145.1	1,192	1,134	n.q.	n.q.	n.q.	1,192	1,735
1968	437.4	429.4	170.8	165.6	1,171	1,131	n.q.	n.q.	n.q.	1,171	1,945
1969	577.5	568.0	222.3	219.9	1,539	1,512	n.q.	n.q.	n.q.	1,539	2,289
1970	462.5	454.1	180.4	175.1	1,244	1,193	n.q.	n.q.	n.q.	1,244	2,001
1971	399.0	388.6	143.7	139.2	1,016	925	n.q.	n.q.	n.q.	1,016	1,746
1972	402.1	381.8	147.7	141.9	935	881	n.q.	n.q.	n.q.	935	1,782
1973	785.1	753.4	300.2	287.0	1,655	1,567	1,680	1,587	1,580	1,667	2,614
1974	868.0	803.6	342.4	318.7	1,794	1,605	1,901	1,626	1,614	1,820	2,800
1975	658.9	633.7	287.5	276.5	1,357	1,300	1,406	1,328	1,214	1,346	2,930
1976	872.3	837.6	475.0	460.2	1,991	1,897	2,126	1,908	1,895	1,931	4,340
1977	916.9	880.3	508.6	493.4	2,028	1,940	2,129	1,969	1,958	2,007	4,530
1978	1,108.1	1,072.6	552.7	540.4	2,700	2,225	2,341	2,166	2,156	2,256	n.a.

n.a. Not available.
n.q. Not quoted.
Sources: International Rubber Study Group, Rubber Statistical Bulletin (various issues); John Keells, Rubber Statistics (of Sri Lanka), various issues.

References

•••

The word *processed* is used in this list of references to indicate that a work has been reproduced by a process other than con-
ventional typesetting and printing, whether it be xerography, mimeog-
raphy, or some other method.

Allen, P. W. "Natural Rubber: Prospects and Requirements for Growth."
Polymer Institute Symposium. Akron University, September 1975.
Processed.
————. *Natural Rubber and the Synthetics.* London: Crosby Lockwood,
1972.
————, P. O. Thomas, and B. C. Sekhar. *The Techno-Economic Poten-
tial of Natural Rubber in Major End-Uses.* MRRDB Monograph 1. Kuala
Lumpur: MRRDB, 1973.
Atkinson, G. W. "Polyisoprene—Present Status and Future Prospects."
*Proceedings of the IRSG Symposium on the Present Position and Pros-
pects for Newer Rubbers,* Sao Paulo, Brazil, October 1967 (London:
IRSG, 1968).
American Chemical Society. *Chemistry in the Economy.* Washington,
D.C.: American Chemical Society, 1973.
Anderson, J. G. "The Rubber Manufacturers' Choice: Natural or Syn-
thetic Rubber." *Plastics and Rubber International* (July/August 1977).
Bateman, L. "Natural Rubber in 2000 AD." *Rubber Age* (May 1967).
————. "Natural Rubber Can Meet the Synthetics Challenge." *Rubber
Developments,* no. 23 (1970).
————. "The Rubber Market in Historical Perspective." *European Rub-
ber Journal* (February 1978).
Bauer, Peter T. *The Rubber Industry: A Study in Competition and Mo-
nopoly.* Cambridge, Massachusetts: Harvard University Press, 1948.
Bennett, D. A. "Changes in Markets for Synthetic Rubber and Its Raw
Materials." *Proceedings of the ECMRA Conference,* Madrid, 1976.
Processed.
Burgess, C. E. *Polymers in the Western European Car Industry.* Lon-
don: Shell International Chemical Company, April 1976.
Campos Lopez, E., M. A. Ponce Neaves, and B. Canales. *Rubber from*

200

Guayule: Research Activities in Mexico. Centro de Investigación En Quimica Aplicada, December 1976.

Charles Rivers Associates and Wharton Econometric Forecasting Associates. *Forecasts and Analysis of the Rubber Market.* Submitted to the Office of Stockpile Disposal, GSA, Washington, D.C., 1974. Processed.

Chow, G. *Demand for Automobiles in the United States: A Study in Consumer Durables.* Amsterdam: North Holland Publishing Company, 1957.

Diamond, J. E. "Tyres and Natural Rubber." *Proceedings of the* NRPRA *3rd Rubber in Engineering Conference,* London 1973.

Diekmann, A. "Future Trends in the Motor Industry." Study prepared for the Verband der Automobilindustrie, Frankfurt. 1974. Processed.

Dissanaynake, A. B. "Supply of All Elastomers." ANRPC Discussion Paper, undated. Processed.

Dunham, D. M. *Spatial Implications in the Competition between Natural and Synthetic Products with Special Reference to the Case of Rubber.* ISS Occasional Paper, The Hague, 1970.

Dworkin, David. "Changing Markets and Technology for Specialty Elastomers." *Rubber World* (February 1975).

Energy Economics Research, Ltd. *International Crude Oil and Product Prices,* various issues.

Engineering News Record.

Evans, M. *Macroeconomic Forecasting.* New York: Harper and Row, 1969.

Federal Energy Administration. *Monthly Energy Review* (December 1976).

Food and Agriculture Organization of the United Nations (FAO). *Agricultural Commodity Projections, 1970–1980.* Volumes I and II. Rome: FAO, 1971.

―――. *Production Yearbook,* various issues.

―――. *Trade Yearbook,* various issues.

Grilli, Enzo, R. Helterline, and Peter Pollak. "An Econometric Analysis of the World Rubber Economy." World Bank Staff Commodity Paper, no. 3. Washington, D.C.: The World Bank, 1978.

Grosh, K. A. "Natural Rubber in Tires." *Proceedings of the Natural Rubber Conference, Kuala Lumpur, 1968.* Processed.

Haque, I. "Analysis of Natural Rubber Market." World Bank Staff Working Paper, no. 113. Washington, D.C.: The World Bank, 1972.

―――. "Efficiency in Resource Allocation: The Case of Natural Rubber." World Bank report no. EC-179. A restricted-circulation document. Washington, D.C., July 1971. Processed.

Harrington, C. J. "Ethylene-Propylene Elastomers." *Proceedings of the* IRSG *Symposium on the Present Position and Prospects for Newer Rubbers,* Sao Paulo, Brazil, October 1967 (London: IRSG, 1968).

't Hooft-Welvaars, Maria. "The International Organization of Commodity Trade: Case Study of Natural Rubber." UNCTAD document TD/B/AC.2/4. January 1966.

———. "The Natural Rubber Problem." World Bank background paper, CSSS-9-A. A restricted-circulation document. Washington, D.C., 1969. Processed.

———. "Profitability of New Investments in Rubber Plantings in Malaysia." UNCTAD document TD/B/C.1/SYN/52. Geneva, June 1971. Processed.

———. "The Profitability of NR and SBR Investments." World Bank Staff Commodity Paper (draft). Washington, D.C.: The World Bank, 1978.

Hymans, S. "Consumer Durable Spending: Explanation and Prediction." Brookings Papers on Economic Activity, vol. 2 (1970).

International Institute of Synthetic Rubber Producers (IISRP). Proceedings of the 15th, 16th, 17th, and 18th Annual Meetings. New York: IISRP Inc., 1974 to 1977.

———. Description of Synthetic Rubbers and Latices. New York: IISRP, Inc., 1968.

International Rubber Quality and Packing Conference. "International Standards of Quality and Packing for Natural Rubber." 1969.

International Rubber Study Group (IRSG). "The Polyisoprene Rubber Situation: A Report by the Ad Hoc Advisory Panels." London, March 1977. Processed.

———. "Report of the Ad Hoc Advisory Panel on the Prospects for Rubber." Jakarta, October 1975. Processed.

———. "Report of the Committee of Experts." London: IRSG, June 1973.

———. "Report on the IRSG Meeting in London, June 20–24, 1977: Discussion Forum to Consider Supply Demand Situation for Rubber through 1990 in the Light of the Report Presented in 1975 by the Group's Ad Hoc Panel." London: IRSG, December 1977.

———. Statistical Bulletin, various issues.

Juster, F. T., and P. Wachtel. "Anticipatory and Objective Models of Durable Goods Demand." Exploration and Economic Research, MBER, vol. 1 (1974).

Keck, Noble. "EPDM Elastomers." Rubber Age (September 1973).

Keells, John. Rubber Statistics (of Sri Lanka), various issues.

Kolbe, H. and H. J. Timm. Factors Determining Price Movements on the World Market for Natural Rubber: Analysis of an Econometric Model. Hamburg: Institut fur Wirtschaftsforschung, 1972 (original in German).

Lamberson, R. "The Economics of Establishing Synthetic Rubber Factories in Developing Countries." UNIDO Document ID/WG.34/50. July 1969.

Landon, J. W. "The Prospects for Rubber." *Symposium on the Outlook for Commodities*, Royal Lancaster Hotel, London, July 1976. Processed.

Leyden, J. J. "Radial Tire Compounding." *Rubber Age* (1972).

National Academy of Sciences. *Guayule: An Alternative Source of Natural Rubber*. Washington, D.C.: National Academy of Sciences, 1977.

Nerlove, M. "A Note on Long Run Automobile Demand." *Journal of Marketing* (July 1957).

Ng, E. K., and Teck Yew Pee. "Innovations in Natural Rubber Technology: Some Malaysian Lessons." Rubber Research Institute of Malaysia, Kuala Lumpur, 1976. Processed.

OECD. *Trade by Commodities: Exports*, various issues.

O'Herlihy, J. "Demand for Cars in Great Britain." *Applied Statistics*, vol. 13 (1964).

Pee, Teck Yew. "Economics of Field Collection." *Planters' Bulletin of the Rubber Research Institute of Malaysia*, no. 110 (September 1970).

————, and Ani bin Arope. *Rubber Owners' Manual*. Kuala Lumpur: RRIM, 1976.

Rhoad, M. J. "Isoprene Worldwide." *Proceedings of the 15th Annual Meeting*. New York: IISRP, 1974.

Rubber Research Institute of Malaysia (RRIM). *Proceedings of the RRI Planters' Conference*. Kuala Lumpur: RRIM, 1971–1976 (annual).

Ruebensaal, C. F. *Changing Markets and Manufacturing Patterns in the Synthetic Rubber Industry*. New York: IISRP, Inc., 1973 to 1977 and 1978 (draft).

————. "The Rubber Industry Statistical Report." Annual report of the International Institute of Synthetic Rubber Producers. New York, 1974–1978.

————. "World Synthetic Rubber—Its Manufacture and Markets." *Rubber and Plastic Age* (1960 and 1965, various issues).

Smith, R. P. *Consumer Demand for Cars in the United States*. London: Cambridge University Press, 1975.

————. "A Note on Car Replacement." *Review of Economic Studies*, vol. XLI, no. 128 (October 1974).

Sonneken, E. H. *Statement to the United States Cost of Living Council Tire Hearings*. Akron, Ohio: Goodyear Tire and Rubber Co., September 1973. Processed.

Sooi, Ng Choong, Colin Barlow, and Chan Chee-Kheong. "Factors Affecting the Profitability of Rubber Production in West Malaysian Estates." *Proceedings of Natural Rubber Conference*, Kuala Lumpur, 1968. Processed.

Stone, Ralph and Company. "The Impact of Pollution Control on the Production Costs of Selected Natural and Synthetic Material." Reference no. ENV/73/007. Draft final report to UNCTAD. September 1975. Processed.

Suits, D. B. "The Demand for New Automobiles." *Review of Economics and Statistics* (August 1958).

United Nations Conference on Trade and Development (UNCTAD). *International Rubber Agreement, 1979* (Document TD/Rubber/15). New York, October 17, 1979.

UNCTAD-GATT International Trade Center. "Report on Some Aspects of Promotion and Marketing of Rubber." Document ITC/PP/11. June 1973.

United Nations, Secretariat, Population Division. Unpublished data.

United Nations Economic and Social Commission for Asia and the Pacific. Report on Projections of Demand for Rubber, Bangkok, Thailand, November 1978. Processed.

United States Department of Commerce. *U.S. Exports, Commodity, by Country*, Schedule B (annual), various issues.

United States International Trade Commission. *Synthetic Organic Chemicals: United States Production and Sales* (annual), various issues.

United States Motor Vehicle Manufacturers Association. *World Motor Vehicle Data* (1977).

Wallis, K. R. "Lagged Dependent Variables and Serially Correlated Errors," *Review of Economics and Statistics* (1967), pp. 555–67.

Workshop on Alternative Energy Strategies (WAES). *Energy: Global Prospects to 1985 and 2000.* New York: McGraw-Hill, 1977.

The full range of World Bank publications, both free and for sale, is described in the *Catalog of World Bank Publications,* and of the continuing research program of the World Bank, in *World Bank Research Program: Abstracts of Current Studies.* The most recent edition of each is available without charge from:

PUBLICATIONS UNIT

THE WORLD BANK

1818 H STREET, N.W.

WASHINGTON, D.C. 20433

U.S.A.

International Sales Representatives

•─•

THE UNITED KINGDOM, CONTINENTAL EUROPE, THE NEAR EAST AND MIDDLE
EAST, AND AFRICA
   The Johns Hopkins University Press, Ltd., 2-4 Brook Street, London
   W1Y-1AA, England

CANADA
   University of Toronto Press, 5201 Dufferin Street, Downsview,
   Ontario, M3H 5T8, Canada

AUSTRALIA AND NEW ZEALAND
   Australia and New Zealand Book Co. Pty. Ltd., P.O. Box 459,
   Brookvale, N.S.W. 2100, Australia

INDIA
   Prentice-Hall International, Inc., Englewood Cliffs, N.J. 07632,
   U.S.A.

SOUTHEAST ASIA
   Prentice-Hall of Southeast Asia, Pty. Ltd., 4-B, 77 Ayer Rajah
   Industrial Estate, Ayer Rajah Road, Singapore 5.

JAPAN
   United Publishers Services Ltd., Shimura Building, 4-1 Kojimachi,
   Chiyoda-Ku, Tokyo, Japan
   Maruzen Co., Ltd., P.O. Box 5050, Tokyo International 100-31,
   Japan, and bookstores of the Maruzen Co. throughout Japan.

LATIN AMERICA AND THE CARIBBEAN
   Unilibros, 5500 Ridge Oak Drive, Austin, Texas 78731, U.S.A.

THROUGHOUT THE REST OF THE WORLD, orders can be sent directly to
   The Johns Hopkins University Press, Baltimore, Maryland 21218,
   U.S.A.

Published by The Johns Hopkins University Press
Baltimore and London